SINGING
the LITURGY

SINGING the LITURGY

A PRACTICAL MEANS OF CHRISTIAN LIVING

+ + + + + + + + + + +

SISTER MARIETTA, S.N.J.M.

+ + + + + + + + + + +

THE BRUCE PUBLISHING COMPANY
MILWAUKEE

NIHIL OBSTAT:

AUGUSTINUS JOHNSON
MARTINUS THIELEN
Censores Deputati

IMPRIMATUR:

✠ EDUARDUS D. HOWARD
Archiepiscopus Portlandensis in Oregon
September 3, 1955

Catholic University of America Classification:
Lynn, BQT4620 Dewey, 246.8

Library of Congress Catalog Card Number: 56–6700

"All the earth shall worship thee and shall sing unto thee: they shall sing to thy name": from all that is created there goes up in His hearing a great chorus of song, "Holy, Holy, Holy, Lord God Almighty," for "as truly as I live all the earth shall be filled with the glory of the Lord." To pray to God is to take one's place in a mighty choir, to add one's voice to a chant which has mounted up to Him since the beginning "when the morning stars sang together, and all the sons of God shouted for joy," and will continue for all time and for all hereafter circling from God through the works of His hands and back again to Himself world without end.

(R. H. J. Steuart, S.J., *Temples of Eternity* [New York: Longmans, Green and Company])

ACKNOWLEDGMENTS

I WISH to acknowledge my indebtedness to my religious Superiors whose authority brought this text to its present state, and who with many other religious of my community encouraged and assisted me in countless ways. Especial appreciation is due to Sister Claire Marie, former Provincial Supervisor of Music, whose zeal and love of the Church has made her an ardent and untiring worker for the Mystical Body of Christ, particularly for all that furthers the worship paid to God by that Body.

Heartfelt thanks are extended to the Right Reverend Monsignor Thomas J. Tobin, S.T.D., J.C.D., LL.D., Vicar-General of the Archdiocese of Portland in Oregon, whose gracious criticism and suggestions were of prime assistance in the development of this text. I also wish to thank the Reverend Austin S. Johnson, former Archdiocesan Music Supervisor, for his kind and continued encouragement.

To the pupils of my liturgical music classes, whose comments and evaluation of its various chapters have contributed to make the work practicable, I owe sincere gratitude.

Acknowledgment is made to those publishers who so kindly gave me permission to quote from their publications. Their names and the books from which I have quoted are listed in the footnotes and in the bibliography. In particular, I extend sincere thanks to those authors and publishers who personally signified their pleasure in sharing their works that God might be further glorified through the sung liturgy.

FOREWORD

THIS present century may well go down in history as the Age of the Laity. The huge growth in population, the spread of irreligion, the complex social problems that confront us, make it apparent that the Church will not fulfill her mission to this generation, unless the laity share in greater degree the burden of their priests.

It has been said correctly that the laity will play a greater role in the Church's social action if they enter more fully into her life of prayer. One cannot read the text of sacred liturgy each Sunday, nor join in the offering of the Mass, without feeling the urge to unite with Christ in extending that kingdom which He is one day to give to His Father.[1] When Pius X called the liturgy the "first and indispensable source of the true Christian spirit,"[2] he had in mind a spirit which would indeed "renew the face of the earth."[3]

In writing her book SINGING THE LITURGY, Sister Marietta has more than done her part in helping laymen understand the liturgy. The interlinear translation of the prayers, and the simple explanations of the chant will benefit many whose student days are long past. Parish priests should find in this book a fund of information for instructing their people.

Sister Marietta's main objective is to translate into fact the fervent wish of the Holy See that the "chant be restored to popular use."[4]

[1] 1 Cor. 15:24.

[2] Pius X, *Motu Proprio on Sacred Music.*

[3] Ps. 103:30.

[4] Pius XI, Apostolic Constitution, *Divini Cultus Sanctitatem.*

When the people sing Mass they no longer "attend as outsiders, or mute onlookers, but fully appreciate the beauty of the liturgy."[5]

We hope that SINGING THE LITURGY will enjoy a wide circulation. Its use as a textbook should give us Catholic graduates better instructed in the sacred rites and better equipped for Christian social action.

✠ EDWARD D. HOWARD
Archbishop of Portland
in Oregon

[5] *Ibid.*

PREFACE

"FOR to me, to live is Christ" (Phil. 1:21). This claim of St. Paul is also the claim of every true follower of Christ. Christ continues His Incarnation and Redemption in us, His members in grace. He wills that each of us be an expression of Him in some finite way. It is our duty and privilege to study His will in our regard and to allow Him to have His way in us freely.

In the liturgical cycle and in the liturgy itself we see Christ expressing Himself in a perfect, human way in His own life.

> No sooner, in fact, "is the Word made flesh" than He shows Himself to the world vested with a priestly office, making to the Eternal Father an act of submission which will continue uninterruptedly as long as He lives: "When He cometh into the world He saith . . . 'behold I come . . . to do Thy will.'" This act He was to consummate admirably in the bloody Sacrifice of the Cross: "In the which will we are sanctified by the oblation of the Body of Jesus Christ once." He plans His active life among men with no other purpose in view.[1]

Here we find Him as our Model. It is through the liturgy, our contact with Him offering Himself for and with us, our contact with Him in the Sacraments and in prayer, that we obtain from Him the grace to co-operate with His action in and through us. The desire of Christ (desired also by the society founded by Him) is "achieved when Christ lives and thrives, as it were, in the hearts

[1] Pius XII, *Mediator Dei* (New York: The America Press, 1948), No. 17.

of men, and when men's hearts in turn are fashioned and expanded as though by Christ."[2]

True participation in the liturgy is the offering of ourselves freely and completely to Christ that He may glorify the Father with and through us. This is above all an internal participation, but it is expressed and affected by an external participation. Nor is it complete unless it is a participation of the whole man, body and spirit, of man as an individual and as a member of society, particularly of the Mystical Body of Christ. This external participation admits of various degrees according as we are more active in our expression of it. A bodily presence at the liturgy, the use of a liturgical book in the offering of it, the voiced offering of it with others in word, the voiced offering of it with others in song, all these may be considered degrees of active participation which are meant to express and make possible a complete return of ourselves to God.

Canon Masure, considering the need of man to return to God, says:

> To achieve the conquest of its being and its destiny it [that is, humanity] casts itself upon Him who, by filling it completely, gives it the power to be its real self. At once and in a single movement it recognizes all the rights of God and bows before His transcendence: it adores and prays. And at the moment when these two beings meet and embrace, God's glory and love are satisfied and also man's restlessness and insufficiency.
>
> In fine, sacrifice is the entire movement of our created nature. This makes us personified tendencies, subsisting relations to God; it demands our attainment of Him like the flight of the arrow to the mark. Sacrifice consists in translating the direction of this living shaft into appropriate symbolic gestures and in giving impetus to the inward drive by the very expression of it in outward form.[3]

The modern movement called the *liturgical movement* was begun a century ago. From its small beginnings it has developed and expanded through the efforts of many loyal and devoted members of Christ's Mystical Body, under the guidance and direction of His

[2] *Ibid.,* No. 20.

[3] Eugene Masure, *The Christian Sacrifice,* translated with a preface by Dom Illtyd Trethowan (London: Burns, Oates and Washbourne, Ltd., 1944; New York: Kenedy and Sons, American Edition, 1947), p. 48.

vicars on earth, and has now spread throughout the Western World. The papal documents of Pius X and of Pius XI concerning sung participation in the liturgy, and particularly the encyclicals of Pius XII on the Mystical Body, *Mystici Corporis,* and on the worship of God by that Body, *Mediator Dei,* have made the liturgical movement a matter which no faithful follower of Christ can ignore. Nor do we wish to do so.

As we look back over these one hundred years and particularly over the past fifty of them, we may wonder that active participation in the liturgy, sometimes even the liturgy itself, is not of more vital importance to us. It is not difficult to learn to sing the liturgy, as we well know. But even among those who have learned to sing it, we sometimes find a real apathy toward doing so in their parish churches. Searching for the causes of this apathy and striving to meet them and, if possible, to forestall them brought into being this handbook entitled SINGING THE LITURGY: A PRACTICAL MEANS OF CHRISTIAN LIVING.

Although inertia on the part of some who could easily sing the liturgy may be due to the conditions under which they learned to sing it, or to the lack of co-operation in others, these factors do not entirely explain its existence. The most outstanding causes seem to be a lack of understanding of the meaning of sanctifying grace, of the doctrine of the Mystical Body, of what the liturgy is and what it is meant to express, of its place in the plan of God for man, and of how necessary is active participation in it if man would have the true Christian spirit. SINGING THE LITURGY is one attempt to furnish at least the germ of the necessary understanding. It has seemed good to present it as a supplementary text for the use of those who are striving to make their participation in the liturgy more active and intelligent. We have tried to make each chapter of this handbook as complete and effective as possible; therefore, of necessity, there has been some repetition of what is fundamental in our study. The following pages have reached their present form after much use and many revisions in the course of the past eighteen years.

While this book has been devised as a text to be in the hands of students of the sung liturgy and used by them according to a four-year class plan, it can also be used for general reading or as a helpful reference. It was intended for, and has been used by, young adults but we trust that it is practicable for adults of any age. With its assistance we are aiming to prepare to "translate the direction of this living shaft" of ourselves, and to give "impetus to the inward drive by the very expression of it in outward form" in as complete a way as circumstances permit. May God bless our efforts and grant us His Spirit which we thus seek.

Feast of Pope St. Gregory the Great, and
The Sixteenth Anniversary of the Coronation of
His Holiness, Pope Pius XII
March 12, 1955

CONTENTS

SINGING
the LITURGY

CHAPTER I

INTRODUCTION TO GREGORIAN CHANT

MUSIC which is worthy of its place in the liturgy of the Church is called liturgical music. Liturgical music differs from other music in spirit and in expression. To understand why this is so, we shall need to understand the liturgy itself.

The Greek word, *liturgy,* referred to any work from which the general public profited. The Church uses this word to refer to its public official prayer. The liturgy is the prayer of the whole Mystical Body, Head and members.[1] It is continually offered in our name and continually represents us all as Christ's Body before the throne of God.

In its Christian use, the word *liturgy* may be understood in two ways. (1) The liturgy is, primarily, that "work of redemption which Christ our Lord first carried out by the sacrifice of the Cross, and which He now continues and applies through Holy Mass, the sacraments, and the office." (2) Liturgy, in its secondary meaning, is the "official collection of prayers, readings and hymns by means of which Christ's liturgy is continued: in fact, the *text* of Mass, sacraments, and office."[2]

Our official prayer represents the adoration, thanksgiving, reparation, and petition of the whole Church. The music which accompanies this official prayer must also have the spirit of the prayer of the whole Church. If the music has this spirit, it is correctly called liturgical music. Although any music can have this spirit, Gregorian

[1] See the encyclical of Pope Pius XII, *Mediator Dei* (New York: America Press, 1948), No. 20.

[2] Clifford Howell, S.J., "The Blessed Virgin in the Liturgy," *Orate Fratres,* 24:1, p. 1.

Chant, which exists primarily for liturgical use, has the spirit of the liturgy as no other music has. Therefore, Gregorian Chant, above all other music, is official or liturgical music.

A. The Language

The Church has not only an official form of worship, but also an official language. This language is Latin. Official transactions of the Western Church are in Latin. Her official prayers are offered in the same language. If we know Latin, then, no matter where we go, we will be able to join our voices in offering the official prayers of the Church. If we know the Chant, we shall be able to join our voices in singing the official prayers of the Church in her official music and in her official language.

B. The Chant

As we have said, Gregorian Chant is the official music of the Church. No other music expresses the thought and feeling of the prayers of the Church as does the Chant.

In early Christian times the prayers of the Church were declaimed on a singing tone. This gave an added beauty and solemnity to the prayers and at the same time made it possible for the congregation to participate more easily. The declamation followed the natural rise and fall of the voices of those who said the words.

In a later chapter we shall consider the origin of these sung prayers. We shall see that early Christians used music that was a heritage of the Hebrew liturgy, influenced by the Graeco-Roman culture. As Christian liturgy developed, however, members of the Church began to compose melodies of their own which were also used by the Church in her worship.

The Church has only one purpose for the use of music in her worship and that purpose is to praise God and to assist us to unite ourselves with Him. The phrase, "To sing once is to pray twice," is commonly attributed to St. Augustine. If singing once is praying twice, then the music itself must pray. The music which prays the best is the Gregorian. It is called Gregorian Chant because of the great services rendered to it by St. Gregory the Great who reigned as pope from 590 to 604. Gregorian Chant is also known as *plainsong, plainchant,* or simply *the chant.*

The *unity* of the Catholic Church is expressed musically through her chant. The Church provides official music for each sung prayer of the various feasts of the year. What unity of worship would be expressed if the Proper of the day were sung in this same official music in all the churches of the world. What unity of worship is expressed in any sung prayer, but particularly if the prayer is sung in Gregorian Chant. It is inspiring to join voices with the Catholics of our parish as we sing our prayers in our official music. It is inspiring to go from city to city or from country to country, and join voices with other members of Christ, singing our official prayers in our official music. It is also very inspiring to think of the countless saints of the past, with whom we are one in Christ, singing these official prayers in this same official music.

REVIEW QUESTIONS

1. In what respect does liturgical music differ from other music?
2. Give a present-day example of the original (Greek) meaning of the word *liturgy.*
3. In what two ways may the Christian use of the word *liturgy* be understood?
4. What is the official music of the Church?
5. Why is this, above all other music, liturgical music?
6. What is the official language of the Church?
7. Discuss the origin of the melodies of the Church's sung prayer.
8. Why does the Church use music in her liturgy?
9. Why is the chant called Gregorian Chant?
10. What other terms are often used to refer to the official music of the Church?
11. "The unity of the Church is expressed through her chant." Discuss briefly.

C. Mechanics of the Chant

I. THE STAFF

The official music of the Church is not difficult to read. The Gregorian staff has four lines. We may be more accustomed to read from a five-lined staff, but the principle of reading either from a four-lined or from a five-lined staff is the same. When Gregorian music was at its height (600–950) there was no staff at all, nor was there a notation, such as we know it, to record the music. When the manuscripts were prepared, signs were placed near the words of the prayers. These signs indicated to the choir leader only the general rise and fall of the melody which he had already learned from memory. The choir members learned the melodies by rote as they followed the hand gestures, or *chironomy,* of the leader. Various systems of notation had been experimentally used. Guido, a monk of Arezzo, Italy, in the eleventh century brought one of these systems to a more perfect form. The four-lined staff has been attributed to Guido and has been in use since his time.

The Gregorian staff uses two clefs: the C or *do* clef and the F or *fa* clef. These clefs mark, respectively, the first and the fourth tones of the scale used in the melodies. Note that it is always a half step from the clef line to the space below.

II. THE NOTES

The notes may look strange to us but they are really very simple to read. We read the one that appears to the eye first when reading from left to right. If one is directly above another, we read the bottom one first.

The notes are: the **punctum,** the **virga,** the **rhombus,** the **quilisma,** and the **liquescent** note. All these notes receive an equal amount of time — one count — but only the punctum may be written alone.

Groups of notes are called **neums.** Neums may be simple or compound. We shall study the simple neums; the others are based on these. Simple neums have either two or three notes and are counted, respectively, "one-two" or "one-two-three."

1. Simple Neums

(1) *pes* (or *podatus*) — an ascending melody of two tones — count "1-2."

(2) *clivis* — a descending melody of two tones — count "1-2."

(3) *scandicus* — an ascending melody of three tones — count "1-2-3."

(4) *climacus* — a descending melody of three tones — count "1-2-3."

(5) *torculus* — a three-note neum of which the middle tone is the highest — count "1-2-3."

(6) *porrectus* — a three-note neum of which the middle tone is the lowest — count "1-2-3."

2. Special Neums

(1) *quilisma* — an ascending melody of three tones of which the first is slightly prolonged — count "1̂-2-3."

(2) *salicus* — an ascending melody of three tones of which the second is marked with an *ictus.* The second tone is counted "1" and is slightly prolonged. The first tone is counted with the preceding time-group — count "m-1̂-2."

(3) *pressus minor* — formed by placing a punctum before a neum on the same pitch as the first note of the neum; the punctum and the first note of the neum must be sung on the same syllable of the Latin word. The punctum is counted "1" and is accented. Count of the given group: "1̂-2-3."

(4) *pressus major* — formed by the conjoining of two neums. The last tone of the first neum and the first tone of the second neum must be on the same pitch and must be sung on the same syllable of the Latin word. The first tone of the pressus itself is, again, counted "1" and is accented. Count of the given group: "m-1̂-2-3."

We also have (5) the *oriscus,* which is a punctum added to a neum; (6) the *distropha,* which is a strophicus of two notes on the same pitch and sung on the same syllable of the Latin word; (7) the *tristropha,* which is a strophicus of three notes on the same pitch and sung on the same syllable of the Latin word; (8) two virga on the same pitch and sung on the same syllable of the Latin word form what is called the *bivirga;* (9) three virga on the same pitch and sung on the same syllable of the Latin word form a *trivirga.*

Some mention should be made of the *liquescent* note as it is used with the neums. "Liquescent" means "melting" or "smooth-flowing." A liquescent note is written smaller than other notes. Although it is held as long as other notes it is sung more lightly. "In reading, the liquescent syllable, which is called semi-vocal, is to be treated softly, and the consonant, so to speak, finished on it. The effect has been described as of an indefinite sound introduced between two consonants, a very slight resonance separating the syllables. In singing, this resonance is supplied by the liquescent note, and an abrupt transition to the new syllable is avoided."[3] Note the frequent use of liquescent notes on "Hosa*n*na," "mu*n*di," "exa*u*di." Liquescent notes, if sung well, are very expressive.

The half-size note which is found at the end of each staff is called a *custos* or guide. This guide indicates the pitch of the first note of the next line. Since it is not considered a note in itself but only a "signpost," it is never counted.

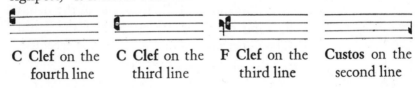

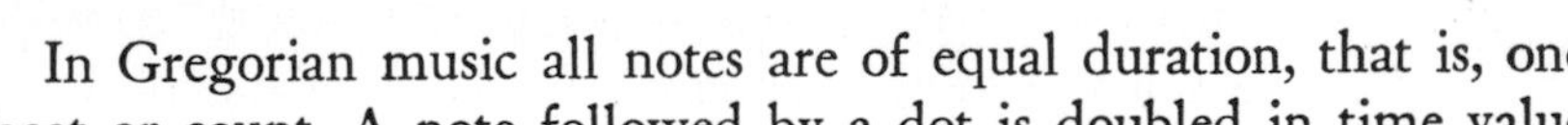

C Clef on the fourth line — **C Clef** on the third line — **F Clef** on the third line — **Custos** on the second line

III. THE TIME

In Gregorian music all notes are of equal duration, that is, one beat or count. A note followed by a dot is doubled in time value and thus receives two counts. A note is never divided into half-

[3] Benedictine of Stanbrook, *A Grammar of Plainsong* (Liverpool: Rushworth and Dreaper, 1934), p. 32.

beats, quarter-beats, etc., nor ever given one-and-a-half-beats, one-and-a-quarter-beats, etc.

Time groups of two or three notes may follow each other freely. This free alternation of binary and ternary groups is always found in free rhythm. The relationship which exists between the time and the rhythm of the music will be studied in greater detail in a later chapter. For our present purpose, it is sufficient to say that the count of "1," or the ictic note, is the point of support of the melody, while the other counts are the up-beats leading to the following count of "1." (The rhythm of a time-group of two notes, counted "1-2," is "down-up." A time-group of three notes, counted "1-2-3," has a rhythm of "down-up-up.") Unless we sing the up-beats as up-beats moving to another down-beat, that is, to the following count of "1," our music has no life. The final group of the musical phrase is always a prolonged support of the melody, a point of rest, and therefore is a dotted note — counted "1-2."

It is easy to count the time of Gregorian music. The rules are simple.

Rules for Counting

1. Every time-group is counted either "1-2" or "1-2-3."
2. Every dotted note is counted "1-2."
3. Every note marked with an ictus is counted "1." (The count of "1" is always the ictic note even when the ictus is not marked.)
4. The first note of a pressus is counted "1."
5. Generally speaking, the first note of a neum is counted "1." (The salicus and the pressus are exceptions to this rule.)
6. A single punctum between two neums is counted with the neum which precedes the punctum.
7. A single punctum after a full bar is counted "2." (As we note below, every full bar allows at least a one-count rest for a breath. If the melody after a full bar begins on the count of "1," the rest is understood *before* the bar and is counted as "3" in the time-group which begins on the last dotted note. If the melody after a full bar begins on the count of "2," as is the case which we are considering under this Rule No. 7, the rest is understood *after*

the bar and is counted as "1." The first note is then the second of a time-group and is counted as "2." In modern notation the rest is printed in its place either before or after the full bar. In the Gregorian notation, the rest is understood but is not printed.)

We have spoken of the ictic note and we know by now that the ictus marks the count of "1." The ictus also marks the place of the down-beat, or the *thetic* note, which is the rhythmic support of the melody. The ictus is sometimes referred to as the *vertical episema.*

Generally speaking, however, the word *episema* is used to refer to the *horizontal episema.* This is the long straight line drawn either over the entire neum or only over the first note of it. This episema means that the notes or note over which it is written should be slightly prolonged. If the horizontal episema is placed *over* a pes, generally both tones are slightly prolonged. If it is placed *under* a pes, generally only the first tone is prolonged.

On a four-line and a five-line staff below, you will find a table of the ordinary neums[4] with a few of their variants. Can you count each?

Pes or *Podatus*

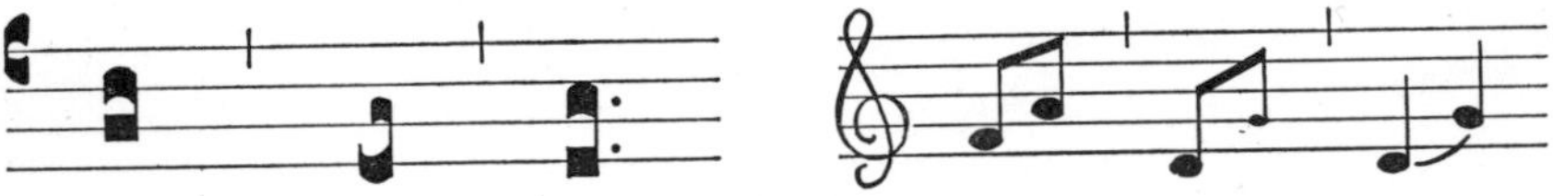

Clivis

Scandicus

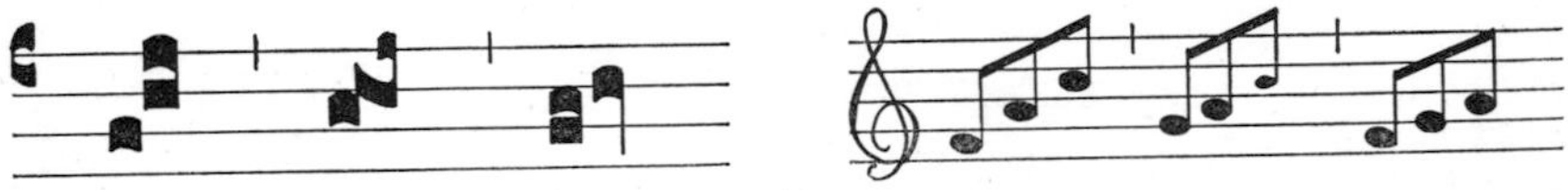

Salicus

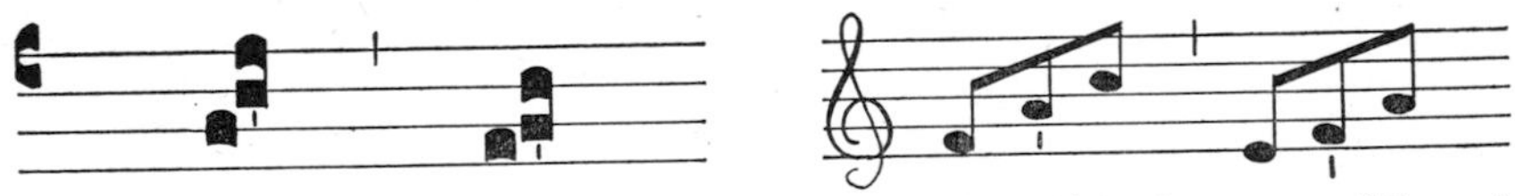

[4] The rhythmical signs are used with the permission of Desclée and Company of Tournai, Belgium.

Quilisma

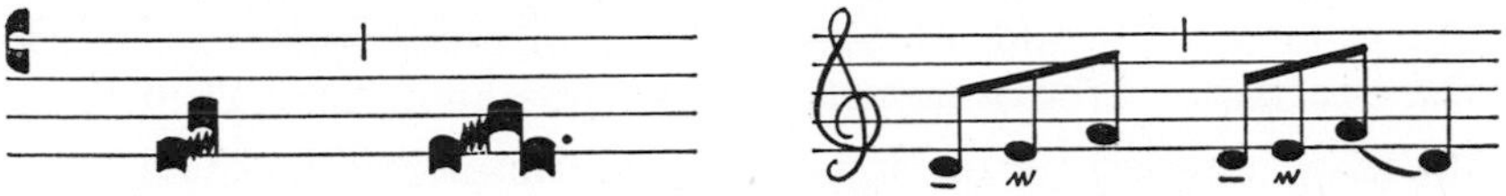

Climacus

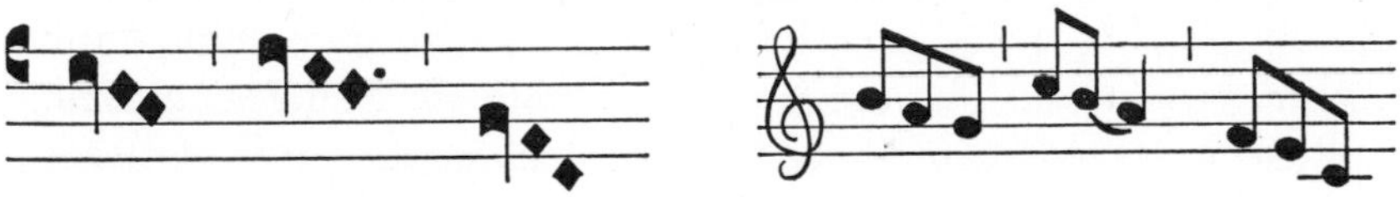

Torculus

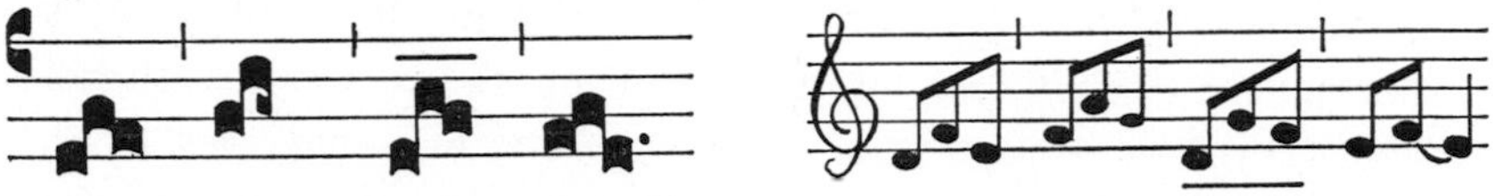

Porrectus

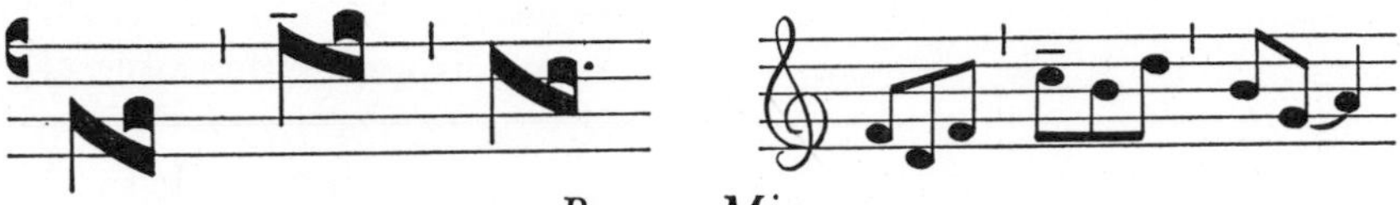

Pressus Minor

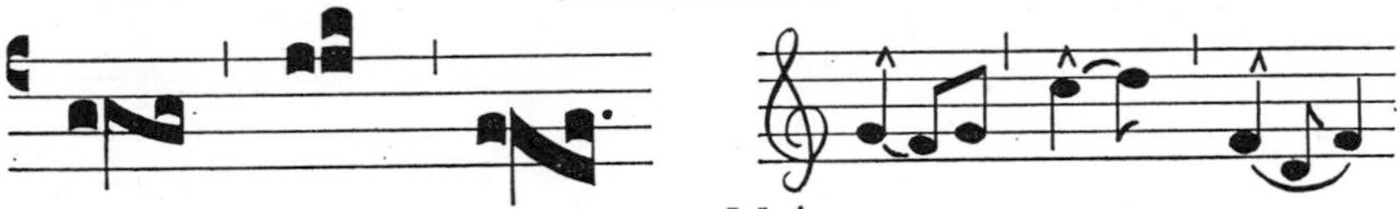

Pressus Major

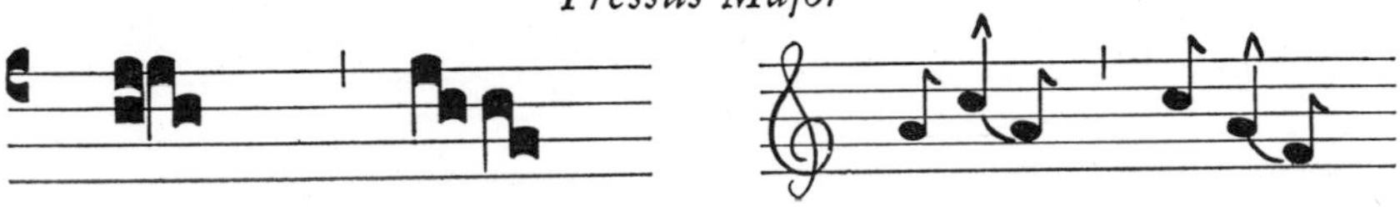

The *Agnus Dei* from *Mass IX*

5.
A- gnus De- i * qui tol- lis pec-ca- ta mun- di:
5.

IV. THE BARS

Music is a language; therefore, like other languages, its symbols must have a punctuation. The punctuation of Gregorian chant is found in the bar lines. The treatment of the musical punctuation found at the bars (and at the dotted notes) is discussed in the chapter on rhythm. There we compare the rhythmic movement in a melody to the movement of an automobile along an ordinary street. The energy of the motor is changed and controlled by a good driver at all pauses — alleyways, ends of blocks, and red lights at arterial highways. (See pages 204–205.)

1. A *quarter bar* cuts only the fourth line of the staff. It marks the end of the smallest section of the music, the *incisa.* Breath may be taken at the quarter bar, but since the melody may not be delayed, it is better not to take a breath here unless the text calls for a break in the tone. The quarter bar is like the comma in literary composition. In the chapter on rhythm we consider this bar as a "side street" or as "the end of a block."

2. A *half bar* cuts the third and second line of the staff. It marks the close of a larger section of the music, the *member.* A breath may be taken at the half bar, but the melody may not be delayed unduly; it should emphasize the text sung at that spot. Sometimes the punctuation of the text admits of a longer breath; sometimes the text permits only a very short "stolen" breath. Rhythmically, this is the "red light" which suddenly changes to "green" for the next phrase.

3. A *full bar* is drawn from the fourth to the first line. It marks the end of a *phrase.* Here we have a pause for a deep breath — a pause equaling at least one full count of silence. The rest or pause is not written on the Gregorian staff, but we are expected to know that it is understood there and are to observe it — a full count of silence. (Some authors even suggest a silence of two counts.) This silence must not disturb the flow of the rhythm. Rhythmically, this is the "red light" at which we pause but at which we keep the "engine" pulsing.

4. Two full bars form what is called a *double bar.* The double

bar is always used at the close of a composition, or, in the course of a composition, at the close of an important section.

V. THE SCALES

We generally speak of scales as being *chromatic* or *diatonic.* (1) A chromatic scale is a scale of half steps only. (2) A diatonic scale is a scale which uses whole and half steps in their natural order, that is, with no chromatics or accidentals. The scale made up of whole and half steps as they are found on the white keys of the piano is diatonic.[5]

Modern music uses two modes of the diatonic scale, the *major* and the *minor*. The major mode begins on **C** and uses the white keys of the piano to the octave **C**, that is, **C–D–E‿F–G–A–B‿C′** or 1–2–3‿4–5–6–7‿i̇. The minor mode (the natural minor) begins on **A** and uses only the white keys of the piano to the octave **A.** It is true that we have fifteen major scales, but they are only the scale of **C** transposed. We also have fifteen scales of the natural minor which are still the **A Minor** transposed. By using accidentals we may vary the minor scales a little, but we still have only the natural minor with accidentals.

The chromatic scale, which is a series of half steps, was considered by the plainsong writers to be too weak for Church music. Gregorian uses only the diatonic scale. Gregorian music, however, has not only two modes of the diatonic scale but eight. These modes can be considered as four different scales but since in the official music books of the Church they are marked as eight we shall consider them as eight. They are:

the scales of **D** and **A** (Modes 1 and 2) with the final on **D**,
the scales of **E** and **B** (Modes 3 and 4) with the final on **E**,
the scales of **F** and **C** (Modes 5 and 6) with the final on **F**, and
the scales of **G** and **D** (Modes 7 and 8) with the final on **G**.

A later chapter will discuss each mode in more detail.

The Gregorian scales have no accidentals except that of **B-flat.**

[5] We will use the usual sign of the whole and half steps. A whole step is signified by a straight line: —. A half step is signified by a curved line: ‿.

The accidental of **B-flat** is allowed in any mode but it appears very commonly in the Gregorian scale of **F** and is often used in the scale of **D**. The sign of the accidental is a rhombus-shaped figure (♭) which changes the **B** in the melody to **B-flat** (1) until the Latin word which is being sung is completed, (2) until the next bar line on the staff, or (3) until a natural sign cancels the flat.

Every time we sing Gregorian melodies we are singing in the Gregorian modes whether we know it or not. The Arabic numeral at the beginning of each composition tells us in which mode it is. As we said above, these modal scales all fit the white keys of the piano. Beginning on **C** and following the white keys of the piano to the octave **C′** we may sing *do–re–mi‿fa–sol–la–ti‿do*. Singing thus we will have whole steps between each degree of the scale except between *mi* and *fa* and *ti* and *do*. *Mi* to *fa* and *ti* to *do* are half steps. Gregorian notation is always written on the staff "in the key of **C**." If, therefore, in all Gregorian scales we always call the **C**, *do*, it will be easy for us to find the melody since the pattern between the tones remains the same. Thus:

C – D – E ‿ F – G – A – B ‿ C′

1 – 2 – 3 ‿ 4 – 5 – 6 – 7 ‿ $\dot{1}$

do – re – mi ‿ fa – sol – la – ti ‿ $\overline{do}$

B-flat we call *te* (pronounced as an Italian or Latin word); it is written in numbers as $\not{7}$. **If we have A, B-flat, C,** the place of the half steps is changed.

A – B ‿ C′	is changed to	**A ‿ B-flat – C′**
6 – 7 ‿ $\dot{1}$		6 ‿ $\not{7}$ – $\dot{1}$
la – ti ‿ $\overline{do}$		*la ‿ te –* $\overline{do}$

REVIEW QUESTIONS

1. Describe the Gregorian staff.
2. How were melodies learned before the staff was invented? What is chironomy?

3. Who was Guido of Arezzo? For what is he noted?
4. Name and describe the Gregorian notes.
5. What is a neum?
6. Name, describe, and give the count of the simple neums.
7. Name, describe, and give the count of the first four special neums.
8. Describe an oriscus, a distropha, a tristropha, a bivirga, and a trivirga.
9. How are the liquescent notes to be sung?
10. What is the purpose of a *custos?*
11. What is the duration of all Gregorian notes?
12. What is the rhythm of a two-note time-group? What is the rhythm of a three-note time-group?
13. Give the rules for counting the time of Gregorian music. Can you apply them?
14. What is the ictus?
15. Describe the horizontal episema. What does this sign mean?
16. Explain the significance and treatment of each of the bar lines used on the Gregorian staff.
17. Describe the chromatic scale. Describe the diatonic scale.
18. Which kind of scale is used in Gregorian melodies?
19. How many scales are used in Gregorian music? Name them.
20. Which accidental appears in Gregorian music? For how long is it effective?
21. Beginning on **C** and following the white keys of the piano, build the Gregorian scale (1) in letter names, (2) in numbers, and (3) in *sol-fa* syllables.
22. Begin on **D** and do the same; begin on **E**; begin on **F**; begin on **G.**
23. Prepare to sing the answers to Questions 21 and 22.
24. Where are the half steps in the scale of **C?** Answer in letter names, in numbers, and in *sol-fa* syllables.
25. What *sol-fa* syllable is given to the **B-flat?** How is it written in numbers?
26. How does a **B-flat** in the melody change the scale pattern of whole and half steps?
27. How can we tell the mode of the melody even before we prepare to sing it?

D. The Pronunciation of Church Latin

In the Gregorian, the language of the music, the spirit of the music, the rhythm of the music, all arise from the language of the words, the Latin. We could hardly say too much about what Latin means to our official worship. In any good vocal music the words are of first importance and this is especially true of the words in the sung prayer of the Church. Latin in itself is by no means a dead language, though it may be dead as far as we are concerned if we know nothing of it. To fully understand it we should have to give it real study and much would be gained by so doing. It is quite easy, however, to get at least an idea of the Latin by learning the meanings of words which are commonly used in our prayers. For this reason some interlinear translations have been placed in the appendix. These are translations with the English equivalent written below the Latin words.

We must be able to pronounce the words if we are to sing them. With a certain amount of study this is quite easy to do.

I. THE VOWELS

All words have vowels and consonants. The vowels in Latin and English are the same—*a, e, i, o,* and *u.* Unlike the English vowels, however, each vowel in Latin has only one sound. This sound is best learned by imitation. General directions for vowel pronunciation follow.

a is as the *a* in the English word "father" — P*á*ter
e is as the *e* in the English word "red" — Am*é*n
is sometimes sounded more like the "eh" in the initial sound of the English *a* — D*é*us
i is as the *i* in the English word "police" — F*íli*um
o is as the *o* in the English word "for" — D*ó*minus
u is as the *oo* in the English word "moon" — *ú*num

Special cases:

y is like the Latin *i* — márt*y*rum
ae and *oe* are diphthongs and are like the Latin *e* — c*aé*li, p*oé*na
au is like the vowel sound in the English word "house" (*au* is never separated) — l*au*dámus
— *au*xílium

II. THE CONSONANTS

Most consonants have the same sound in Latin and English. Exceptions:

Before *e, ae, oe*	(1) *c* is like *ch*	— caéli
i and *y*	(2) *cc* is like *tch*	— écce
	(3) *sc* is like *sh*	— descéndit

	(4) *g* is a soft *g*	— regína
Otherwise	(1) *c* is like *k*	— cáro
	(2) *cc* is like *k*	— ecclésiam
	(3) *sc* is like *sk*	— discussúrus
	(4) *g* is a hard *g*	— glória
(5) *ch* is always like *k*		— chérubim
(6) *th* is always like *t*		— thrónum, Sábaoth
(7) *gn* is like the *ny* in the English word "canyon"		— ágnus
(8) *h* is like *k* in the words *mihi* and *nihil*		— míhi
otherwise *h* is silent		— hónor
(9) *ti* before any vowel and after any letter except *s, t,* or *x,* is like *tsi*		— grátia, laetítia
ti before any vowel but preceded by *s, t,* or *x* is regular		— hóstia
(10) *j* is like the English *y*		— Jésus
(11) *xc* before *e* is like a soft *x* (or *k*) with *sh*		— excélsis
otherwise *xc* is treated regularly (*x* with *k*)		— excussórum

III. SYLLABICATION

It is much easier to pronounce a word if we can sound it in syllables. Breaking a word into syllables is called syllabication. In the syllabication of Latin words we shall follow the rules given in the *C.C.C.* of the Gregorian Institute of America[6] quoted below:

> The following rules are flexible enough to allow an exception here and there for the benefit of the singers who must think of both *diction* and *tone production.* [These rules, for the most part, follow the general classical rules of syllabication.]
>
> Rule 1. Every Latin word has as many syllables as it has vowel sounds or diphthongs, e.g., *De-us, cae-lum, vi-si-bi-li-um, fi-li-i.*
>
> Rule 2. A single consonant between two vowels is written and pronounced with the following vowel. . . .
>
> Rule 3. Double consonants are separated. . . .
>
> Rule 4. Where two different consonants occur together, the first is pro-

[6] *Catholic Choirmasters Course,* Clifford Bennett, editor (Toledo: Gregorian Institute of America, 1945), C.L., 25.

nounced with the preceding vowel, e.g., mu*n*-*di*, e*r*-go. *Exceptions:* the consonants *ct, cr, gn, mn, pt, pr, sc, st, tr,* generally commence a new syllable, especially in the liturgical texts. . . . Generally *cl* is written and pronounced together. Naturally, the diphthongs *th, ph, ch,* and *sh* are not separated.

Rule 5. Where three consonants occur together, the first is pronounced with the preceding vowel, e.g., co*n*-spe-ctu, se-pu*l*-cra, e*x*-spe-cto.

Rule 6. Compound words are divided according to derivation into their original parts. . . . However, there are cases to prove that the exception may be the case when the preposition ends in a single consonant and the next letter of the compound is a vowel, e.g., *per-e-o,* usually *pe-re-o; trans-i-re, tran-si-re.*

REVIEW QUESTIONS

1. In vocal music, of what importance is the word? Is this true of a text meant to be sung to Gregorian music?
2. What is an "interlinear translation"?
3. Study the directions given for the pronunciation and articulation of the vowels and consonants of Latin words.
4. Study the rules for syllabication.
5. Which consonants are not separated?

E. Conclusion

It is the wish of the Church that we study both the liturgy and the music to which the liturgy is sung. That we learn the music of the liturgy has been solemnly requested of us many times, particularly in the *Motu Proprio on Sacred Music* of St. Pius X (1903); the apostolic constitution of Pius XI, *Divini Cultus Sanctitatem* (1928); and the encyclical, *Mediator Dei,* of Pius XII (1947).

What the Church asks us to do, she asks because she knows that thus God's glory and the sanctification of souls will be advanced. We have been asked to learn to sing the official worship of the Church so that we may take a very active part in this worship. We cannot learn all that we should about this important subject in a short time, but by continued study and prayer and with the assistance of the Holy Ghost, we shall grow constantly in the knowledge and understanding of whatever contributes to our active share in the worship of the Body of Christ. With the help of the Holy Spirit let us prepare ourselves to fulfill the desires of Pius XII stated in the *Mediator Dei:* "Let the full harmonious singing of our people rise to heaven like the bursting of a thundrous sea and let them testify by the melody of their song to the unity of their hearts and minds as become brothers and the children of the same Father."[7]

GENERAL AIMS

1. Steady growth in the knowledge of the liturgy of the Church and in the appreciation of what the liturgy means to God, to the Mystical Body, and to us individually as members of that Body.
2. Steady growth in the understanding of the theory of the chant — the neums, the counting, the rhythm.
3. Steady development of facility in reading the music of the chant — the modes and their characteristic melodies.
4. Steady development of correct pronunciation — vowels and consonants.
5. Steady growth in the understanding of the prayers of the Mass and of the Latin hymns.
6. Enough knowledge and appreciation of what the liturgy means to make us individually apostles of active participation in it.

REVIEW QUESTIONS

1. Give the titles, dates, and authors of the recent papal documents concerning the liturgy and its music.
2. Why have we been asked to study liturgical music?

[7] Pius XII, *Mediator Dei* (New York: America Press, 1948), No. 194.

CHAPTER II

OUR SACRED LITURGY

A. The Creation of Man

GOD is essentially perfect. Since He is in Himself all Wisdom, Goodness, Beauty, Love, Power, nothing can increase His happiness. Because of His goodness and love He wishes other beings to share the possession of His happiness. That is why God made angels and men.

To man, as we know, God gave natural gifts, preternatural gifts, and supernatural gifts. The natural gifts which God gave to man are wonderful, as were also the preternatural gifts, but surpassing all creation are the supernatural gifts. By them man is enabled to share in the very life of God Himself; he is brought into intimate union with the Divinity, and is empowered to do acts that increase this union and merit the vision of God for all eternity.

On this earth man is not given the beatific vision but rather the power, through God's grace, to merit it. Yet, in Eden, the companionship of Adam and Eve with God was most intimate. To continue in this state of wonderful happiness and to attain finally to the eternal face-to-face possession of God, only one thing was asked of them — that they should not eat of the Tree of Good and Evil. God required one sign by which they were to acknowledge their complete dependence on Him, one denial which would signify their giving of themselves to Him in loving submission. Satan deceived our first parents into acting as if God's will and their happiness were not two aspects of the same truth, as if their happiness would not be found in the union of their wills with God's will.

REVIEW QUESTIONS

1. What was God's purpose in creating angels and men?
2. What do we mean by God's "extrinsic glory"?
3. Explain the relationship between God's extrinsic glory and the happiness of men.
4. What gifts did God bestow on man? Explain each.
5. What was the form of the official sacrifice God required of Adam and Eve?
6. In what did Satan deceive our first parents?
7. Is it still true that man's happiness is to be found in the union of his will with God's will?

B. After Man's Sin

Because of sin, not only were man's natural gifts weakened, but the preternatural and supernatural gifts with which man had been originally endowed were lost to him. Nevertheless God did not change His desire for man's true happiness, and man still could find his restlessness satisfied only in loving union with God. Of himself man was, as always, incapable of effecting this union. As we know, God in His great mercy and goodness intervened and the only-begotten Son of God was given to man as Head and Redeemer.[1] The only-begotten Son of God would take to Himself a human nature, come to earth, and re-establish the bond between God and man by repairing the injustice done to God and restoring the supernatural life to man. What had been at first freely given by God to man was purchased now with great cost by the God-Man for all who would unite themselves to him.

The effect in our souls produced by this union with Christ is a mystery upon which we cannot meditate too much. Although it is a mystery, prayer and study will assist us to grow in its understanding.[2] With the restoration of our supernatural gifts in Christ,

[1] Thus the Church on Holy Saturday sings: "O happy fault, that merited so great a Redeemer!" "The second stage in God's economy for man's salvation was not merely a healing of the first but was as high above the first as Christ, the second Adam, is above the first Adam."

[2] Suggested popular readings on this subject are:

Francis P. Le Buffe, S.J., *Let's Look at Sanctifying Grace* (St. Louis: Queen's Work Press).

Most Rev. A. Noser, S.V.D., S.T.D., *Living With God in My Heart* (Techny: Mission Press).

the possibility of heaven and the face-to-face possession of God is also restored. Our union with Christ can be so close that we can become to Him "other Christs." And in proportion to our union with Him, we, "other Christs," "share in the eternal love of God that descended through Christ into this world of time in order that through Christ God might even in time give unto men a share in the eternal life of the Triune God."[3]

This share in the eternal life of the Triune God is personal to each, yet it is far more than that. The Holy Spirit, the Substantial Love of the Father and the Son, is one and the same Spirit in the Head and the members. Through this Spirit we enter the Christ-life. Through this Spirit the Christ-life grows within us. This personal sharing in the Christ-life joins us ever more closely in membership with Him and with all others joined with Him. "The mystical body here on earth is therefore a constantly growing fellowship of souls, in whom the Christ-life becomes ever more real."[4]

REVIEW QUESTIONS

1. How did sin affect the relationship of man with God?
2. Discuss shortly the effect of the supernatural gifts restored in Christ.
3. What is the office of the Holy Spirit with regard to the Christ-life within us?
4. How does Dom Virgil Michel characterize the Mystical Body?

C. Sacrifice

Sacrifice is an exterior sign of the interior return of ourselves in love to God; it is (1) the offering of something as a sign of our loving acknowledgment of God's dominion over us and (2) His acceptance of our offering. Or in the words of Canon Masure: "Sacrifice is the movement or action by which we try to bring our-

---

Raoul Plus, S.J., *God Within Us* (London: Burns, Oates and Washbourne, Ltd.), and *In Christ Jesus* (New York: Benziger Brothers).

Daniel A. Lord, S.J., *Our Part in the Mystical Body* (St. Louis: Queen's Work Press).

Dom Columba Marmion, O.S.B., *Christ in His Mysteries* (London: Sands and Company, Ltd.).

M. Eugene Boylan, O.Cist.R., *The Mystical Body* (Maryland: Newman Book Shop).

[3] Virgil Michel, O.S.B., *Our Life in Christ* (Collegeville: The Liturgical Press, 1939), p. 33.

[4] *Ibid.*, p. 36.

selves to God, our end, to find our true beatitude in our union with Him."[5] It will always be true that "to recognize the rights of God, to make an apparent renunciation of ourselves, is to attain our end and to achieve ourselves."[6]

Of its very nature, sacrifice expresses adoration, thanksgiving, and petition. Because of sin, sacrifice must also include reparation.

Any act or sign by which man signifies a return of himself in love to God is, in a general sense, a sacrifice. A sacrifice, to be one in which all share, that is, a liturgical sacrifice, must be offered by an official delegate (a priest) according to a rite which the senses can follow. In a sacrifice of propitiation for sin, the victim must be completely surrendered to God in the name of the sinner (or sinners) and destroyed according to the rite commanded by Him. Any sacrifice, to be complete, must be accepted by God. "Sacrifice is in the end union with God."[7]

REVIEW QUESTIONS

1. What is sacrifice?
2. What sentiments of worship are expressed in sacrifice?
3. A liturgical sacrifice of propitiation may be defined in five points. What are these points?

D. Sacrifice in the Old Law

As we have said, because of sin man's sacrifice, of itself, could never be acceptable to God. Yet in virtue of the Sacrifice of the Redeemer to come, men who lived between the time of the sin of Adam and Eve and the Redemption could offer gifts signifying the gift of themselves, and be acceptable to God. As a matter of fact, God Himself established the rites according to which certain sacrifices had to be offered to Him at specified times.[8] The account of the establishment of these sacrifices is found in the Old Testament books of Leviticus, Numbers, Deuteronomy, and others. Many

[5] Eugene Masure, *The Christian Sacrifice,* translated with a preface by Dom Illtyd Trethowan (London: Burns, Oates and Washbourne, Ltd., 1944; New York: Kenedy and Sons, 1947), p. 41.

[6] *Ibid.,* p. 54.

[7] *Ibid.,* p. 152.

[8] Read *Mediator Dei* (New York: The America Press, 1948), No. 16.

of these sacrifices prefigured in signs Christ's own sacrifice of Himself. They were acceptable to God and effective for the people because of the grace of the coming Redeemer.

REVIEW QUESTIONS

1. Discuss the necessity and origin of the sacrifices of the Old Law.
2. Were these sacrifices truly acceptable to God? Why were they accepted by Him?

E. The Sacrifice of Christ

"Sacrifice and oblation thou wouldst not: but a body thou hast fitted to me: Holocausts for sin did not please thee. Then said I: Behold I come: in the head of the book it is written of me: that I should do thy will, O God" (Hebr. 10:5–7).

Everything in the life of the eternal Son of God become man was a perfect sacrifice, for everything in His human life was absolutely given to the Godhead within Him. Unceasingly He expressed the return of Himself to His Father in love, and unceasingly He was united with Him.[9]

We can be sure that the forms of liturgical sacrifice decreed by God for His chosen people were perfectly observed by Christ in virtue of whom they were pleasing to the Father. "Do not think that I am come to destroy the law, or the prophets. I am not come to destroy, but to fulfil" (Mt. 5:17).

We cannot expect to understand the mystery of Christ fully. With prayer and study we shall grow in this understanding. For our present purpose we must remember that although as the Sacrifice of the only Son of God made man, Christ's Sacrifice would not have had to express reparation, yet as the Sacrifice of the Head of all humanity, Christ's Sacrifice had to express reparation as well as adoration, thanksgiving, and petition. These sentiments were expressed through all His acts, but they came to a climax and were particularly expressed in His Sacrifice of Himself on the cross. Finally, here was the Sacrifice which took the place of, and completely suppressed, the symbolic liturgies of the past.

[9] Read No. 17 of the *Mediator Dei*.

REVIEW QUESTION

1. What does this handbook tell us of the sacrifice of Christ?

F. Christ's Sacrifice in Our Liturgy

Christ's Sacrifice was perfect and complete.[10] By It He offered to His heavenly Father in the name of mankind a worship worthy of the Godhead; by It He made possible a return of man to God and the union of man with God which would result. "I am come that they may have life" (Jn. 10:10).

Christ did even more than offer His Sacrifice for us. He made it possible and even commanded us to offer His Sacrifice (and our sacrifice through, with, and in His). This He did in establishing the liturgy. He established a rite by which we may renew His sacred Passion, Resurrection, and Ascension, and He instituted sacred signs through which we may enter the life He purchased for us, or through which this life is increased in our souls. Thus He made His Sacrifice more completely ours.[11] Truly He is our Way, our Truth, and our Life. "No man cometh to the Father, but by me" (Jn. 14:6). All our liturgy is *per Christum Dominum nostrum*. It is only through Christ that we are brought into the current of the life of God; it is only through Him that His life in us is increased.

Pius XII thus summarizes what we have been considering:

> . . . the divine Redeemer has so willed it that the priestly life begun with the supplication and sacrifice of His mortal body should continue without intermission down the ages in His Mystical Body which is the Church. . . . In obedience, therefore, to her Founder's behest, the Church prolongs the priestly mission of Jesus Christ mainly by means of the sacred liturgy. She does this in the first place at the altar, where constantly the sacrifice of the cross is represented and, with a single difference in the

[10] Read "The Only Son's Return" in *The Christian Sacrifice* of Canon Masure (New York: Kenedy and Sons, 1947).

[11] Our sacrifice offered in the liturgy of the Mass is a Perfect Sacrifice since (1) at the Last Supper, as in the Mass, Christ makes His Sacrifice ours, and (2) in the Mass Christ makes our sacrifice His since He changes the very sign of our sacrifice into Himself. Nevertheless our part of this Perfect Sacrifice must ever increase in perfection.

manner of its offering, renewed. She does it next by means of the sacraments, those special channels through which men are made partakers in the supernatural life. She does it, finally, by offering to God, all Good and Great, the daily tribute of her prayer of praise.[12]

The life of Christ in us, our eternal life begun even here on earth, increases as long as we are on earth if we so desire. This Christ-life is dependent on the offering of ourselves to God in love according to His will, and on His acceptance of our offering. "If any one love me, he will keep my word, and my Father will love him, and we will come to him, and will make our abode with him" (Jn. 14:23).[13] The grace of sharing in His life is obtained for us in our Redemption by Christ, and is renewed and applied to our souls by His Redemption continued in the sacred liturgy.

All the liturgy is sacrificial. We realize in part how this is true of the Eucharist. We shall increase our preparedness for the graces offered us if we consider further the sacrificial aspects of the Eucharist and the sacrificial aspects of the other Sacraments and of the Divine Office as well.[14]

REVIEW QUESTIONS

1. Why did Christ establish the liturgy?
2. What does the liturgy effect in our souls?
3. All our liturgy is "through Christ our Lord." Explain.
4. How does the Church prolong "the priestly mission of Jesus Christ"?
5. On what does the Christ-life in us depend? Why does this give us the "right" to the Christ-life?

G. The Offering of the Whole Man

When we make a return of ourselves to God we should make a

[12] *Mediator Dei,* Nos. 2 and 3.

[13] Our turning to God is by our free will but it is also the result of God's grace. (See *Summa Theologica,* Part II [First Part], Q. 109, A. 6, Obj. 1 and 4.) "Without me you can do nothing" (Jn. 15:5). "No man can come to me, except the Father, who hath sent me, draw him" (Jn. 6:44). "By this hath the charity of God appeared towards us, because God hath sent his only begotten Son into the world, that we may live by him. In this is charity: not as though we had loved God, but because he hath first loved us, and sent his Son to be a propitiation for our sins. . . . Let us therefore love God, because God first hath loved us" (1 Jn. 4:9–10, 19). How grateful we should be to Infinite Love incessantly seeking us!

[14] See Dom Virgil Michel's *Our Life in Christ* and the *Proceedings for the Liturgical Week* for 1943.

complete return of ourselves, just as we are in relation to God. To Him each of us is an individual, a personally adopted son of God; therefore, our return to Him must be a personal, individual offering. Because of our union with all who possess the Christ-life, we are also members of His Body, members of His members. Consequently our return to Him must be made visibly with them; our worship must be co-offered, or, as we generally say, it must be corporate. The liturgy fulfills both the individual and the corporate need of man for his complete return to God.

REVIEW QUESTION

1. Discuss "the offering of the whole man" to God.

H. Conclusion

All the points in this chapter could be developed more fully. Yet from this short study we may easily see the importance and the need of the liturgy for the glory of God and the sanctification of souls.[15] And we shall see more easily why it is that our Holy Father urges us to learn all we can about the liturgy[16] and to participate in it as fully as we are able.[17]

[15] See *Mediator Dei,* No. 26.
[16] *Ibid.,* No. 202.
[17] *Ibid.,* Nos. 23–24, 98–128, and 192–194.

CHAPTER III

PARTICIPATION IN THE LITURGY

A. The Liturgy Itself

THE liturgy is the official prayer of the Church. Through the ministry of those ordained by the Church for this end, it is the prayer of Christ, the Head, and of His whole Church,[1] no matter where it is offered or when it is offered.

Christ came on earth to repair the wrong that man had done to God, to open heaven for us, and to win for us the graces we need to get there. These graces are ours if we but use the means Christ has given us to gain them. The chief means of gaining these graces are the Sacraments and prayer.

There are two kinds of prayer in the Church, two aspects under which we may consider the worship paid to God by His Mystical Body: liturgical or public prayer, and private prayer. (1) Liturgical prayer is *official* prayer. It is offered by and in the name of the whole Church, Christ and His members, regardless of the number present at that prayer. In the Roman Rite, the term *liturgical prayer* includes the Sacraments, the Mass, and the Divine Office. (2) Private prayer is *unofficial* prayer. It is not offered in the name of the whole Church but in the name of those praying it at the time. The whole Church profits by any prayer offered by any of her individual members, but not in the same way that she profits by the offering of her official prayer.

When we were baptized we became members of Christ; we entered into communication with His life in each individual member of His Church. This Christ-life is developed in us particularly

[1] See *Mediator Dei,* No. 20.

through the liturgy. Our Holy Mother the Church knows this and takes care of us as her dear children. Thus we are bound in conscience for our own spiritual good to offer the liturgy at specified intervals. We realize this with regard to the reception of the Sacraments. The same is true with regard to offering the Mass. We are compelled to offer this liturgy, under pain of mortal sin, on Sundays and holydays of obligation; we are urged to offer it more frequently. Priests offer the liturgy of the Divine Office daily.

We say "offer Mass" and not "hear Mass." It is possible that the common and acceptable phrase "hear Mass" may convey a very wrong impression to us. For the Mass is the renewal of the Sacrifice of Calvary; in It Christ offers Himself for us, and we offer ourselves with Him to the eternal Father.

REVIEW QUESTIONS

1. What is the liturgy?
2. Distinguish between liturgical prayer and private prayer.
3. How does the liturgy affect the Christ-life within us?
4. Why is it to be preferred that we say "offer Mass" instead of "hear Mass"?

B. Private Prayer

We are treating particularly of liturgical prayer, but we do not disclaim the need for private prayer. Private prayer is very necessary for us and we must not neglect it. Pius XII, in his encyclical on the *Mystical Body,* says: "It is true that public prayer, prayers, that is, that are offered by Mother Church, because of the dignity of the Spouse of Christ, excel any other kind of prayer; but no prayer, even the most private, lacks its own dignity and power, and all prayer is immensely helpful to the Mystical Body."[2]

Private prayer and liturgical prayer should be united in our personal prayer life. In his encyclical on the sacred liturgy, *Mediator Dei,* Pius XII "warmly recommends" devotions "not strictly liturgical."[3] He discusses this in Numbers 172 to 185 of the encyclical and asserts that "there could be no real opposition between the

[2] Pius XII, *Mystici Corporis* (New York: The America Press, 1943), No. 105.
[3] *Mediator Dei,* see No. 172 ff.

sacred liturgy and other religious practices."[4] The Holy Spirit must be given freedom to work in us as He wills. He will not work oppositely in our private and our liturgical prayer.[5] Therefore we may judge whether or not He is inspiring our "devotions" by whether or not they are effective in making the liturgy "loved and spread daily ever more widely, and in making the faithful approach the sacraments with more longing desire, and in obtaining for all things holy due respect and honor."[6]

With regard to "devotions," the encyclical previously declares: "Moreover, by nourishing the spiritual life of the faithful they prepare them to take part in the sacred public functions with greater fruit."[7] "Sacred public functions" is another way of saying "the sacred liturgy." As we saw in Chapter II, the liturgy is absolutely necessary for us if we would enter upon or live the Christ-life. All that we do should, hand in hand with the liturgy, increase the Christ-life within us.

REVIEW QUESTION

1. Discuss the relationship which should exist between liturgical and private prayer in our individual prayer life.

C. Recent Papal Acts Regarding Participation in the Liturgy

I. ST. PIUS X

St. Pius X, who was pope from 1903 to 1914, took as his motto "to restore all things in Christ." This was in August, 1903. On November 22, 1903, in the *Motu Proprio on Sacred Music,* he made it a matter of obligation that we strive toward the ideal in regard to participation in the liturgy. The ideal is that each person have as full a participation in the liturgy as possible, according to the plan of the Church. St. Pius X made this a matter of obligation because of its importance to our souls now and for eternity.

[4] *Ibid.,* No. 173.
[5] *Ibid.,* No. 37.
[6] *Ibid.,* No. 181.
[7] *Ibid.,* No. 175.

In the introduction to this *Motu Proprio,* St. Pius X says:

> It being our most eager wish that the true Christian spirit may flower again in every way and be upheld by all the faithful, before anything else it is necessary to see to the holiness and dignity of the temple, where the faithful gather to gain that spirit from its first and indispensable source: the active participation in the sacred mysteries and the public and solemn prayer of the Church.[8]

These direct words of St. Pius X are commonly expressed thus: "Active participation in the sacred mysteries and in the solemn public prayer of the Church is the primary and most indispensable source of the true Christian spirit."

Pius X fostered active lay participation in the liturgy by (1) making it *possible* and a matter of *obligation* to sing at High Mass; (2) by making it *possible* and *praiseworthy* to receive Holy Communion frequently — even daily; and (3) by making it *possible* for the laity to have the missal.[9]

As pastor at Salzano, at Treviso, as bishop of Mantua, and as patriarch of Venice, Joseph Sarto saw the good resulting from participation in the liturgical prayer life of the Church. It was natural that when he became Pope Pius X he would endeavor to bring as many as possible to this source of sanctity. As he said in his catechism:

> The feasts were instituted for the very purpose of rendering a common supreme worship of adoration to God in His temples. The ceremonies, words, melodies, in a word, all the externals, have been so well assembled and adapted to diverse circumstances that the mysteries and truths of the events celebrated cannot but penetrate into the soul and there produce the corresponding acts and sentiments. If the faithful were well instructed, and celebrated the feasts in the spirit intended by the Church when she instituted them, there would be a notable renewal and increase of faith, piety, and religious instruction: the entire life of the Christian would thereby become better and stronger.[10]

[8] *The Motu Proprio of Church Music of Pope Pius X,* translation and commentary by C. J. McNaspy, S.J. (Toledo: Gregorian Institute of America, 1950), Introduction.

[9] Gerald Ellard, S.J., *The Dialog Mass* (New York: Longmans, Green and Company, 1942), p. 8. This paragraph is almost completely Father Ellard's expression.

[10] Pius X, cited by Lambert Beauduin, O.S.B., *Liturgy the Life of the Church,* translated by Virgil Michel, O.S.B., 2nd edition (Collegeville: Liturgical Press, 1929), p. 47.

II. POPE BENEDICT XV

Benedict XV was pope from 1914 to 1922. We would not expect that the European situation during those years would be of much natural assistance in continuing to develop the ideas and desires of St. Pius X. Yet we find Benedict XV praising and blessing those who were holding a congress to increase in the faithful the knowledge of the liturgy and the desire to take an active part in it. "All this cannot but serve admirably to bring the faithful into closer union with the priest, to lead them back to the Church, to nourish their piety, to give renewed vigor to their faith, to better their lives."[11]

III. POPE PIUS XI

Pius XI was elected pope in 1922. In the *Apostolic Constitution, "Divini Cultus Sanctitatem,"* he reaffirms the desires of St. Pius X concerning the active participation of the laity:

> It is most important that when the faithful assist in the sacred ceremonies . . . they should not be merely detached and silent spectators, but . . . they should sing alternately with the clergy or the choir as it is prescribed.[12]
>
> In order that the faithful may more actively participate in divine worship, let them be made once more to sing the Gregorian Chant, as far as it belongs to them to take part in it.[13]

Other passages from this document could be quoted. Let us note that Pius XI is not here regulating only the part of a special choir, but also the part of the congregation. If we read the words with which he closes the *Apostolic Constitution,* we shall realize the importance of his prescriptions.

IV. POPE PIUS XII

Concerning the importance of the liturgy itself, Pius XII says: "It should be clear to all, then, that God cannot be honored worthily

[11] Benedict XV through the letter of Peter Cardinal Gasparri, Papal Secretary of State, cited in *Orate Fratres,* Vol. IX, No. 7, p. 325.

[12] Pius XI, *Apostolic Constitution,* No. 9, as in *Sacred Music and the Catholic Church,* George V. Predmore (Boston: McLaughlin and Reilly, 1936).

[13] *Ibid.*

unless the mind and heart turn to Him in quest of the perfect life, and that the worship rendered to God by the Church in union with her divine Head is the most efficacious means of achieving sanctity."[14]

We would only have to scan the encyclical *Mediator Dei* to see how much of it deals with participation in the liturgy. Pius XII could not more definitely urge us to increase our appreciation of the liturgy and our participation in it. Let us read the encyclical itself. Read Numbers 80 to 128, 150, 192 to 194, 201, and others.[15] Let us, above all, co-operate with our pastors in their response to this request made of them:

> Try in every way, with the means and helps that your prudence deems best, that the clergy and people become one in heart and mind, and that the Christian people take such an active part in the liturgy that it becomes a truly sacred action of due worship to the eternal Lord in which the priest, chiefly responsible for the souls of his parish, and the ordinary faithful are united together.[16]

REVIEW QUESTIONS

1. What is the ideal of the Church with regard to participation in the liturgy?
2. What importance did St. Pius X attach to active participation in the liturgy?
3. Give the title and date of the document of St. Pius X on the liturgy and its music.
4. State three ways in which St. Pius X fostered active lay participation in the liturgy.
5. Cite an instance in which Benedict XV expressed his attitude toward active participation in the liturgy. What did he say?
6. Give the title and date of the document of Pius XI concerning the liturgy and its music.
7. Quote words of Pius XI which show his concern for the active participation of the laity.
8. Give the title and date of the encyclical in which Pius XII treats of the sacred liturgy.
9. Quote words of Pius XII, which express his desire for the fuller participation of the people in the corporate worship of the Church.

[14] *Mediator Dei,* No. 26.
[15] All the numbers given here are from the edition published by the America Press.
[16] *Mediator Dei,* No. 199.

D. Our Personal Need for Participation in the Liturgy

"The cooperation of the faithful is required so that sinners may be individually purified in the blood of the Lamb."[17] The eternal Father gave His only-begotten Son to ransom man from the consequences of his sin. "He who buys is Christ; the price is His Blood."[18] All that we could possibly need for our redemption and sanctification was obtained for us in the Sacrifice of Calvary. But it is not given to us unless we individually come into contact with Calvary; it is not given to us unless we co-operate with the means of grace our Lord provides. Therefore Pius XII reminds us: ". . . Christ, after redeeming the world at the lavish cost of His own blood still must come into complete possession of the souls of men. Wherefore, that the redemption and salvation of each person and of future generations unto the end of time may be effectively accomplished, and be acceptable to God, it is necessary that men should come into vital contact with the sacrifice of the cross, so that the merits which flow from it, should be imparted to them."[19]

It is particularly in the liturgy that we "come into vital contact with the sacrifice of the Cross." Pius XII says elsewhere: "The greatest, the most efficacious, and the holiest of all practices of piety is the participation of the faithful in the Holy Sacrifice."[20]

REVIEW QUESTIONS

1. With His Blood, Christ redeemed the souls of men. Are all souls then necessarily redeemed? Explain.
2. What does Pius XII say of participation in the Holy Sacrifice?

E. In What Active Participation Consists

The purpose of the liturgy is the purpose of Christ Himself: to give glory to God directly through a worship worthy of Him and

[17] *Ibid.*, No. 78.
[18] *Ibid.*, No. 76.
[19] *Ibid.*, No. 77.
[20] Pius XII to Rome's Lenten preachers in 1943, cited by Gerald Ellard, S.J., in the foreword to the *Mediator Dei* (New York: The America Press, 1948).

indirectly through the salvation and sanctification of men. The liturgy gives glory to God by expressing exteriorly and corporately the interior worship of the Church and by effecting in the souls of men a fuller Christ-life.[21] The purpose of participation in the liturgy must be the same as the purpose of the liturgy itself. "While the sacred liturgy calls to mind the mysteries of Jesus Christ, it strives to make all believers take their part in them so that the Divine Head of the Mystical Body may live in all the members with the fulness of His holiness."[22]

Pius X has told us that active participation in the liturgy is the foremost and indispensable source of the true Christian spirit. Pius XII says: ". . . all the faithful should be aware that to participate in the eucharistic sacrifice is their chief duty and supreme dignity."[23]

If to participate in the liturgy is so important, it is important that we know in what "participation" consists and how we may become more "active" in it. In Numbers 23 and 24 and Numbers 80 to 128 of the *Mediator Dei,* we are given definite papal instructions on this matter. We will attempt to summarize some points which may help us to follow these injunctions. We shall discuss particularly our participation in the Sacrifice of the Mass, for this is the liturgy at which we assist most frequently. The *Mediator Dei* also discusses and urges participation in the Divine Office, as we may read in Numbers 138 to 150. What we say with regard to participation in the Mass may be applied to participation in all the liturgy.

All exterior worship demands interior worship, or it is not worship at all. In the liturgy both these elements must be "intimately linked."[24]

Our participation in the worship of God may be called active inasmuch as we are active in expressing exteriorly our interior participation. Pius XII tells us that we participate in the liturgy inasmuch as we offer it with the priest and inasmuch as we offer our-

[21] As we have noted, God's glory and our happiness are two aspects of the same truth.
[22] *Mediator Dei,* No. 152.
[23] *Ibid.,* No. 80.
[24] *Ibid.,* Nos. 23–24.

selves as victims with the divine Victim.[25] In our active exterior participation in the liturgy, we aim to express the interior participation which is ours — the complete return of ourselves to God in union with Christ's own Sacrifice of Himself. Our active exterior participation should not only express our interior participation, but should act as a stimulus to a fuller interior participation.

"Participation involves several factors. It makes separate, practical demands of each person. The starting point for participation is holiness, the possession of sanctifying grace and its constant increase in the soul."[26]

Sanctifying grace gives us membership with those offering the liturgy, that is, with Christ and His Mystical Body. This membership must be expressed exteriorly. Thus the Church demands attendance at Mass on all Sundays and holydays of obligation, and the receiving of the Sacraments of Penance and Holy Eucharist at least once a year. She urges us to express our union with Christ through these means much more frequently than the law prescribes.

To receive Holy Communion during the Sacrifice of the Mass is our great privilege. In the Sacrifice of the Mass we express our interior desire to make a complete return of ourselves to God and to be united with Him. In the Consecration He changes the signs of the offering of ourselves (bread and wine) into Himself. Through these signs which have become Himself He unites Himself to us in Holy Communion. Thus the complete sacrifice is expressed exteriorly. This, surely, is "active participation."

The words *active participation* are often used to refer to a more or less actively *voiced* participation. Pius XII warns us that since our talents and characters, our needs and inclinations are varied, our response to a voiced participation will necessarily be varied also.[27] Yet he praises those who strive that "the faithful, united with the priest, may pray together in the very words and sentiments of the Church," as well as those "who strive to make the liturgy

[25] *Ibid.* Read Nos. 80–104.

[26] Robert E. Brennan, *The Apostolate of the Liturgy, A Commentary on Mediator Dei* (Washington, D. C.: N.C.W.C., 1948), p. 5.

[27] *Mediator Dei,* No. 108.

even in an external way a sacred act in which all who are present may share."[28]

The means of participation mentioned in *Mediator Dei* suggest more than a bodily presence at the liturgy, more than participation by intention only. The encyclical refers to the use of the Missal as an active means of promoting true interior participation. Voiced active participation includes (1) the singing of "hymns suitable to the different parts of the Mass";[29] (2) the "Missa Recitata" or dialog Mass; (3) the "Missa Cantata" or sung Mass; and (4) the High (or Solemn) Mass,[30] which is a sung Mass with three officiating priests or ministers, the celebrant, deacon, and subdeacon. Pius XII particularly recommends the High Mass.[31] The bishop is the celebrant of a Pontifical Mass. The pope is the bishop who is the celebrant of a Papal Mass.

REVIEW QUESTIONS

1. Discuss the relative importance of interior and exterior worship of God.
2. What, essentially, is holiness?
3. How does our holiness affect our participation in the liturgy?
4. According to the *Mediator Dei,* what should be our interior expression of our participation in the liturgy?
5. By what exterior means may we express and stimulate our interior participation?
6. What is a "Missa Recitata"? a "Missa Cantata"? a Solemn Mass? a Pontifical Mass? a Papal Mass?

F. The Place of Music in Participation in the Liturgy

Music has a very important place in participation in the liturgy. We have quoted from the *Motu Proprio* the desires of St. Pius X for the fuller active participation of the people in the liturgy. Yet we note that the *Motu Proprio* is entirely directed to the regulation of the music used in the liturgy.

A later chapter will discuss the music used in the liturgy. For the present, let us reflect that the interior return of ourselves to God is expressed exteriorly through prayer in word and prayer in act.

[28] *Ibid.*, No. 105.

[29] *Ibid.*

[30] In the United States both the Missa Cantata and the Solemn Mass are referred to as "High Mass."

[31] *Mediator Dei,* No. 106.

The music to which we sing the words must follow the spirit of the words themselves. Thus we may say that the purpose of music in the liturgical prayer of the Church is (1) to clothe with a suitable melody the words of the prayer (2) so that the faithful may enter more easily into the spirit expressed in the prayer, and (3) thus be more ready to receive the graces that Christ wills we receive through this prayer.

REVIEW QUESTIONS

1. What papal document suggests that music is intimately connected with a fuller participation in the liturgy? Explain.
2. How do we commonly express exteriorly the interior return of ourselves to God?
3. What is the purpose of music in the liturgical prayer of the Church?

G. Living Our Participation in the Liturgy

Strictly speaking, we do not participate in the liturgy when we offer the Masses which are being offered throughout the world. Yet in another freer sense we do participate, for these Masses are the Sacrifice of Christ offered by the Church in the name of all who are one in Christ, which we offer and have offered with the Church, and with which we have offered ourselves. We are told that there are on an average of four elevations of the Sacred Host every second. Joining ourselves with the offering of Christ's Sacrifice should enable us to live in the spirit of sacrifice and should increase our interior participation in the liturgy which we shall express exteriorly as circumstances permit.

The liturgy, as we have seen, is the source of our life in Christ. It is also meant to be a guide of Christian living. As we said above, we express our prayer in word and in act. Looking at the Mass alone it is easy to see how this prayer in word and in act could and should be both a model and guide for all the prayers and actions of our day.[32]

The Fore-Mass, or Mass of the Catechumens, is almost completely

[32] This idea was developed by Father Richard Rooney, S.J., of the Queen's Work, in a class, "The Mass, the Source and Guide of Christian Living," S.S.C.A., Spokane, Wash., 1951.

expressed in words. In this part of the Mass, God teaches us, not only through His inspired words in the Epistle and Gospel and through His Church speaking in the sermon, but also through the Psalms which He provided for our use in addressing Him and through the prayers which the Church has formulated to assist us to express our worship. God has here given us a definite model for the way we should express our worship of Him throughout the day.

In the Fore-Mass we learn by listening. In the Sacrifice-Banquet, or the Mass of the Faithful, we learn by doing. For in this part of the Mass, action predominates. Christ Himself takes the gift of bread and wine in which we offer ourselves, and changes it into His own Body and Blood. The bread and wine thus becomes the Perfect Love-Gift of man to God, the Man-God offered in sacrifice for man. The Perfect Love-Gift is also the Gift of God to man, and God Himself invites man to receive this Gift in Holy Communion. In the sacred action of the Mass, man renders to God perfect homage in, with, and through Christ, and as a result God gives Himself to man more fully. Here, also, God gives us a Model and Guide for our further acting and He shows us that as we give ourselves to Him with and in Christ, He will come to us.

In the Sacrifice of Calvary renewed in the Mass, Christ expresses not only the attitude of man to God Himself, but also the attitude that man should have toward his fellow man and through him to God. If the offering of ourselves with and in Christ is sincere and true, we will express our love for the Father as Christ expressed His, that is, by preferring in the circumstances of our lives to do and to accept what God wills for us; by striving to live, according to Calvary's example in the Mass, the Man-God's attitude toward God and man.

Our participation in the Mass increases the Christ-life within us. Our participation also increases the grace to live according to the model of Christian living presented to us in the Mass. A fuller Christian living is again a more complete participation in the liturgy which we have offered and a preparation for a still greater participation in the liturgy which we will offer.

REVIEW QUESTIONS

1. Discuss our participation in the liturgy which is being offered constantly throughout the world.
2. By what means does the Fore-Mass teach us how to pray in word?
3. By what means does the Fore-Mass teach us how to pray in act?
4. Considering the guidance given us in the Sacrifice-Banquet of the Mass, how should we act (1) with regard to God; (2) with regard to those who have authority over us; (3) with regard to our companions; (4) with regard to our enemies or those who have wronged us? (5) What should be our attitude toward our work; (6) toward our recreation?
5. What relation is there between participation in the liturgy and Christian living?

THOUGHT QUESTIONS

1. Does it make any difference to God if I participate in the liturgy as fully as circumstances permit? Explain.
2. Does it make any difference to the Church as a whole? Explain.
3. Does it make any difference to me personally? Explain.

CHAPTER IV

THE LITURGY AND ITS MUSIC

TO UNDERSTAND the spirit and expression of liturgical music we must understand the spirit of the prayer of which it is an integral part, that is, we must understand the spirit of the liturgy itself. *Liturgy* means official *public work* or *public service.*[1] When we use this word in connection with the worship of God, we mean that the liturgy is the public and external expression of the internal homage of the Mystical Body of Christ. In the words of Pius XII, "the Christian liturgy is the worship rendered by the Mystical Body of Christ in the entirety of its Head and Members."[2]

Man's innate tendency to express toward God sentiments of praise, adoration, thanksgiving, petition, and reparation, becomes even more natural for him as man becomes more and more aware of what he is before God, of what God is in Himself, of all that God has done for him, and of how much love he owes to God. The expression of praise, adoration, thanksgiving, petition, and reparation to God is worship of God.

The very highest form of worship is sacrifice. Sacrifice is "a dramatic, and intensely natural way of saying that we belong wholly to God."[3] In a sacrifice we offer a vicarious gift, the symbol of ourselves. When we sacrifice something to God, we are by this act seeking our greater union with Him. If God accepts the offering,

[1] The fact that prayers are said aloud and in public does not make them public in the sense used here. A *public* or liturgical *act* is done in the name of and for many. A *public* or liturgical *prayer* is offered in the name of and for many; the public and liturgical prayers of the Church are offered in the name of all the Church, Head and members.

[2] *Mediator Dei,* No. 20.

[3] Reynold Hillenbrand, "The Meaning of the Liturgy," *National Liturgical Week* (Conception: Liturgical Conference, 1942), p. 22.

the object itself becomes sacred and immediately becomes for us a means of the greater union we were seeking.

A. Mediator Dei

From the first moment of His Incarnation, our Lord, the God-Man, was a perfect Mediator between God and Man. As the Head of all mankind, He offers to God a perfect worship in the name of mankind; as the Head of His Mystical Body, He worships God in the name of His Body. Christ's worship culminated in the highest form of worship, the sacrifice of Himself on the cross. In this sacrifice, Priest and Victim are identified; Christ is both. In this sacrifice Christ, the Mediator, becomes a divine liturgist, for on the cross Christ acts in the name of all, and He signifies by this external sacrifice the internal homage of all who are one with Him.

On Calvary we have the two moments of all sacrifice: the Perfect Victim, offered to God and accepted by Him, become for us for whom it was offered a perfect means of Communion with the Divinity.

"These two moments — and we must never separate them in our thought — are, of course, found again in the Mass: one and the same sacrifice with that of the Cross, differing only in the mode of its offering. The Mass is not just a memorial of Calvary; not a repetition of Calvary; but the same essential act. The physical pain and the mental dereliction, these are over; but the Cross was the expression, through the humanity, of the eternal will-to-share; and the Mass is the same essential expression of the same will-to-share. God's cross goes on. Not a sparrow falls to the ground, today as yesterday, but our heavenly Father has care of it. And through the humanity of the Son, it is a *redeeming* care.

"But as the Pope has made very clear to us, in this redemptive process which goes on day by day, the Head of the Mystical members, needs the prayer and penance of the faithful.[4] By sharing in

[4] Pius XII in the encyclical *The Mystical Body of Christ* says, "this too, must be held, marvelous though it appear; Christ requires His members. . . . in carrying out the work of Redemption He wishes to be helped by the members of His Body." *Mystici Corporis* (New York: America Press, 1943), Nos. 54 and 55.

the Mass we share in the Cross and the fruits of the Cross."[5]

At the Last Supper our Lord instituted a rite in which He offered Himself in sacrifice to God for man, the sacrifice of His Life which would be accomplished on the morrow. In this rite were apparent all the requirements of a truly liturgical (but bloodless) sacrifice of propitiation:[6] (1) there was the action which indicated the complete surrender of the victim, (2) the offering was made by a duly authorized Priest, and (3) it was an offering that the senses could follow.

Our Lord, after instituting the rite at the Last Supper, said: "Do this for a commemoration of me" (Lk. 22:19). At every Mass since, this command has been fulfilled; the priest at each Mass makes the offering, as our Lord commanded and in the same manner as He did, of the Victim immolated on Calvary.

In the ancient sacrifices, the sacrifice-banquet held a very important place. In the sacrifice-banquet, the victim — offered, immolated, and accepted by God — was consumed. Partaking of the victim was a sign that by the sacrifice man was admitted to the participation of divine things. How especially true is this in the Sacrifice-Banquet, Holy Communion, in which the Victim received is God Himself. (Read St. Paul's First Epistle to the Corinthians, 10:14–29.)

We would consider ourselves privileged to be present when our Lord, the God-Man, prayed to His eternal Father. In truth we were and are present, for in all His prayer, but particularly in the Cenacle and on Calvary, we were present to Christ as members of His Mystical Body, and even now His prayer is continued in the world in the liturgy of His Church.

It may be said in two senses that Christ instituted the Christian liturgy. (1) He, Himself, was the first to offer it, and (2) He left to His Church directions as to how it should be offered. Although He did not regulate details of the liturgy, Christ clearly indicated

[5] Gerald Vann, O.P., *The Sorrow of God* (Oxford: Blackfriars Publication, 1946), p. 13. This pamphlet has been incorporated in *The Pain of Christ* by Father Vann and is published by Blackfriars.

[6] Cf. De La Taille, *The Mystery of Faith,* Bk. I (New York: Sheed and Ward, 1940), especially pp. 10–23.

the essentials. Pius XII calls the essentials the "divine elements."[7] Around the divine elements are human elements. These are the prayers and ceremonies which the Church has admitted to her liturgy and which may be changed by her authority under the guidance of the Holy Spirit. In a later chapter we shall see, in part, how the Church has modified and adapted the human elements of the liturgy according to the needs of the age and as circumstances and the good of souls required. In all the rites of the Church, the divine elements are the same, while the human elements vary.

The whole Christ offers liturgical worship to God; when we participate in the liturgy we must do so as members of the whole Christ. "It is the mystic Christ, the whole Christ — Jesus, the Life, the Head, and men, His living members; the divine Vine and His divinized branches — who re-enact this perfect liturgy."[8] "Nor should Christians forget to offer themselves, their cares, their sorrows, their distresses and their necessities in union with their divine Saviour upon the Cross."[9] All of the liturgy is ours. The Sacrifice of the Mass is *our* Sacrifice; ours to offer and with it to be offered. In the Sacrifice of the Mass we are, in a certain sense, to be both priest and victim. Our unity with the true Priest and Victim increases constantly as we make use of the graces given to us through the Cross. God gives these graces to us as we offer ourselves with the Sacrifice of the Cross.

REVIEW QUESTIONS

1. What is the meaning of the word "liturgy" as it applies to worship?
2. What fundamental attitudes of man's heart and mind are expressed in worship?
3. What is the highest form of worship?
4. What is sacrifice?
5. Why is Christ a perfect Mediator between God and man?
6. Why is Christ called a "divine liturgist"?
7. Explain the phrase "eternal will-to-share."
8. What does Pius XII mean when he says that Christ needs us, His members?

[7] *Mediator Dei,* No. 50.
[8] Reynold Hillenbrand, *loc. cit.*
[9] *Mediator Dei,* No. 104.

9. In the ancient sacrifices, what was the significance of the sacrifice-banquet?
10. Prove that Christ instituted the Christian liturgy.
11. What do you mean by the divine elements of the liturgy? What do you mean by the human elements?
12. Who participate in the liturgy?

B. Living the Liturgy Enables Us to Live Christ

As we have said, the perfect worship of God by Christ culminated in His complete Sacrifice on the cross. His worship, however, was constant from the first moment of His Incarnation and found expression in the varying circumstances of His human life.

Why did the Son of God become man? This demands a twofold answer.[10] He became man *primarily* to restore to God the extrinsic glory that had been lost by original sin — to carry out the divine glory perfectly in a human life. He became man *secondarily* to enable us to partake of the divine nature and thus, through us, to continue to carry out the divine glory.

Christ's only purpose in life was to do His Father's will; all He did is included in this. Thus He says of Himself, "I came down from heaven, not to do my own will, but the will of him that sent me" (Jn. 6:38), and, "I do always the things that please him" (Jn. 8:29).

Christ proclaimed publicly that Mary was blessed because she was His Mother, but even more blessed because she fulfilled the will of His Father. "Yea rather, blessed are they who hear the word of God, and keep it" (Lk. 11:28). When Mary said, "Be it done to me according to thy word" (Lk. 1:38), Christ began His human life in her. By doing and accepting His will, we permit Him to live and grow in us also, in grace.

Because of baptism, Christ lives in each of us living our human life. Because of Baptism, Christ walks again on earth glorifying and praising God in human circumstances.[11] Through the grace of Baptism we become divinized; God deifies us through a partici-

[10] Read Chapters XII–XVI of *The Mysteries of Christianity* by Matthias Joseph Scheeben (St. Louis: B. Herder, 1946). Note particularly pp. 418–430.

[11] This thought and its mode of expression is taken from lectures of Father Francis J. McGarrigle, S.J. For a fuller discussion of this and also of the will of God, see Father

pated likeness.[12] The Incarnation is continued in us. "I am the vine; you the branches" (Jn. 15:5). Therefore Christ tells us to say "Our Father" (Mt. 6:9), and He says, "I ascend to my Father and to your Father" (Jn. 20:17).

This Christ-life, begun in Baptism, should grow and fructify as does all life. All that we do in grace affects the Christ-life in us, but this life is particularly aided by the means Christ Himself ordained, that is, by the Sacraments. Christ has merited for us the grace of divinization. He is also our Model and Guide and the Source of our life in Him. Sanctifying grace is entirely the gift of God. The necessary condition for sanctifying grace is the fulfillment of the will of God. The chief and ordinary means of sanctifying grace is the liturgy, particularly the Sacraments.

We find in Christ a human life perfectly lived — a perfect human life according to the plan of God. He has left us, in the Scripture and in the traditions of His Church, a sure way of knowing the principles of a perfect human life. Moreover, the Church in the liturgical year presents to us the various occasions and circumstances of Christ's human life, those circumstances in which He manifested in detail the sentiments of filial love, preference for His Father's will, and seeking of His Father's glory which He expressed so intensely on Calvary. If we act according to the Spirit of Christ shown to us in the liturgy of the year, we will gradually "put on Christ," we will tend toward a perfect human life as God sees it.

Living according to the principles shown us in the liturgy and co-operating with the grace of which the liturgy is the source, is living the Christ-life. Living the Christ-life we participate in the mysteries of Christ. For "the mysteries of Christ are our mysteries."[13]

McGarrigle's *My Father's Will,* published by The Bruce Publishing Company, Milwaukee, Wis.

[12] St. Thomas Aquinas, *Summa Theologica* (London: Burns, Oates and Washbourne), Part II (First Part), Q. 112, Obj. 3 (American edition — New York: Benziger Bros.).

[13] This is the title and subject matter of the first chapter of *Christ in His Mysteries* by Dom Columba Marmion (London: Sands and Company, 1931), p. 3. In the summary heading of this chapter Marmion notes the "threefold reason whereby Christ's mysteries are ours: — Christ lived them for us; in them He shows Himself to us as our Exemplar; in them He unites us with Himself as the members of His Body."

But "participation in the mysteries of Jesus requires the cooperation of the soul. If God reveals the secrets of His love towards us, it is in order that we may accept them, that we may enter into His views and designs, and adapt ourselves to the Eternal Plan, apart from which neither holiness nor salvation are possible."[14]

The Church desires to assist us individually to become perfect human beings according to God's plan for us.[15] She desires that we find in the liturgy the *means* of living a perfect human life, and the *example* of this life as lived by Christ and His saints. Pius XII reminds us: ". . . the most pressing duty of Christians is to live the liturgical life, and increase and cherish its supernatural spirit."[16] He states further: ". . . the liturgy shows us Christ not only as a model to be imitated but as a Master to whom we should listen readily, a Shepherd whom we should follow, Author of our salvation, the Source of our holiness, the Head of the Mystical Body whose members we are, living by His very life."[17] The liturgy shows us the principles of a perfect human life and aids us by grace to apply these principles to our lives. The grace to live these principles is obtained especially through the liturgy of the Eucharist — considered both as sacrifice and sacrament — connected to which are all the sacraments and around which is placed the liturgy of the Divine Office.[18]

The liturgical year has been compared to a great gem in the center of which is a large priceless jewel presenting a varied appearance as it is seen in various lights.[19] Surrounding the jewel are lesser jewels, chosen because they reflect in a particular way the beauty of the center and attract one's attention to it. It is evident that the large priceless jewel in the center is the Temporal Cycle — the life of Jesus Christ which "the liturgy at stated times pro-

14 Dom Columba Marmion, O.S.B., *Christ in His Mysteries,* translated from the French by a Nun of Tyburn Convent (London: Sands and Company, 1931), p. 19.

15 *Mediator Dei,* No. 101.

16 *Ibid.,* No. 197.

17 *Ibid.,* No. 163.

18 *Ibid.,* Nos. 163–164.

19 Rev. John Dunne, S.J. From notes in his class on "Liturgy."

poses . . . for our meditation,"[20] and which it presents to us in various lights throughout the year.[21] The lesser jewels are the saints included in the Sanctoral Cycle. The saints are there because they lived, as we too can live, with the grace and according to the principles of the inner cycle.

The prayers and readings of the Mass and Divine Office of each day of the Temporal Cycle and each day of the Sanctoral Cycle reflect the spirit of Christ, exemplified in His own life and in the lives of His saints. Each day presents to us particular aspects of the Christ-life. While the Divine Office and the Mass express the spirit of the day in its fullness, the kernel of this spirit is found in the Propers of the Mass alone.[22] Let us take our missals, choose a certain day, and from the prayers and readings of the Mass of that feast, see how the Church presents to us the principles of a Christian life.

REVIEW QUESTIONS

1. Why did the Son of God become man?
2. How did Christ summarize the all-embracing spirit of His human life?
3. To what did Christ attribute the blessedness of Mary?
4. "Because of Baptism Christ walks again on earth glorifying and praising God in human circumstances." Explain.
5. What is the necessary condition of sanctifying grace? the chief and ordinary means?
6. What do you mean by the "Christ-life"?
7. Where are the principles of a perfect human life presented to us?
8. How does our text describe the Temporal and the Sanctoral Cycles?

C. The Music of the Liturgy Is One With the Liturgy

All that we have said about the liturgy must be kept in mind if we would understand liturgical music, for music that has not the spirit of the liturgy has no place in it. "If the Catholic liturgy is in reality an act of Christ and of the whole Church, the liturgical chant can only fulfill its object entirely when it is connected as closely as possible with this act, when it interprets the various texts

[20] *Mediator Dei,* No. 153.

[21] *Ibid.,* Nos. 153–165.

[22] In this chapter, as in preceding chapters, we are considering the liturgy of the Mass particularly. What we say of it should be applied equally to all the liturgy.

in accordance with the thoughts and sentiments that move Christ and the Church in their united action."[23] Music is a language in itself. Liturgical music must express the thoughts that Christ and His Church are expressing in offering the liturgy.

Why is music used in the liturgy? If we study the history of any religion, pagan or Christian, we shall see that music has always held a prominent place in the worship; thus we conclude that the need to worship in song is natural for man. Indeed St. Augustine says: "It is the part of love to sing." "The man of nature quite freely sings out the intenser moods of his heart; and the liturgy, as we have seen, does not suppress nature, but elevates and perfects it."[24]

Music has played a vital part in developing the form of the liturgy. As a matter of fact, unless we consider the liturgy as meant to be sung, as it was originally, we shall not understand the form of its human elements. The music used in the liturgy of the early days of the Church was one in spirit with the liturgy. The same must be true now.

"Sacred music as an integral part of the solemn liturgy shares in its general purpose, which is the glory of God and the sanctification and edification of the faithful."[25]

The Church uses only vocal and organ music in her liturgy.[26] In this handbook we are considering only the sung prayer of the Church.[27] "Sung prayer" means "prayer that is sung." Vocal music is always word music. This means that the words are always very important and must be considered both in the composing of the

[23] Dom Dominic Johner, *A New School of Gregorian Chant* (New York: Pustet, 1914), p. 237.

[24] Dom Virgil Michel, *The Liturgy of the Church According to the Roman Rite,* p. 321. With permission of The Macmillan Company of New York.

[25] Pius X, *Motu Proprio of Church Music,* translation and commentary by C. J. McNaspy, S.J. (Toledo: Gregorian Institute of America, 1950), No. 1.

[26] See No. 15 of the *Motu Proprio,* as well as Nos. 7, 8, and 9 of the *Apostolic Constitution* of Pius XI. In Section VI of the *Motu Proprio* St. Pius X discusses the use of other instruments than the organ. Some of these instruments, at the discretion and with the permission of the bishop, may be exceptionally permitted; others, as noted, are never permitted.

[27] Although we are not here considering organ music, we must realize that this music too must express the spirit of the liturgy.

music to which the words are sung and in the singing itself. Again, quoting St. Pius X in his *Motu Proprio:*

> Sacred music . . . contributes to the increase of decorum and splendour of the ecclesiastical ceremonies, and since (1) its principal function is to adorn with suitable melody the liturgical text proposed to the understanding of the faithful, (2) its proper purpose is to add greater efficacy to the text itself, so that (3) by this means the faithful may be more easily moved to devotion, and better disposed to gather to themselves the fruits of grace proper to the celebration of the sacred mysteries.[28]

REVIEW QUESTIONS

1. Discuss the purpose of music in the liturgy.
2. When is music liturgical music?
3. What is meant by "sung prayer"? Explain.

D. Criteria of Sacred Music

The Church has not only the right and the authority but she also has the duty to decide what qualities are necessary for the music of her liturgy. Otherwise the good which the liturgy should effect in souls might easily be lessened. The Church, following the guidance of the Holy Spirit and in the name of the authority she has received from God, has expressed very clearly the necessary principles of music used in the service of the liturgy. These right principles have been defined in the decrees of general and provincial councils, and in the repeated commands of the Sacred Congregations and of the Popes who have been Christ's vicars on earth. St. Pius X, however, realizing that there is a "constant tendency to go aside from correct norms"[29] promulgated his *Motu Proprio on Sacred Music,* and he imposed upon all its "most scrupulous observance."[30] In this *Motu Proprio* he stated definitely the criteria, or necessary qualities, of sacred music.

The criteria of the music of the liturgy are *holiness, beauty,* and *universality.* "It must be *holy,* and therefore avoid everything that is secular, both in itself and in the way it is performed. It must be

28 Pius X, *Motu Proprio,* No. 1. The parenthetic numerals are ours.

29 *Ibid.,* Introduction.

30 *Ibid.*

really an *art,* since in no other way can it have on the mind of those who hear it that effect which the Church desires in using in her liturgy the art of sound. But it must also be *universal* in this sense, namely, that although each country may use in its ecclesiastical music whatever special forms may belong to its own national style, these forms must be subject to the proper nature of sacred music, so that it may never produce a bad impression on the mind of any stranger who may hear it."[31] Let us discuss each principle here promulgated and see how it applies.

1. *The music must be holy.* As Dom Michel has said: ". . . liturgical music must be more than art. It is both art and liturgy, and therefore also religion in practice."[32] Since music is an integral part of liturgical worship, it must, like all the liturgy, be obedient to the demands of the Church; it must be pious, noble, holy, sanctifying. Since it is an integral part of liturgical worship, music must increase the solemnity of the sacrifice and emphasize the particular mood of the liturgical season. The music itself must always pray, must "point to God." It must have no suggestion of the secular in it. Pius XII in the *Mediator Dei* says: "It is not merely a question of recitation or of singing which, however perfect according to norms of music and the sacred rites, only reaches the ear, but it is especially a question of the ascent of the mind and heart to God so that, united with Christ, we may completely dedicate ourselves and all our actions to Him."[33]

In performance also, we must keep the spirit of the liturgy. In the way we sing we must "point to God"; we must center the attention on the Sacrifice at the altar and not draw attention in the slightest degree to ourselves as individuals, nor even to the choir as a group of individuals.

2. *The music must be true art.* This point is easily misunderstood and consequently may be easily ignored. Mrs. Justine Ward reminds us that it is very difficult to establish standards of taste because

[31] *Motu Proprio,* No. 2.

[32] Dom Virgil Michel, *The Liturgy of the Church According to the Roman Rite,* p. 324. With permission of The Macmillan Company.

[33] *Mediator Dei,* No. 145.

these standards are not obvious.[34] True beauty appeals to the soul. As long as man is on earth, beauty must reach his soul through his senses, but the senses are only a means of communication. For beauty is "a communication between God and the soul; the revelation to the soul of something of the proportion and order, the majesty, the grandeur and nobility, of God Himself."[35] Therefore true beauty is imperishable; although it presents different aspects at different times, beauty is in itself unchangeable. The more perfectly a work of art has in itself the underlying principles of beauty, the greater it is as art.

We realize that we need training to make an intelligent choice on most forms of art. Yet with regard to music we sometimes think that "I like it" is the final answer to "Is it good?" or "Is it acceptable?" We forget that our taste can be improved and that we should strive to improve it. "To bring to the worship of God less than the best is to offer the sacrifice of Cain."[36]

"A clear distinction must be made between prettiness and beauty. A pretty object is not beautiful; a thing of beauty cannot be pretty. Prettiness tickles the untrained ear and eye, but leaves the soul untouched. It is wholly superficial: it goes no deeper than the senses, to which it affords a passing pleasure, but nothing more."[37] If a thing is truly beautiful it is true art. Therefore we must conclude that the music used in the liturgy must appeal not merely to the senses but to the soul; it must be, not "pretty," but "beautiful," or true art as St. Pius X declared.

The music used in the liturgy must be in accord with the general standards of art and with the liturgical standards of art. "Art to be true art must fulfill the function for which it is destined."[38] But we must consider the liturgy to decide what music fulfills the

[34] Justine B. Ward, "Liturgical Music, How to Bring About Its Reform," *The Catholic Choirmaster,* 28:9.

[35] Beatrice Bradshaw Brown, "The Sacrifice of Cain," *The Catholic Choirmaster,* 28:156, p. 155.

[36] *Ibid.,* p. 156.

[37] *Ibid.,* p. 155.

[38] Dom Stephen Thuis, "Parish Worship, Its Artistic Expression," *National Liturgical Week* (Conception: Liturgical Conference, 1941), p. 194.

function of the liturgy. Music which is true art from the liturgical point of view must be one in spirit with the liturgy in inspiration and expression. If we fail to see why certain pieces of musical art are banned from use in the liturgy it is because we either forget the purpose of music in the liturgy or because we fail to distinguish between music that is religious in a general sense and music that is religious in a liturgical sense.

Spiritual Music

Generally Religious	*Liturgically Religious*
1. "The expression of the personal emotional reaction in the soul of an individual."[39] This music may be quite self-conscious.	1. The expression of the prayer of the whole Mystical Body.
2. Subjective in character and expression.	2. Objective in character and expression.
3. Free in character and sentiment.	3. According to the liturgy in character and sentiment.
4. The composer is unrestricted in the interpretation of the text.	4. The composer must follow the spirit of the text as the Church is praying it.
5. This music may verge on a worldly expression.	5. This music must pray.
6. This music may be personally dramatic, even theatrical.	6. This music must always pray; it must not even suggest the theater.
7. The accompaniment may be chromatic, very colorful in harmony, even sensuous.	7. The accompaniment must be simple, artistic, and prayerful; never sensuous.

Composers have a right to compose music that is spiritual in a general religious sense; and we have a right to perform it for our personal enjoyment. But it has no place in the liturgy, as we can easily see.

When we consider the works of the great masters of music from certain standpoints, we find them to be "true art" for they are truly beautiful in themselves. This is the case of the "Masses" of Bach, Beethoven, Mozart, etc. But as Masses intended for use in

[39] *Ibid.*

the liturgy they are evidently not "true art" for they do not fulfill the requirements of the liturgy itself. Free, subjective, and unrestricted in text, as they generally are, they do not "fulfill the function for which they were destined" if they are sung at the Holy Sacrifice of the Mass.

Let us consider the Bach *B Minor Mass* as an example. This composition is beautiful choral music and is a masterpiece. (1) But the words of the liturgy, as set to this music, are not given the place that should be theirs. Here the words are simply a means of carrying to us beautiful music — the music is of first importance and the words are merely an accompaniment. As a matter of fact, this music does not need the words of the liturgy at all. Yet in the liturgy, spoken or sung, the words are always of first importance. (2) The text is repeated as many times as the composer desired. Yet the *Motu Proprio* states explicitly: "The liturgical text must be sung as it stands in the books, without alteration or inversion of words, without undue repetition, without breaking syllables, and always in a way intelligible to the faithful who listen."[40] The RCA Victor chorale and orchestra has made a recording of this "Mass" on 12-inch (78 r.p.m.) records.[41] The first group of "Kyrie eleison" covers three sides; the "Christe eleison" covers two more sides; the last "Kyrie eleison" covers one more side — in all, six sides or three full records (each side of this type of record takes from four to five minutes to play). Can we think that there is no "undue repetition" of words in this composition? Note that the part of the celebrant on the intonation of the *Gloria,* that is, "Gloria in excelsis Deo," is sung by the choral group and covers nearly two thirds of a side. (3) Verses of the chants are treated as individual pieces and are given complete musical treatment so that they appear as various movements of a composition. This also the *Motu Proprio* forbids in liturgical music.[42]

If we listen to the recording of this composition and judge it from the general standards of musical art, we easily recognize its beauty.

[40] *Motu Proprio,* No. 9.
[41] Victor DM-1145 and DM-1146.
[42] *Motu Proprio,* No. 11.

We also easily recognize that it would be a misfit in a liturgical service.[43]

3. *The music must be universal.* We can easily see that the liturgy which is *catholic* or *universal* demands also a music which is catholic, or at least a music which excludes no one in the Mystical Body.

Conclusion. With some training we would not find it difficult to decide which music is highly liturgical and which is highly non-liturgical, for the extremes are apparent. But as we come from the extremes toward the center of the scale, we are less able to decide. Here we need more than mere training, we need the special guidance of the Holy Spirit who is very interested in our choice because it is music to be used in the liturgy and consequently will either advance or hinder our growth in Christ. It would be a matter for serious prayer if the choice were ours to make.

But the Church has established Diocesan Music Commissions for this very task. Its members have the necessary training; and since they are appointed by the authority of God in His Church, they can depend on His guidance. Thank God, we have only to let the Diocesan Music Commission decide for us what is His will in this respect.

In the discussion of the criteria of sacred music, we have been

[43] Perhaps we should here consider other "hymns" which sometimes come under discussion: (1) the *Ave Maria* of Schubert, (2) the *Ave Maria* of Bach-Gounod, (3) the *Wedding March* from *Lohengrin* by Wagner, and (4) Mendelssohn's *Wedding March.* (1) Schubert might be surprised to think that we would even consider his *Ave Maria* as Church music. He wrote that lovely melody and accompaniment to Ellen's prayer in Scott's *Lady of the Lake* (Canto III, XXIX). If we read the words we will find that they are not the words of the "Hail Mary" either in English or in Latin, nor do the words of the "Hail Mary" and this melody fit artistically together. (2) In Bach's *Well-Tempered Clavichord,* which he wrote illustrating that the then new method of tempering the scale was practicable, is a prelude in C major. Using this prelude as an accompaniment, Gounod wrote a melody to which the Latin words of the "Hail Mary" have been "placed." Note, too, that the words *Mater Dei* are omitted in this "hymn." Can we really feel that this *Ave Maria* is in any sense acceptable as Church music? (3) We are not here discussing organ music, yet we cannot avoid noting from the title *Wedding March* from *Lohengrin* that this march suggests a theater, not the liturgy, as (4) does also Mendelssohn's *Wedding March* from *Midsummer Night's Dream.* Anyone who has ever seen the drama *Midsummer Night's Dream* would not be too much complimented at the implication if this music were played for his wedding.

considering the music and not the text. Yet the importance of the text has been in our thought constantly. The text expresses our worship, our corporate worship, in words chosen by our Mother, the Church, herself. Thus the *Motu Proprio* states:

> As the texts that can be rendered in music and the order in which they are to be performed are fixed for every liturgical function, it is not allowed to change this order or to change the prescribed texts into others of one's own choice, or to omit them either entirely or even only in part.[44]

All music used in the liturgy must aid in the fuller expression of the spirit already expressed in the *words* of the liturgy.

Prayers expressed in words not taken directly from the liturgy are more or less "liturgical," inasmuch as the words more or less express the thought of the liturgy. This is our criteria in judging the text of hymns in the vernacular. In such cases both the words and the accompanying music must fulfill the function for which they are destined.

REVIEW QUESTIONS

1. Why must the Church decide the necessary qualities of Church music?
2. What are these qualities? Discuss each.
3. Discuss the two kinds of religious or spiritual music.
4. Discuss the "Masses" of Bach, Mozart, etc., from the standpoint of art. Why are they not suitable as liturgical art?
5. Discuss the Bach *B Minor Mass.* Explain, under three headings, why it is not liturgical.
6. Is the *Ave Maria* of Schubert or that of Bach-Gounod suitable for liturgical use? Explain.
7. What is the purpose of the Diocesan Music Commission?

E. Types of Music Allowed in the Liturgy

With some reservations, it may be said that all types of music are allowed in the liturgy as long as they fulfill the requirements of holiness, beauty, and universality. As we would expect, the *chant* possesses these qualities perfectly. The chant was born of the liturgy and is inseparably connected with it. Consequently, St. Pius X says

[44] *Motu Proprio,* No. 8

that it has always been looked upon as the highest model of Church music, and that to the degree other music is like it in movement, inspiration, and feeling, the more other music is acceptable.[45] *Classic polyphony,* especially the polyphony of the Roman School, which Palestrina brought to perfection in the sixteenth century, also possesses these three requisite qualities in a high degree. It is, therefore, most acceptable. We may also use *modern music.* The Church has always favored the progress of the arts and consequently not only allows, but encourages the use of modern music which fulfills the requirements of the liturgy.[46] It is with regard to modern music, however, that we may have to use some reservation, for modern music had a secular and not a religious birth, and this secular source must not be allowed to express itself in any way. All the music used in the liturgy must be holy, true art, and universal.

REVIEW QUESTION

1. Discuss the three types of music permitted for use in the liturgy.

F. Rendition of the Music of the Liturgy

We shall discuss particularly the rendition of the chant, since the chant is our model in all liturgical music. What we say of its rendition may be applied to all other music which may be considered liturgical.

> . . . these Gregorian melodies are the very melodies that have been loved and sung down the ages by the most noble souls that have ever graced this sinful world of ours, sung with ecstatic joy by the countless Saints — nay, possibly even, as in the psalmody, made sacro-sanct by the very lips of our Divine Saviour Himself and His Apostles. Laden with such soul-fragrance and such sanctity, these chant melodies must surely yield some of their potency also to our souls as we struggle on in our efforts for the better things.[47]

Although we should prepare ourselves to sing the prayers of the Church as well as we can, we must realize that the musical side of our offering is not as important as the prayer itself. Thus we will

[45] *Ibid.* Read Nos. 3, 4, and 5.
[46] See the *Motu Proprio,* No. 5, and the *Mediator Dei,* No. 193.
[47] Thuis, *loc. cit.,* p. 194.

agree that the difficulty of singing well is a spiritual rather than a material difficulty.[48]

That music is used in the liturgy for prayer's sake must be kept constantly in mind. (1) Thus we will remember that our sung prayer is addressed completely to God and not to the congregation. It is sung primarily for the ear of God alone, and only secondarily to assist others to take part in the sacred action at the altar. (2) The music must be true art, but it is art for the sake of prayer or it is not true art when it is used in the liturgy. It is a prayer that is sung and not a song that is prayed. (3) In the plan of the liturgy, each co-offerer has a special participation which should be expressed in a sung prayer. Thus the ministers at the altar are to be the only real soloists;[49] the choir, a specially trained group of men and boys, is to sing the sung parts of the Proper of the Mass, that is, the Introit, Gradual and Alleluia, and the Offertory and Communion Antiphons; the congregation is to sing with the choir the short responses, and to alternate with, or join with, the choir singing the Common of the Mass, that is, the Kyrie, Gloria, Credo, Sanctus and Benedictus, and Agnus Dei. (The congregation may also sing the Responsories of the Proper either alternately or with the choir. The plan for choir and congregation here outlined is not a hard and fast rule, but both the choir and congregation should participate vocally.)

In preparing to sing a particular piece of the liturgy, there are several fundamental points which should be given consideration.[50] (1) We should study the text of the piece from as many aspects as possible: what it expresses, why the Church finds it fitting on this feast and at this point of the liturgy, etc. (2) We should prepare the melody well so that our prayer will find its fuller expression through this medium. (3) We should remember to pray as we sing and in no sense to strain for "effects."[51] (4) The tempo of the sung

[48] Dunford, translator of Sunol, *Text Book of Gregorian Chant* (Boston: McLaughlin and Reilly, M. & R., edition No. 988), p. vij.

[49] See the *Motu Proprio,* No. 12.

[50] See Johner, *A New School of Gregorian Chant,* pp. 281–298.

[51] Although, again, it is sung prayer and not organ music that is being discussed here, the more complete expression of this sung prayer demands the relationship of text to music

prayer should be determined by the character of the melody, of the text, and of the feast; the number of singers and the character of their voices; the acoustics of the building. (5) The smaller and greater rhythms of the music, making evident the thought of the text, must never be neglected. The sung prayer must have proportion and balance but it must be sung as a whole.

REVIEW QUESTIONS

1. What do you mean when you say that the difficulty of singing well is a spiritual rather than a material difficulty?
2. The music of the liturgy is music for prayer's sake. Discuss under three headings.
3. Name the sung parts of the Mass. Who should sing each part?
4. Summarize the five fundamental points to be considered in preparing to sing a prayer of the liturgy.

G. Corporate Worship and the Music of the Liturgy

Since man is both an individual and a member of society, he must express his worship of God both individually and socially.[52] The liturgy, as no other prayer, completely satisfies this need of man. Worship through the liturgy, however, must by its very nature be predominantly social, or corporate, for the liturgy is the worship of the whole Christ, Head and members. The expression of our worship in the liturgy, therefore, must also by its very nature be predominantly social, or corporate.

We should not be satisfied with an implicit participation in the liturgy. St. Pius X wished the faithful to participate *actively* in the sacred liturgy and he declared, as we have often quoted, that active participation in the sacred liturgy is the primary and indispensable source of the true Christian spirit.[53] As we saw in Chapter II, the popes since St. Pius X have continued his plea for active participa-

---

in the following order: "The words, the melody under the words, the accompaniment under the melody, the organ under the accompaniment, and the organist under the organ." (Notes from a class with Dr. H. Becket-Gibbs.)

[52] See Chapter II, page 27 of this text. Dom Virgil Michel (*The Liturgy of the Church According to the Roman Rite,* p. 54) reminds us that even in our individual prayer life, we, as members of the Body of Christ, should not separate ourselves in thought from the prayer of our Head.

[53] See also *Mediator Dei,* Nos. 78, 80, 194, 201, 204, and others.

tion in the liturgy, and Pius XII, in his encyclical *Mediator Dei,* not only urged participation, but stated definitely in what active participation consists.

As we said, the liturgy, and therefore our participation in it, fulfills both the individual and social need of man. Thus we actively participate by our bodily presence at the liturgy in which we offer Christ and ourselves with Him to the heavenly Father. Still more do we participate when we express the offering of ourselves with Christ in gifts (Mass stipends and contributions to the collection), and certainly by the reception of Holy Communion.[54] Man ordinarily uses his voice in expressing externally his thoughts and intentions. A normal and ordinary way of taking an active part in any social gathering is to say aloud what we are thinking. This vocal expression in the Mass, whether spoken or sung, is very important. It is meant as a means to an end. It is meant to assist us, and should assist us, to participate more fully in every other way, particularly in the offering of ourselves to God with, through, and in Christ, and in the reception of Him in Holy Communion.

The value of corporate worship may be considered from three standpoints: (1) the value of corporate worship before God, (2) its value to me as an individual and as a social being, and therefore (3) its value to society in general. These standpoints may be considered individually, but they are really inseparably united. For although Christ's offering of Himself is always essentially perfect, yet the offering of His Body changes as the holiness of His Body, that is, of us His members, changes. Therefore the perfection of the homage rendered to God through the Mass may also vary. God in His goodness has so designed it that His glory and our perfection are bound as one. My external participation in corporate worship should assist others with whom I am one spiritually to increase their participation. If our individual and united offering is greater because of our corporate worship, as it should be, then we are more prepared for the streams of grace with which God desires to flood our souls. Our increase in holiness adds to God's

[54] See D. Leo Rudloff, "Meaning of Participation in the Mass," *National Liturgical Week* (Conception: Liturgical Conference, 1942), pp. 28–29.

greater extrinsic glory. Also our increase in holiness makes us more one with Him and with each other. Thus the circle of His grace continues, and is intensified because of our corporate worship.

Our Lord Himself said: "For where there are two or three gathered together in my name, there am I in the midst of them" (Mt. 18:20). Surely the singing of the chants of the Mass should bring us more "together" in our worship. Also, this "togetherness" has for its only object the more complete worship of God, helping us to enter into the offering which He makes for and with us in His own name and in the name of us who are one with Him.

"As Christians we find the only effective means for individual growth and social progress in the teachings of Jesus Christ. No other teacher has presented the lessons of justice and charity as they were taught by the Son of God. No other teacher has lived the lessons of sacrifice and obedience as they were lived in Bethlehem and Nazareth and on the Hill of Calvary. They are lessons of love for God and neighbor which the world must learn if there is to be justice and charity, peace and order among men."[55] It is particularly through the liturgy that we come into contact with Christ in Himself and in His teaching, both individual and social.

"I believe," said Donosco Cortes, Spanish ambassador in Paris, "that those who pray do more for the world than those who fight, and if the world goes from bad to worse, it is because there are more battles than prayers. If we could penetrate into the secrets of God and of history, I am convinced that we should be struck with amazement on beholding the tremendous effect of prayer, even in quite ordinary matters."[56] How true this must be of the prayer of those actively associated with the action of Christ. Surely, here we may find Catholic Action: for the corporate offering of the liturgy is *the* Catholic Action.

The remedy for the evils of the world "must be the restoration of the common bond uniting the world into one brotherhood under God, the common Father. The *I* must be blended into the *we.*

[55] Rev. George Johnson in *Guiding Growth in Christian Social Living* (Washington, D. C.: Catholic University of America Press, 1946), p. 1.

[56] Cited by Lefebvre, *Catholic Liturgy* (London: Sands and Company, 1924), p. 9.

We must pray together, sacrifice together, sing together—as one united common family under the common Heavenly Father. And where is this better realized this side of Heaven than when gathered together before the altar, which is Christ, using our powers of the priesthood, praying, offering, receiving, singing our Mass together in that unison song of Christ's Mystical Body, the Church."[57]

REVIEW QUESTIONS

1. Why is corporate worship essential to man?
2. How can we actively participate in the Mass?
3. What is the purpose of singing the Mass?
4. Name four popes who have lately urged congregational singing. Can you name the documents in which they did this?
5. In what way may corporate worship affect the worship of God by the Mystical Body?
6. How does the liturgy cause the principles of social justice and charity to grow in us?
7. What would you suggest as the best means of securing peace to the world?

H. The Moral Aspect of Church Music Legislation

Some Church music regulations, that is, those which are *preceptive,* are binding in conscience; those which are *directive* are meant to be counsels or recommendations and therefore are not binding in conscience although they are to be respected. *Preceptive regulations* are definite and employ such terms as: "it is to be observed," "so we write anew and command observance," "the custom is to be eliminated," etc. *Directive regulations* generally use such terms as: "it is praiseworthy," "we recommend," etc.[58] Both St. Pius X's *Motu Proprio on Sacred Music* and Pope Pius XI's *Apostolic Constitution "Divini cultus sanctitatem"* are preceptive as we may see from the following phrases:

[57] Thuis, "Parish Worship, Its Artistic Expression," p. 197. Father Thuis is, of course, speaking as a priest when he says "using our powers of priesthood." With regard to what is sometimes called "the priesthood of the laity" read the statement and warning of Pius XII in the *Mediator Dei,* Nos. 80–84.

[58] George V. Predmore, *Sacred Music and the Catholic Church* (Boston: McLaughlin and Reilly, 1936), p. 21. The following phrases from the *Motu Proprio* and the *Apostolic Constitution* are quoted from this source.

Motu Proprio:

(1) Such is the abuse affecting sacred chant and music. . . .

(2) We consider it our first duty without further delay to raise our voice at once in reproof and condemnation of all that is seen out of harmony with the right rule . . . in the functions of public worship and in the performance of the ecclesiastical offices.

(3) We do therefore publish, *motu proprio,* and with certain knowledge, our present instruction, to which, as to a *juridical code of sacred music,* We will with the fulness of Our Apostolic Authority that the force of law be given, and we do by Our present handwriting impose its scrupulous observance on all.

Apostolic Constitution:

(1) In order to urge the clergy and faithful to a more scrupulous observance of these laws and directions which are to be carefully observed by the whole Church, We think it opportune to set down here something of the fruits of Our experience during the last twenty-five years.

(2) These things We command, declare and sanction, decreeing that this Apostolic Constitution be now and in the future firm, valid, and effective, so as to obtain full and complete effect, all things to the contrary notwithstanding. Let no man therefore infringe this Constitution by Us promulgated, nor dare to contravene it.

These expressions are very strong. Yet they teach us a lesson in regard to the importance of the liturgy and the music used in it. For the Church, as a loving, careful, and solicitous mother, speaks so firmly only with regard to what is of importance to the glory of God and the salvation of souls. These regulations on sacred music and its use in the sacred liturgy must mean a great deal to God and His Church and to us who are members of His Church.

REVIEW QUESTIONS

1. What is the difference between the preceptive and directive regulations of the Church?
2. Is the *Motu Proprio* of St. Pius X and the *Apostolic Constitution* of Pius XI concerning sacred music of preceptive or of directive force? Quote phrases in proof.

I. Conclusion

Christ promised that His Spirit would guide His Church on earth even to the end of time. As we study our liturgy and its music we should strive to enter more completely into the mind of Christ concerning both. We should intelligently co-operate with those who are the authority of God on earth so that we may think and act as the Holy Spirit directs us through them. Let us do all in our power that the prayer of Pius XII may be fulfilled:

> May God, whom we worship, and who is "not the God of dissension but of peace," graciously grant to us all that during our earthly exile we may with one mind and one heart participate in the sacred liturgy which is, as it were, a preparation and a token of that heavenly liturgy in which we hope one day to sing together with the most glorious Mother of God and our most loving Mother, "To Him that sitteth on the throne, and to the Lamb, benediction and honor, and glory and power for ever and ever."[59]

[59] *Mediator Dei,* No. 209.

CHAPTER V

HISTORY OF THE SUNG LITURGY

Introduction

INTELLIGENT man feels a need for the worship of God. His very nature demands that he express this worship both individually and socially, that is, that his worship be both private and public (or as we say, using a Greek word for public, that it be liturgical). The Church, following Christ's example, has in the development of her liturgy filled this need of man. "The Church's life is centered in her liturgy — that wonderful cycle of prayer and praise."[1] The more a man becomes truly Christian, the more he finds the center of his life where the Church centers hers.

Although we are sketching the history of liturgical music, we cannot dissociate it from the history of the liturgy itself; for music and liturgy developed hand in hand. Indeed, Lang in *Music in Western Civilization* says: "Rites and music influenced each other to such an extent, in the liturgy of Christian antiquity, that a history of music cannot be written separately from a history of religion."[2]

The Purpose of Music in the Liturgy

The liturgy of the Church prays and teaches. Therefore the music used in the liturgy must also pray and teach. St. Paul wrote thus to the Colossians: "Teaching and admonishing one another in psalms, hymns, and spiritual canticles, singing in grace in your hearts to God" (Col. 3:16). Words alone cannot express the great

[1] Benedictine of Stanbrook, *A Grammar of Plainsong,* 3 ed. (Liverpool: Rushworth and Dreaper, 1934), p. 3.

[2] Paul Henry Lang (New York: W. W. Norton, 1941), p. 42.

spiritual realities of life. The language of music expresses what words alone cannot say, for "music is a revelation of the illimitable which lies behind all the barriers of time."[3]

He who loves will naturally sing. "Music is the language of love. Hence the Church, as the Bride of Christ, has always sung the praises of her Divine Lover, Jesus Christ. Her praises, in turn, are the echo of that ineffable canticle sung in the Godhead from all ages."[4]

Dom Thuis maintains that the status of Gregorian Chant through the years may be considered a barometer of the religious fervor through these years. Since active participation in the liturgy has thus far presupposed the use of the chant, we are not surprised at his opinion. For the true Christian spirit is expected as a result of active participation in the liturgy.

Music in the liturgy is a means to an end. Music is always subordinate to the purposes of the liturgy; nevertheless it is inseparable from its solemn celebration. For this reason Pius X demanded that all liturgical music possess qualities proper to the liturgy itself: the music of the liturgy must be *holy* and *universal,* and it must be *true art.*

Particular Aims of This Study

We are going to sketch the history of the music of the liturgy. We will note the forces that affected the music as they affected the expression of the people in other forms, and consequently as they affected the expression of the people in their worship. This short study should assist us to understand better the present state both of the liturgy and of the music of the liturgy. It should enable us to co-operate more intelligently now and in the future in the return of the laity to a fuller participation in their official worship.

In our study we will also note that the Church has taken into her liturgical life, into her corporate worship, means of expression which have been vital to her members as a group. We will consider, for example, forces in the development of the liturgical year, the

[3] Benedictine of Stanbrook, *op. cit.,* p. 3.

[4] Dom Stephen Thuis, O.S.B., *Gregorian Chant A Barometer of Religious Fervor* (St. Meinrad: Abbey Press, 1931), p. 3.

celebration of the feasts of martyrs, etc. Pius XII has said: "Every single period in the Church's history has contributed to enrich those sacramental rites, as the Missal and the Roman Ritual (to cite well-known instances) clearly manifest. From the progressive development of any of the rites one easily sees the Church's care in searching out the form best suited to their purpose."[5] Thus the consideration of our rite should help us to understand our liturgy better. For it is only in the light of the past that we can understand the present and the future.

As we study the Church in the various periods of her history, in the various periods of her liturgical development, we shall appreciate and learn to love her more. Edward Dickinson, a non-Catholic, says: "It [that is, the music of the early Church] was an outgrowth of the conditions of the age, of the necessities of devotional expression, and of that peculiar phenomenon symbolic of the spiritual life within. The Catholic Church develops, but, in essence, she does not change. The history of her music is likewise typical of her whole history."[6] Our faith should grow stronger as we watch her develop but in essence never change.

Our appreciation of our liturgy should grow as we study its history. We should become more and more aware of what taking an active part in it can do for us as individual and corporate members of Christ's Body. For as Dom Johner says: "Our liturgy is an inseparable, uninterrupted communing of Christ with His Bride, His visit by grace and His tarrying with us — a blessed union, like the familiar intercourse of the Master with His disciples in the days of His sojourn on earth, and in many respects closer, firmer and more effective."[7]

Study is necessary, but it alone is not sufficient. To make our knowledge affect our lives, we need the action of grace. "We may know the liturgy through association, we can appreciate it through

[5] Pius XII in his charge to Lenten preachers for 1945, cited by Gerald Ellard, S.J., *Mass of the Future* (Milwaukee: The Bruce Publishing Company, 1948), p. xii.

[6] Cited by Dom Thuis, *Gregorian Chant A Barometer of Religious Fervor*, p. 9.

[7] Dom Dominic Johner, *A New School of Gregorian Chant*, 2 Eng. ed. (New York: Pustet, 1914), p. 236.

study, but we will never *understand* the liturgy until we have *lived* it."[8] As we study, then, let us beg the Holy Spirit to enlighten our minds, but most of all to inflame our hearts with the love and faith that *lives* the liturgy as Christ, its Divine Founder, wills we should.

Rites

Before we begin our study, it may be well that we discuss briefly the meaning of the word *rite*.[9] In all the various liturgies the essentials are the same. But around the essentials there have developed, in various centers, customs which gradually became settled and crystallized. For example, since the prayers were at first extemporaneous, they may have had a different order and a different mode of expression, even if, perchance, the prayers offered at various places were for the same intention. "Insistence on one part at one place, on another at another, different parts shortened or enlarged, slight re-arrangements of the order, caused for some practical reason, bring about different types of liturgy."[10]

A bishop subject to the patriarchate of Antioch, Alexandria, or Rome naturally imitated his patriarch to a great extent. Yet since uniformity was not expected at first, there was fluidity within each patriarchal rite as well as quite a development in parent and daughter rites. Although not all authorities agree as to the number of parent rites, generally four are given:[11] that of Antioch, of Alexandria, of Rome, and of Gaul. Derived from the Antioch-Jerusalem Rite is the great Byzantine Rite. The Roman and Gallican Rites were followed in the West. Under the term *Roman Rite* may be included (1) the original pure Roman Rite and the African Rite (neither used today), (2) the present Roman Rite with its Gallican additions, and (3) various modifications of this last as used by

[8] Marie Pierik, *The Spirit of Gregorian Chant* (Boston: McLaughlin and Reilly, 1939), p. 202.

[9] Book Two of *Our Quest For Happiness* by Clarence Elwell and others (Chicago: Mentzer, Bush and Company, 1945), on pp. 525–527, gives a concise and exact summary of the various rites of the Church.

[10] Adrian Fortescue, *The Mass* (New York: Longmans, Green and Company, 1912), p. 77.

[11] *Ibid.*, pp. 76–109. See also Joseph A. Jungmann, S.J., *The Mass of the Roman Rite*, translated by Francis A. Brunner, C.SS.R. (New York: Benziger Brothers, 1951), pp. 33, 44.

religious orders such as the Dominicans and Carmelites, and diocesan modifications for the most part now abolished. The Gallican Rite has two remnants only — the Ambrosian and the Mozarabic.[12]

PERIODS OF THE MUSIC OF THE LITURGY

First Period — Formative Period — From the Year A.D. 33–600.
Second Period — Period of Diffusion and Perfection — 600–1300.
Third Period — Period of Decadence of the Chant — 1300–1517.
Fourth Period — Period of Loss of the Chant — 1517–1850.
Fifth Period — Period of Restoration of the Chant — 1850–the Present.

REVIEW QUESTIONS

1. Why must we study the history of the liturgy as we study the history of its music?
2. Give an example of the liturgy praying and teaching.
3. How does music help the liturgy in its praying and teaching?
4. State the qualities required of liturgical music.
5. Explain what Dom Thuis means when he calls Gregorian the barometer of religious fervor.
6. State three results which are to be expected from the study of the history of the liturgy and its music.
7. When will we understand the liturgy? Explain your answer.
8. How did the various rites come into existence?
9. To which rite do you belong?
10. Give the titles and dates of the periods of the music of the liturgy.

FIRST PERIOD — FORMATIVE — UNTIL A.D. 600

A. The Time of Christ to the Edict of Milan — A.D. 1–313

HISTORICAL SETTING

The beginning of the Christian Era saw the life of Christ and the founding of His Church. After His death, His teachings were spread through His Church, His Mystical Body, which won converts and grew in spite of persecution and early heresies (Donatism

[12] Fortescue, *op. cit.*, pp. 108–109.

and Manichaeism). The Church in this early age is the Church of the Apostles, martyrs, and early apologists. Here, too, we see the founding of monasticism in the East.

THE LITURGY OF THE FIRST THREE CENTURIES

1. IN THE TIME OF CHRIST

Although our Lord as Author of the Law was surely not subject to it, yet He fulfilled its precepts as though He were. He says of Himself: "Do not think that I am come to destroy the law, or the prophets. I am not come to destroy, but to fulfil" (Mt. 5:17). As a true Israelite He followed the "custom of the law" (Lk. 2:27). Therefore we may say that He and His disciples followed the form of the Hebrew liturgy. Several times a year they went to the Temple at Jerusalem and every Sabbath to the Synagogue.

The service at the Synagogue was a prayer service. In it we distinguish a form which affected the form of the first part of the Mass in our own rite. This Synagogue service consisted of (1) prayers — of adoration, praise, thanksgiving, petition, atonement (reparation); (2) readings from Scripture; (3) singing of psalms between readings; and (4) a sermon by one of the rabbis or elders of the people.

As we have said, this Synagogue service has affected our own liturgy. The manner of singing the psalms in both this and the Temple service has also affected the manner of doing the same in our liturgy. Here are found the forerunners of the Christian antiphonal and responsorial psalmody. Both of these will be explained later.

Certainly we wish we could have seen and heard our Lord when He took part "according to the law" in the worship of His Father. We wish we could know with certainty what melodies He sang as He chanted the prayers of the Hebrews. Modern Jewish writers, such as Idelssohn and Zaminsky, find a relationship between some Hebrew and Gregorian melodies. We cannot claim that Christ sang melodies which we sing now. Nevertheless, it is safe to say that He may have sung melodies which would sound familiar to us.

And we do know that the psalms held a prominent place in His prayer life as they did in the life of all His chosen people. We also know that after the first Mass, the Last Supper, our Lord sang a hymn, for so the New Testament tells us. We are told that the psalms customary after the paschal banquet are Psalms 113 to 118. One of these we sing at the close of Benediction of the Most Blessed Sacrament. The *Laudate Dominum* is Psalm 116. We cannot but agree with Gastoué when he says: "Jesus! The first chanter of the new law! The first liturgical Christian chant accompanies the first Eucharist! For a truth, the musical life of the Church commences in thanksgiving at the Last Supper, and it springs from the heart of Jesus."[13]

None of the New Testament accounts of the events of the Last Supper is complete in itself. But by putting the four together we find in the liturgy of the Last Supper the nucleus, if not the order, of our liturgy in the present day. Our Lord (1) took bread and wine separately, (2) said a prayer of thanksgiving, (3) through words of Consecration changed the bread into His Body and the wine into His Blood, (4) broke the Bread, (5) gave the Apostles Holy Communion, and (6) addressed to them a loving and solemn sermon.[14]

II. IN THE TIME OF THE PERSECUTIONS – A.D. 33–313

For a time the Apostles and their converts to Christianity continued to follow the form of the Hebrew liturgy with the addition of their own prayer service and the offering of the Eucharist, as our Lord had commanded them: "Do this for a commemoration of me" (Lk. 22:19). We are not surprised to see that they still frequented the Temple and took an active part in the service of the Synagogue. Yet at the same time we know that the first Christians met together, probably in private homes, for a distinctly Christian service of prayer and for the "breaking of the bread" (*fractio panis*).

[13] M. Gastoué, quoted by Rene Aigrain, *Religious Music* (London: Sands and Company, n.d.), p. 11.

[14] Read Chapters 14 to 16 of the Gospel of St. John. Read also Christ's prayer for His disciples, therefore for us, in Chapter 17 of St. John.

Although the word *Synaxis* means a meeting of any kind, it is often used to refer to the Christian prayer service. The Christian Synaxis was based in form on the Synagogue service. Here, as in the Synagogue service, we have the praying together, the singing of psalms and hymns, readings from Scripture to which is added the reading of letters (or epistles) of absent leaders of the early Church, and sermons (or homilies). Yet there is a vast difference between the Synagogue service and the Christian service of prayer, for in the Christian Synaxis all is centered in and radiates from devotion to and through Christ, the God-Man. "In all these rites and prayers Christ is ever present, prompting and operating, so that the expression 'Christian worship' is strictly accurate."[15]

At first, the common "breaking of bread," the offering of the Eucharist, was a separate service, preceded or accompanied by the *agape,* or "love feast," which was soon omitted entirely in this connection. The Eucharistic offering, varying in its expression, tended to the following form: (1) a prayer of thanksgiving, (2) the separate consecration of the bread and wine, (3) prayers (in the early rite, prayers remembering Christ's death), and (4) the reception of Holy Communion. Writings of the third century mention the offering of gifts by the faithful before the prayer of thanksgiving. It is probable that this offering was made from the first days of the liturgy.

Gradually the ordinary Synaxis was followed by the Eucharist but their distinctness remains evident even now in our composite service — the Mass.

The offering of the Eucharist was also held in connection with nocturnal meetings, the night watches or vigils. Christians met during the night hours and spent the time in watching and praying, that is, in prayers, in reading from Scripture, in singing psalms, and in listening to short sermons. Following the watch, in the early morning the Eucharist was offered.

The vigil service, a prayer service again reminding us of the

[15] Dom Fernand Cabrol, *The Prayer of the Early Christians* (London: Burns, Oates and Washbourne, 1930), p. xxiv.

Synagogue service, was later combined in *Matins,* with its three nocturns, which is our Divine Office of the night. A vigil preceding the Sunday Eucharist normally began at midnight. The Easter vigil began even earlier and continued until the morning Eucharist. Perhaps in imitation of this Easter vigil, Christians began to meet on other days at the hour when the lamps were lit (*hora incensi*). This is probably our first form of Vespers.[16] The "hours" of the day were also the occasion for special prayer, as we shall see.

In the Eucharist and in the ordinary Synaxis and vigil services, as well as in the special prayers throughout the day, we see foundations of the liturgy. In the beginnings of the Church there was a remarkable uniformity in the liturgy. Yet it was a "uniformity of type rather than of detail,"[17] although in many cases the actual words were the same. Since no uniformity of detail was demanded during the early centuries and since each bishop could pray as he wished, there were slight variations within a comparative uniformity of outline. These variations of detail led to the development of the various rites of the Church, all based on the early liturgy.

How do we know the early form of our liturgy? What are our sources of information? We have, first of all, the witness of the New Testament. Beyond that, we may refer to other early documents. Those of the *first* century are the *Didache,* which is "apparently the earliest extant work after the New Testament,"[18] and the various Epistles of Clement, Barnabas, and Polycarp. Those of the *second* century are the account of Pliny, the apologies of St. Justin Martyr and of others, and the writings of St. Irenaeus. Those of the *third* century are the *Didascalia of the Apostles* and the *Apostolic Tradition* of St. Hippolytus. The latter document is our most important source concerning the liturgy at Rome in this, the third, century. The *fourth* century saw the beginnings of different liturgies, so from here on we would have to trace each rite separately.

[16] Peter Wagner, *Introduction to the Gregorian Melodies,* translated by Agnes Orme and E. G. P. Wyatt, Vol. I (London: Plainsong and Medieval Society, 1901), p. 109.

[17] Fortescue, *op. cit.,* p. 56.

[18] *Ibid.,* p. 8.

In this study we will but indicate briefly the development of the liturgy and the music of the liturgy of the Roman Rite.

We have mentioned many times the singing of psalms. We know that music was "the handmaid of the liturgy" from the beginning. St. Paul himself urged the Christians at Ephesus and Colossus to sing hymns, psalms, and canticles: "Speaking to yourselves in psalms, and hymns, and spiritual canticles, singing and making melody in your hearts to the Lord" (Eph. 5:19).

To what melodies did they sing their prayers? Since the first Christians were Jews and converted Greeks, we should expect the prayer-music of the early Christians to show a Jewish and Greek influence. "Having been brought into touch with two civilizations and two forms of art—the Hebrew and the Graeco-Roman—with exquisite tact she (the Church) borrowed from each what best suited her ends."[19] "Or, as it has been popularly expressed, the music of Holy Mother has originated in Hebrew sources, has passed through Greek channels, and was finally cast in the Roman mold."[20]

Dom Cabrol summarizes our liturgical indebtedness to the Jews. After mentioning the books of the Jews, particularly the books of Moses, of the prophets, and of the psalms, he says: "The Christian *synaxis* bears an astonishing resemblance to the Synagogue service and is made up of the same elements. The very mould into which their improvised prayers were cast, is borrowed from the Jewish worship. Some of the expressions most frequently met with in Christian worship, such as *Amen, Alleluia, Hosanna, Pax Vobis, Dominus vobiscum*—are found in the Old Testament. The typically Jewish formula—*The God of Abraham, of Isaac and of Jacob*—is still found in Origen and other writers. Ablutions, the imposition of hands, the use of oil and incense, certain attitudes at prayer, viz. standing, kneeling, extending the hands, were features of the Mosaic ritual and the two chief Christian festivals, Easter and Pentecost, take from the Jewish calendar, if not their meaning, at any rate

[19] Benedictine of Stanbrook, *Gregorian Music,* cited by Dom Thuis, p. 16.
[20] Dom Thuis, *Gregorian Chant A Barometer of Religious Fervor,* p. 16.

their name and their place in the course of the year. The form of the litany, of the *anaphora* or preface, of the collect and even that of the doxology is of Jewish origin. The week of seven days, except for the vital change of the Sunday, and the division of the hours of the day into threes [the "Hours" of the Divine Office], have been borrowed in the same way."[21]

From the Greeks came "undoubtedly decisive influences for the fashioning of the Christian rite of initiation with its exorcisms and anointing, and also the idea of celebrating the solemn rite of baptism on the night of Easter. From Hellenism came the 'discipline of the secret,' that is, the Christian obligation to secrecy in regard to the essential acts of worship. From Hellenism came the tendency to submit the Christian formulas of prayer to the rules of ancient rhetoric and especially to the particular rules of symmetry. From Hellenism came many technical terms in the language of the liturgy, such as the word *liturgy* itself and the words *mysterium, anaphora, canon, praefatio, anamnesis,* etc. And finally, from Hellenism came certain patterns of prayer such as that of the litany of All Saints, and acclamations such as *Kyrie eleison* and *Dignum et justum est.*"[22]

Since, as we have noted, the Hebrew liturgy and the Graeco-Roman practices have influenced our liturgy, we may also reasonably expect that our liturgical music was influenced by the music of each.[23] (1) Diatonic melodies, that is, melodies composed of whole and half steps, were used by the Greeks and influenced our early liturgical music. To the Greeks we also owe (2) the art of rhythm, and (3) in all probability, the principle of the undivided beat.

We have already mentioned the influence of the Jews on our psalmody. We also owe them (1) the style of music which we call responsorial, (2) the principle of the close relationship between

21 Dom Fernand Cabrol, *op. cit.,* p. xxi.

22 Theodor Klauser, "A Brief History of the Liturgy in the West," Part I, *Orate Fratres* (Collegeville: St. John's Abbey Press), Vol. XXIII, No. 1, p. 9.

23 Continued research is ascertaining contributions to our liturgy and its music from other sources. This does not lessen the early influence of both the Hebrew and Graeco-Roman cultures.

music and text (this principle involves free rhythm), and the practice of *melismatic* or florid passages sung by a soloist at a verbal and musical cadence. The fact that singing in the early Church was monodic, that is, single-voiced or in unison, can be traced to both cultures.

The Hebrews gave us *responsorial* singing and the congregational use of the *antiphon*. From the first, both in the Mass and in the Divine Office, responsorial psalmody has been associated with solo singing. *Antiphonal singing* was not introduced into the Western Rite until a later date. Antiphonal psalmody, developing differently in the Mass and in the Divine Office, is not a solo but a choir psalmody. Although antiphonal singing was not introduced into the Roman Church until the fourth century, we will consider this style of singing here as we endeavor to make clear how it differs from responsorial singing.

The words *responsorial* and *responsory* practically define themselves; immediately we think of a response or refrain. In responsorial psalmody, each psalm verse, originally sung by a soloist, was followed by a verse which was called the responsory or refrain. The responsory was sung by a group.

Antiphony means "sounding against." In antiphonal psalmody, the psalm verses were sung one after another in alternating choirs. An *antiphon* is an independent piece. Although it did not have to be, its text was often taken from the psalm with which it was associated. Used as a responsory, it "sounded against" the verses sung by the soloist.

Let us use Psalm 64 to demonstrate a type of responsorial and a type of antiphonal singing. We will use only the first six of its fourteen verses. Note that we have chosen the antiphon which the Church associates with Psalm 64 in the Introit of the Requiem Mass. We will sing both the antiphon and the psalm verses to Tone 5a.

Antiphon

Requiem aeternam dona eis, *Do*mine: * et lux perpetua *lu*ceat eis.

Psalm 64

1. Te decet hymnus, Deus in *Si*on: * et tibi reddetur votum *in* Jerusalem.
2. Exaudi orationem *me*am: * ad te omnis *ca*ro veniet.
3. Verba iniquarum praevaluerunt *su*per nos: * et impietatibus nostris tu pro*pi*tiaberis.
4. Beatus, quem elegisti, et assum*psi*sti: * inhabitabit in *a*triis tuis.
5. Replebimur in bonis domus *tu*ae: * sanctum est templum tuum, mirabile in *ae*quitate.
6. Exaudi nos, Deus, salutaris *no*ster, * spes omnium finium terrae, et in *ma*ri longe.

(English Translation)[24]

Antiphon

Eternal rest give unto *them,* O Lord: * and let perpetual light *shine* upon them.

Psalm 64

1. A hymn, O God becometh thee in *Si*on: * and a vow shall be paid to thee *in* Jerusalem.
2. O hear *my* prayer: * all *flesh* shall come to thee.
3. The words of the wicked have prevailed *o*ver us: * and thou will pardon *our* transgressions.
4. Blessed is he whom thou hast chosen and taken *to* thee: * he shall *dwell* in thy courts.
5. We shall be filled with the good things of *thy* house: * holy is thy temple, wonder*ful* in justice.
6. Hear us, O God, our *Sav*iour, * who art the hope of all the ends of the earth, and in the *sea* afar off.

Responsorial Singing

Sung by a Soloist		Sung by the Congregation (or Choir)
Antiphon	— followed by —	Antiphon (used here as a responsory or refrain)
Verse 1	— followed by —	Antiphon
Verse 2	— followed by —	Antiphon
Verse 3	— followed by —	Antiphon
Verse 4	— followed by —	Antiphon
Verse 5	— followed by —	Antiphon
Verse 6	— followed by —	Antiphon

[24] Both the Latin and the English translation are from *The New Psalter,* edited by E. P. Graham (New York: Pustet, 1935), p. 266.

Antiphonal Singing

1st Choir		2nd Choir
Antiphon intoned and completed by both choirs together		
Verse 1	— followed by —	Verse 2
Verse 3	— followed by —	Verse 4
Verse 5	— followed by —	Verse 6
Antiphon sung by both choirs together		

The style of antiphonal singing did not always follow this pattern — for example, the antiphon was sometimes sung by the combined choirs after each alternating verse; nor was the style of responsorial singing always thus — we find others in the Offertory and Communion of the Requiem Mass. This plan, however, will suffice to enable us to understand the fundamental difference between responsorial and antiphonal singing.

"Of less importance was a third kind of psalmody, the *Cantus in directum,* or *directaneus,* which consisted in the psalm being performed from beginning to end without responsorial or antiphonal additions."[25]

The extent of the singing done at the definitely Christian assemblies — for example, at the celebration of the Eucharist — is a matter of which we cannot be certain. Authors take absolutely opposite views on this point. The details of the liturgy, as we know, could be varied in different places. Moreover, wherever Christians were suffering persecution, the liturgy would have to be offered as secretly and as quietly as possible. Thus we may conclude that the singing varied from place to place according to circumstances.

Although some early Church Fathers, for example, Clement of Alexandria, permitted the use of the lyra and the kithara because King David used them, the music of the liturgy was vocal and not instrumental. This was true, first of all, because instruments were associated with pagan life, but above all, because the voice can unite itself completely with the expression of worship in word whereas an instrument cannot.[26]

25 Wagner, *op. cit.,* p. 24.

26 Chapter IV discusses the importance of the words, or text, of the liturgy and the relationship which must exist between the text and the music which accompanies it.

REVIEW QUESTIONS

1. What was the form of the Hebrew Synagogue service?
2. Give proof that our Lord followed this form of worship.
3. Why do you think that our Lord may have sung the *Laudate Dominum omnes gentes* at the Last Supper? When do we sing it?
4. How did the Christian Synaxis resemble the Synagogue service? How did they differ?
5. What was the form of the Eucharist? Where did the early Christians get this form?
6. What early service later developed into Matins? What is the origin of Vespers?
7. Was there uniformity of worship in the first three centuries of the Church? Explain.
8. What influence did the Greeks have on the liturgy itself?
9. What contributions did the Jews make to our liturgy? Name at least five.
10. List four contributions made by the Jews to our liturgical music.
11. List four contributions made by the Greeks to our liturgical music.
12. How does responsorial singing differ from antiphonal singing?
13. What is a responsory? What is an antiphon?
14. To what extent was there singing in the early Christian assemblies? Give proofs that the early Christians did sing their prayers.
15. Why is the music of the liturgy predominantly vocal?

B. Liberated Christendom — A.D. 313–600

HISTORICAL SETTING

In 313, Constantine the Great legalized the Christian religion by the Edict of Milan. After this decree the Church expanded to the boundaries of the Empire, and developed in freedom its body of doctrines and practices. In this growth two influences were outstanding: (1) the prestige of the popes and (2) monasticism.

When Constantine left Rome, taking the government of the Empire to Byzantium, renamed Constantinople, Rome was left to become the City of the Popes. The full significance of this event did not unfold itself until later centuries. The invasions of the barbarians, beginning about the fourth century, presented the Church with the great task of converting and Christianizing them, while she watched the ancient Empire crumble about her. Her "eldest daughter" among the tribes was the Frankish nation, which was converted mainly through the efforts of its king, Clovis, about A.D. 500. During these same years, though the Church was fighting such heresies as Donatism, Arianism, Monophysitism, Monothelitism, Pelagianism, and Nestorianism, she emerged as the greatest political power in Western Europe.

During this same period we see the founders and leaders of monasticism: St. Anthony, St. Pachomius, St. Basil, St. Benedict, and others, as well as those who are classed among the early Doctors of the Church — St. Ambrose, St. Augustine, St. Jerome, and finally St. Gregory I, surnamed the Great.

THE FORMATION OF THE ROMAN RITE

As we have stated, to get a true idea of our liturgy, the development of the liturgy and the music of the liturgy must be considered together. For this study to be complete we should consider the history of each prayer as well as all its attendant ceremonies as the expression of our worship. Chapter VI of this text discusses, in part, the liturgy of the High Mass. Speaking generally, we may say that the form of our present-day High Mass is the form in use at the close of this period, that is, the early seventh century.

I. DOCUMENTARY EVIDENCE

We shall not discuss the origin of the Roman Rite in any detail, for in some respects its origin is not an easy question even for those who have spent years of research on the subject. This rite, which is certainly the most widespread rite of all, is definitely different from all others. "In the second century Rome used much the same liturgy as Antioch and the other Eastern Churches; by the VIIth century she had evolved from that her own particular rite, differing in important points from any other."[27]

During the first three centuries the prayers were extemporaneous and the ceremonial was not fixed, although habit gradually developed customs which became established as such. Little by little it became the rule that the prayer texts should be put into

[27] Fortescue, *op. cit.*, p. 112.

writing. How long before the fourth century this was the practice we do not know. The twenty-fifth canon of a synod at Hippo in 394, which "forbids anyone to use written out prayers of other Churches till he has shown his copy to the more learned brethren,"[28] proves that some prayers were written out and subject to approval at least by this time.

The various kinds of books necessary for the complete ceremonial celebration of the Roman liturgy of this period are explained in Number IX below. There we note that the book which contained the prayers the celebrant needed for his part of the liturgy is called a *sacramentary*. Several ancient sacramentaries are extant. The *Leonine Sacramentary* (named after Pope Leo, 440–461), the *Gelasian Sacramentary* (attributed to the time of Pope Gelasius I, 492–496), and the *Gregorian Sacramentary* (attributed to Pope Gregory I, 590–604) are among the most important sources of information concerning the origin of the Roman Rite. (1) The Leonine Sacramentary, of which we have a manuscript written in the seventh century, "represents a pure Roman use with none of the later Gallican additions.[29] But it is only a fragment. . . . It contains very much old matter and is invaluable as being our oldest source of the Roman Rite."[30] (2) The Gelasian Sacramentary has two forms, yet it is still a Roman book Gallicanized. Its manuscript was written in the seventh or eighth century. It is so definitely colored by usages of years much later than Pope Gelasius, that we cannot secure from it much information regarding the early Roman Rite. (3) Tradition ascribes the Gregorian Sacramentary to Pope St. Gregory the Great. Some late writers dispute its authorship. However, "that the essential part of the Gregorian Sacramentary goes back to St. Gregory's time, indeed to a much earlier period, is certain."[31] This Sacramentary, with additions and modifications, is the foundation of our Roman Missal of today.

[28] *Ibid.*, p. 115.

[29] As we will see later, all additions coming from the countries north of the Alps are styled Gallican additions.

[30] Fortescue, *op. cit.*, pp. 118–119.

[31] *Ibid.*, p. 123.

De Sacramentis, a work probably of the late fourth century or early fifth century, is of particular importance because, with the *Apostolic Tradition* of St. Hippolytus (third century), it is an important witness of the Canon of our Mass.[32] This work is often credited to St. Ambrose, but we cannot be certain of its authorship.

The *Roman Ordines* (*Ordines Romani*) are also documents of importance. These are collections of rubrics and directions for carrying out the Roman ceremonies. Fifteen in number, they give descriptions of Roman usages from the seventh to the fifteenth centuries. We shall see that some of the *Roman Ordines* are not as completely Roman as we might expect from the general title. Ceremonies in use at Rome in a Papal Mass would need adaptation at other Masses elsewhere. This fact, and the custom of liturgical practices differing in part from the practices at Rome, would influence the *Roman Ordo* as it was followed outside of Rome.

Other documents discuss the Roman liturgy of this period. The documents named above are generally considered of the greatest importance.

II. HYMNS

We have not said anything about hymns except to state that they were sung. Even at an early age, new Christian song creations were composed in the poetic form of the times; these were all considered under the general title of *hymns.* The heretics found hymns a wonderful means of spreading their false teachings. In fact, the heretics made such a use of hymns that some Church councils, such as the Council of Laodicea (fourth century), felt obliged to ban from use in the liturgy all hymns using texts not scriptural in origin.[33] The ban was not so general that no hymns were composed, but their development throughout the Christian world as a whole was certainly retarded.

The subject of Christian hymnody is a large and interesting field which we cannot enter in such a short study. St. Ambrose, who

32 The work entitled *Apostolic Constitutions,* dating about 400, is also claimed by some to be an important document of the very early Roman Rite. Opinions on this point vary.

33 Wagner, *op. cit.* Read Chapter X.

introduced antiphony and hymnody into the West (in Milan), is known as the "Father of Ecclesiastical Music." We will but mention certain other great hymn writers, chosen from a long list: St. Clement of Alexandria (150–220), Aurelius Clemens Prudentius (348–413), St. Hilary of Poitiers (fourth century), Sedulius (fifth century), Claudius Mamertus (died 473), Pope Gelasius (died 496), Venantius Fortunatus (530–609), St. Gregory the Great (540–604), Venerable Bede (673–735), Theodulf of Orleans (eighth century), Hermann Contractus (1013–1058), St. Bernard of Clairvaux (1091–1153), and St. Thomas Aquinas (1227–1274).

III. DEVELOPMENT OF THE LITURGICAL YEAR AND SOME OF ITS ACCOMPANYING RITES

1. The Liturgical Year

As the first Christian converts from Judaism "had all their lives been accustomed to observe a weekly day of rest and prayer, it must have been almost inevitable that they should wish so to modify this holiday that it might serve as a weekly commemoration of the source of all their hopes. Probably at first they did not wholly withdraw from the Synagogue, and the Sunday must have seemed rather a prolongation of, than a substitution for, the old familiar Sabbath. But it was not long before the observance of the first day of the week became distinctive of Christian worship."[34] Early writings, even books of the New Testament, seem to indicate that Sunday was the day of the Eucharist: "And on the first day of the week, when we were assembled to break bread . . ." (Acts 20:7).

In Chapter 23 of Leviticus we read of the establishment of the Jewish calendar and of the sacrifices which God required of His chosen people on certain days. In the Christian liturgy, two of these days, Easter and Pentecost, are two of the greatest feasts of the year, because the Resurrection of Christ occurred on the first,

[34] Herbert Thurston, "Calendar," *Catholic Encyclopedia,* Vol. III, p. 159. This copyright is now held by the Gilmary Society of New York.

and the descent of the Holy Spirit upon our Lady and the Apostles on the second.

The feasts of Easter and Pentecost, Jewish feasts which had thus taken on a new meaning after Christ's death, easily became Christian liturgical days. The feast of the Ascension, celebrated between Easter and Pentecost, appears to be the oldest feast of purely Christian origin. It was a normal development that Christmas should also take its place in the liturgical cycle, although this feast did not appear until the fourth century. With the celebration of days preparatory to, and following, these feasts, and with the addition of new feasts, the great liturgical cycle *de tempore* was established, a cycle that has been developing ever since.

The Greeks and Romans had long been accustomed to celebrate the anniversaries of the death of a great man with a joyous banquet held in his honor. Thus, too, in the early days of the Church, the anniversaries of the deaths of martyrs were kept with the offering of flowers and prayers at the tomb, followed by a memorial feast or banquet. Private celebrations easily became liturgical celebrations, and the anniversaries of the deaths of martyrs and outstanding Christian saints were then celebrated with the offering of the Eucharist and the partaking of the Eucharistic Banquet. Though these were at first local celebrations and connected with the tombs of the martyrs, the commemoration of the anniversaries spread with the communication between churches. This communication included not only the interchange of accounts, such as the "Acts of the Martyrs," describing their lives and the circumstances of their deaths, but also the interchange of the relics of the martyrs.

The fourth century witnessed a growth in devotion to the martyrs. Churches began to be built over their tombs, or their relics were inserted in the altar stones. Feasts were established to honor these holy men and women, and these feasts were admitted to the liturgical year in the sanctoral cycle. The calendar of the Church was outlined by the end of the fifth century, and through the years it has been filled in and expanded.

Every calendar, civil or religious, becomes a means of commemorating past events which have special significance for us, events which we relive because of the relationship they bear to us. The liturgical calendar and the events relived by the members of the mystical Christ should mean much to us. As we meditate on them, as we enter into them,[35] the graces secured for us through them should enter into us and reanimate our spirit and change our lives. The liturgy "contains the reality it symbolizes."[36] As our Holy Father declares: ". . . the liturgical year, devotedly fostered and accompanied by the Church, is not a cold and lifeless representation of the events of the past, or a simple and bare record of a former age. It is rather Christ Himself who is ever living in His Church. Here He continues that journey of immense mercy which He lovingly began in His mortal life, going about doing good, with the design of bringing men to know His mysteries and in a way live by them."[37]

2. Some Rites Entering the Liturgy in This Period

The study of the origin and, in particular, of the meaning of the various practices present in our modern-day liturgy is very beneficial and should not be neglected. Only thus will we be enabled to enter into the spirit expressed by these practices and to obtain from them the graces meant for us.

Many of the rites and practices which accompany the celebration of the liturgy were originally forms of expression in the religious and secular life of the people. The Church "Christianized" these natural and habitual forms of expression and took them into the official form of the worship of the Mystical Body. For any pagan interpretation the Church substituted one which would bring her members into a closer relationship with the one true God. She then incorporated the custom in her worship. This is probably the origin of processions, of seasonal observances, e.g., the Ember Days, and of various other practices and customs.

[35] See Marmion, *Christ in His Mysteries* (London: Sands and Company, 1931; American Edition, St. Louis: B. Herder), Chaps. I and II.

[36] "The Apostolate," *Orate Fratres,* April, 1936, p. 269.

[37] *Mediator Dei,* p. 165.

Soon after the Edict of Milan, a large basilica was built at the place of the Holy Sepulcher in Jerusalem; then from the Christian world pilgrimages to the Holy Places began. Pilgrims' accounts of the ritual celebrated at Jerusalem probably influenced the liturgy in the West. It has been thought that at least the Palm Sunday procession and the adoration of the cross on Good Friday were derived from these accounts. We shall see later that our liturgy of Palm Sunday and Holy Week was affected by a strong Gallican activity, itself influenced by early Eastern rites.

IV. THE DIVINE OFFICE

It is not necessary that there be a uniformity of rite throughout the world, for although the liturgy is one, the ways of offering it may, and do, vary. There may have been some who desired a uniformity of rite between East and West, but these desires were not achieved after the rites became established as such. Each rite, however, certainly influenced the other. The influence of the East is very apparent in the development of the Divine Office.

The disciples of our Lord, long accustomed to the Jewish practice of prayer at certain hours of the day, very naturally continued to pray at these times.[38] Thus we know that the Holy Ghost came down upon the Apostles as they were assembled in prayer at the third hour. The Acts of the Apostles bear witness to the fact that it was at the sixth hour (Acts 10:9–10) when Peter was at prayer that he saw the vision of the great sheet let down from heaven to earth. Peter and John went "into the temple at the ninth hour of prayer" (Acts 3:1). At midnight Paul and Silas prayed in prison (Acts 16:25).

Early Christian writings, for example, the writings of St. Paul, St. Clement, Pliny, and St. Hippolytus, testify to the fact that specified Hours of prayer were observed in the course of the first three centuries of the Church. After freedom of worship was officially granted by the Edict of Milan (313), our present Hours of the Divine Office, Matins, Lauds, Prime, Terce, Sext, None, Vespers, and Compline, began to take form.

[38] *Ibid.*, No. 140.

We have already traced the origin of *Vespers* and of *Matins* in the vigil services. Up to the fourth century, daily vigil celebration was considered a private prayer; during the fourth century, the Church recognized it as an official or liturgical prayer. In the Syrian Church at the beginning of the fourth century, there was a service at morn before the Eucharist. This was probably the origin of *Lauds.*

After the Edict of Milan, ascetics (early "religious") who were everywhere in the East, were free to meet together at the third, sixth, and ninth hours (*Terce, Sext,* and *None*) for prayer. These hours, which were the Jewish hours of prayer, hallowed by the occurrences of our Lord's Passion, were now for Christians even more significant. Thus began the day Hours. *Prime,* an early morning day prayer, was introduced at Bethlehem in the late fourth or fifth century. We are not certain of the origin of *Compline,* the Church's official night prayer, although it is believed that it was in use sometime before the fifth century.

We will not consider the subject of the time and circumstances of the introduction of the Hours into the West. We know definitely that the offering of the *Divine Office* — the *Opus Dei* or *Work of God* — was made obligatory for the Benedictines by the year 529 or 530. St. Benedict established the order of the Hours for his own monks, and most authorities agree that the Roman Office was influenced by his arrangement. St. Benedict himself had been influenced in his arrangement by practices at Rome and elsewhere. St. Gregory I, who had been both a monk and an abbot of one of the Benedictine monasteries in Rome and who was pope from 590 to 604, made changes in the Roman Office of his day, leaving it, in broad outline, the Office of the present-day Breviary.

Peter Wagner, in his *Introduction to the Gregorian Melodies,* Chapter VII of Book I, surveys the development of the Office. He considers among other details, the influence of the monastic on the Roman Office.[39] This, again, is a vast and interesting subject which we cannot consider here. There is a difference between the

[39] See also Dom Ernest Graf, O.S.B., *The Church's Daily Prayer* (London: Burns, Oates and Washbourne, Ltd., 1938), Chaps. II, III, and others.

monastic and the Roman Office but "the difference is even now inconsiderable, and does not concern any single form which is of the essence of the Office."[40]

The Office, offered in common, was intended to be sung, not said. This fact explains its form as nothing else can. Saying the Office was sanctioned by the Church in the thirteenth century when circumstances made it impossible for many priests to offer it in common.

Where did the founders of the Office get their prayers? The Psalms form a large part of the Hours. We cannot but agree that the Psalter acquired an importance in the Christian Church that far surpassed the importance it had possessed in Judaism.[41] There was scarcely a Christian practice where the Psalter did not have a place of honor. Consequently, we are not surprised to discover that it was the custom of the faithful to learn the psalms from memory. Early religious communities made this memorization a matter of obligation for their members.[42]

Let us study and sing *Compline for Sundays* in the form in which it is now used in the Roman Rite. Let us notice its use of the lessons, its antiphons and psalms, its hymn, canticle, and responsory. Do we know why each selection bears its particular title? Can we do the same for *Vespers?* for the other Hours?

V. OTHER LITURGICAL DEVELOPMENTS OF THE FOURTH, FIFTH, AND SIXTH CENTURIES

Let us merely summarize three other developments.

1. *The Mass and the Divine Office began to assume a fixed type of song.* The Antiphon, which had hitherto belonged exclusively to the Office, was included definitely in the Mass and became the foundation of the three processional chants during the movements to and from the altar: the Introit chant, Offertory chant, and the Communion chant. The chants during the Offertory and Communion processions were probably instituted in the fourth century.[43]

40 Peter Wagner, *op. cit.*, p. 155.

41 *Ibid.*, p. 5.

42 *Ibid.*, p. 9.

43 Cabrol, *The Mass of the Western Rites* (St. Louis: B. Herder, 1934), p. 29.

The psalm melodies of the early Church were quite simple and truly psalmodic. During the last part of this period the melodies became more florid and richly melismatic. This is especially true of the responsorial psalm between the readings in the Mass, which was thus also abbreviated to one or two verses.

2. *Latin became the liturgical language.* In the beginning there was no thought of a liturgical language. The prayers of the liturgy were said in the vernacular, or language of the people, which originally was Greek or Aramaic. We are not certain when the language of the Roman liturgy became Latin. Most authorities agree that probably both Latin and Greek were used for some time, and that about the fourth century Latin began definitely to supplant the Greek in liturgical use.

We will see that the use of Latin, after it was no longer spoken as a common tongue, contributed its share to the gradual decline of the voiced liturgical participation of the laity. Many of the branches of the Eastern Rite still have the Mass in their tongue. In the West, Latin was for centuries the international language and it was normal that the international, or rather supranational, Church should use this language for the worship of the Western peoples. Perhaps the liturgy of the Western Rite will allow the vernacular language again. There are advantages in the use of the vernacular that balance the use of the Latin. The Holy See will decide which is more beneficial for souls. In the meantime, vernacular translations of the Missal (and the study of Latin or of interlinear translations of the prayers) assist us to follow the thought and to participate actively in the liturgy of our Roman Rite.

3. *The Schola Cantorum was founded.* This will be discussed in some detail later.

VI. THE EARLY FATHERS AND MUSIC IN THE LITURGY

Only a few Fathers will be mentioned here as proof that from the beginning there was an interest in the use of music in the liturgy.

St. Clement of Alexandria (150–220) was noted as a great hymn writer. His most famous hymn is the "Hymn to the Creator." *St.*

Eusebius (260–340) remarks that the voice is to be preferred to instruments in the church. *St. Athanasius* (298–373) strove against the use of overelaborate melodies for the psalms. *St. Basil* (330–379), after whom the *Liturgy of St. Basil* is named, encouraged the vigil celebration in his various churches. He used to visit these churches one after another on the same night to show his approval and to take part in the service.[44] He introduced antiphonal singing at Caesarea.[45] *St. Gregory Nazianzen* (325–390) found it hard to leave Constantinople where the whole congregation chanted the psalms.[46] *St. Hilary of Poitiers* (died 368) unsuccessfully strove to introduce Syrian hymnody into the West. *St. Jerome* (340–420) translated the text of the Bible to the Latin Vulgate. He approved of the singing of the jubilus[47] but opposed the use of instruments.[48] He was the counselor of Pope Damasus, who in his turn did much to organize the Roman liturgy. St. Jerome advised him to add to the Mass the *Alleluia* which was widely used by the people in the East as a refrain to the solo psalmody.[49]

St. Augustine

St. Augustine (354–430), who wrote a treatise on music, introduced psalm singing at the Offertory of the Mass in Africa. He who was able to resist the powerful influence of the sermons of St. Ambrose was not able to resist the effect of the psalmody of the Church, as he himself confesses: "I wept at the beauty of Your hymns and canticles and was so powerfully moved at the sound of Your Church's singing. Those sounds flowed into my ears, and the truth streamed into my heart: so that my feeling of devotion overflowed, and the tears ran from my eyes, and I was happy in them."[50] Later he worried that he took too much

44 Lang, *Music in Western Civilization,* p. 44.
45 Aigrain, *op. cit.,* p. 23.
46 Wagner, *op. cit.,* p. 111.
47 A *jubilus* is a florid melody on a single vowel — as on the "a" of *Alleluia.*
48 Thuis, *Gregorian Chant A Barometer of Religious Fervor,* p. 13.
49 Lang, *op. cit.,* p. 46.
50 From *Confessions of St. Augustine,* p. 193, translated by F. J. Sheed, copyright Sheed and Ward, Inc., New York.

natural joy in hearing psalms sung. However he again reasons thus: "Yet when I remember the tears I shed, moved by the songs of the Church in the early days of my new faith: and again when I see that I am moved not by the singing but by the things that are sung — when they are sung with a clear voice and proper modulation — I recognize once more the usefulness of this practice [of psalmody]."[51]

The words of St. Augustine are often used to justify the jubilus. "He who jubilates utters no words, but a sound of joy without words: for it is the voice of the spirit lost in joy, expressing that joy to the utmost of its power but unable to define its meaning."[52] Elsewhere he says that if we must praise God and we cannot praise Him adequately in words, what else can we do but jubilate.[53]

St. Ambrose

St. Ambrose (340–397), the Bishop of Milan, and Pope St. Gregory the Great (540–604) are particularly to be noted.[54] The hymns of St. Ambrose, profound in meaning and exquisite in expression, were clothed in classic phraseology and yet had great popular appeal. Other writers imitated his style, and their hymns are also called Ambrosian; therefore, it is not possible to determine how many he actually wrote himself. We do know that he composed these four: *Aeterne rerum conditor, Deus creator omnium, Jam surgit hora tertia,* and *Veni redemptor gentium.* St. Augustine tells us that St. Ambrose introduced the Eastern style of hymn and psalm singing among the Milanese, as they spent the night in prayer in the cathedral with him when he was suffering persecution from the Arians.[55] The style of psalm singing that he introduced was antiphonal.

To St. Ambrose is also credited the style of singing called Ambrosian or Milanese. It is characterized by great simplicity —

51 *Ibid.,* p. 243.

52 St. Augustine quoted by Maurice Zundel, *The Splendour of the Liturgy,* p. 84, copyright Sheed and Ward, Inc., New York.

53 Zundel, *The Splendour of the Liturgy* (New York: Sheed and Ward, 1944), p. 85.

54 Read a summary of their lives in your Church History text.

55 *Confessions of St. Augustine,* p. 193.

based on a psalm tone with an occasional inflection and the use of the jubilus on some words. It is a style of chant that is predominantly syllabic. The *Gloria, Alii Cantus ad Libitum* in the *Kyriale* is Ambrosian.

Some authors attribute the adoption of the four authentic modes in plainsong to St. Ambrose, but this claim is generally discredited.

St. Gregory I

In the years during which he reigned as pope, St. Gregory I (590–604), also called the Great, did so much for the liturgy and its music that the official song of the Church has been named Gregorian Chant. (1) He revised, corrected, and completed the work of his predecessors, either by himself or with the aid of chanters of the Roman Schola Cantorum who worked under him. (2) He regulated the use of all the chants of the year according to the Church year then existing. So universally respected was this work that for many years no one changed it. (3) He has been credited with the composition of new chants. (4) He reorganized the Schola Cantorum (this will be discussed later). (5) A *Sacramentary,* as we have seen, and a *Cento,* or compiled *Antiphonale,* are attributed to him. (6) He regulated the part of the deacon as soloist in the liturgy. In Jewish responsorial psalmody, the soloist, who was a trained singer, sang long groups of tones (a *melisma*) at the textual punctuation marks. This improvisation, if sung well, was capable of giving much honor to God. It was both an offering of an art to God and, above all, an expression of interior worship. Here the soloist sang in the name of the people. The same practice had been adopted by the Christians and was considered so important a function in the worship, that only one whose probity of life was recognized by the celebrant (the pope) could sing the solo chant — the Gradual solo in the Mass. The Gradual was the musical climax of the Mass and the honor of being chosen soloist was valued. It is thought that St. Gregory did not wish the singing voice to be considered in the qualifications of the rank of deacon and that he felt that deacons were sometimes distracted from their other rights and duties because of the prestige given to them as soloists. Therefore he forbade deacons to sing as a solo any musical portion of the Mass other than the Gospel.[56]

(7) Other modifications in the pre-existing practices have been attributed to St. Gregory. We can truly admit his action in the following: (*a*) the insertion of a few phrases in the Canon (St. Benedict XIV, 1740–1758, claims that no pope has added to or changed the Canon since Gregory[57]); (*b*) the inclusion of the *Pater Noster* before the breaking of the bread; (*c*) the provision that the *Alleluia* be chanted after the Gradual out of Paschal time; (*d*) the prohibition of the use of the chasuble by the subdeacons assisting at Mass.[58]

VII. STATION PROCESSIONS

The Roman word *station* meant a watch or vigil. In early Christian usage the term was taken to mean a large church assembly, or to designate a day of prayer and fasting. It is used in this latter sense when the Wednesdays and Fridays of Lent are called *Station Days.* But in the sense of the *stational* observance, it referred to the gathering of the faithful offering the Mass celebrated by the pope.[59]

The station observance, which had begun in the fourth and fifth centuries, reached the height of its development under St. Gregory the Great. On certain days of considerable liturgical importance, the celebrant (the pope) and his clergy, with the faithful, met in some church called the church of the assembly.[60] After a Collect recited by the celebrant in the name of the people, they walked in solemn procession to a stational church. During the procession, prayers in the form of litanies were chanted, the people frequently repeating "Kyrie eleison." After a solemn entry into the stational church, the Mass was celebrated.[61]

[56] See Wagner, *Introduction to the Gregorian Melodies,* p. 76; also Fortescue, *The Mass,* p. 266.

[57] Fortescue, *op. cit.,* p. 172.

[58] G. Roger Hudleston, "Gregory I," *Catholic Encyclopedia,* p. 786.

[59] See Cabrol, *Mass of the Western Rites,* p. 45.

[60] Pius Parsch, *The Liturgy of the Mass,* translated by Frederic C. Eckhoff (St. Louis: B. Herder, 1940), p. 54.

[61] The arrangement of the station observance varied somewhat throughout the years.

In the beginning, the place of station was chosen by the pope and announced to the faithful at the previous station observance. Gregory I established an order of stations in Rome, assigning certain days to definite churches or basilicas. This order, which with additions has prevailed until our day, may be ascertained by referring to our missals. At the beginning of about 87 of our Masses, we find the place of station noted. The place of the station, or the saint whose church is thus honored, has at times influenced the Proper for the day, as we may easily see in the missal.

Stational observance was continued until the ninth century. Beginning to decline at this time, it was finally completely discontinued in the fourteenth century.[62]

VIII. THE SCHOLA CANTORUM

Tradition tells us that the first *Schola Cantorum,* or School of Singing, was founded at Rome under Pope Sylvester. It was simply a body of singers who went as a choir to the basilica where the procession or feast was to be celebrated. Since Sylvester was pope (314–336) immediately following the Edict of Milan, we are not surprised that each basilica had not as yet a college of its own singers. Pope Hilary (461–467) established a group of seven subdeacons to be responsible for the music of all the services at which he officiated, and applied the name *Schola Cantorum* to this body.

St. Gregory reorganized the Schola Cantorum. Until then its members had two duties: (1) to produce, improve, and sing the music for all papal functions; and (2) to train perpetuating members. Gregory developed two Schola which had previously existed and which continued to fulfill the first duty. These Schola were practically theological seminaries. He also founded and endowed

---

Father Pius Parsch in his *The Liturgy of the Mass,* pp. 56–59, quotes Father Kramp's description of the Easter stational observance based on the *Ordo Romanus I.* This is generally accepted as the type of stational observance in the time of Gregory I. (See also Fortescue, *The Mass,* pp. 174–176; and Jungmann-Brunner, *The Mass of the Roman Rite* [New York: Benziger Brothers], pp. 67–73.)

[62] Read Parsch, *The Liturgy of the Mass,* pp. 81–82, for a short description of the revival of station observance in our day.

two others of an entirely different character, one at the Lateran Church and the other at St. Peter's. These were also responsible for the choir singing at papal functions, but their particular duty was to train perpetuating members. The students were small boys, mostly orphans. "The lads were given a sound, general, musical, and religious education by the members of the Schola Cantorum which thus became a self-perpetuating body."[63] The Schola Cantorum existed until the fourteenth century. "So highly successful was this foundation in supplying competent musicians that the Schola itself came to be popularly called, after the orphanages, the *Orphanotrophium*. It was the first musical Conservatory."[64]

We will not enter into the discussion of whether or not more is attributed to St. Gregory than is his due in regard to the Schola. We safely claim what is set forth in this section and also what is stated by Rene Aigrain. We quote: "First as deacon, then as archdeacon, he had had the direction of the Roman Church, and came to know better than anyone how to guard against possible abuses." Later the same author says: "Gregory gives to the school [that is, to the Schola Cantorum] its constitution . . . which it retains almost exactly in the following centuries: to this the testimonies are sufficiently numerous and precise. . . . He gave lessons there, probably at the time when he was yet only an archdeacon; he transmitted to the school, therefore an interpretation of the melodies, which we shall be justified in calling, in these conditions, a Gregorian tradition."[65]

We would not easily imagine the importance either of the Schola or of its members in the life of the Church. Peter Wagner supplies us with most interesting details on this point. Most of the popes of the seventh century either were closely connected with it or came from its ranks.[66]

Liturgy and music, unified in the *Antiphonale Missarum* and

[63] Winfred Douglas, *Church Music in History and Practice* (New York: Scribner's Sons, 1937), p. 54.

[64] *Ibid.*

[65] Aigrain, *op. cit.*, pp. 32, 34.

[66] Wagner, *op. cit.* See Chap. VI.

performed and developed by the skill and genius of those connected with the Schola Cantorum, "stood as a complete model and standard for the worship of the Church; and though this work was primarily undertaken for the city of Rome alone, its very excellence brought about a wide dissemination, not only of the actual services and the music, but as well of the method of organization that had made them possible."[67]

IX. ACTIVE PARTICIPATION IN THE LITURGY

In the early days of the Roman Rite, it was customary that the Mass at Rome be celebrated either by the pope or by his representative, and that the clergy and people of Rome be present, all, needless to say, actively participating in the rite. In early times, and throughout the years into the thirteenth century, bishops and their priests celebrated Mass together, either consecrating together (*concelebratio sacramentalis*) or individually fulfilling their own hierarchical functions with the bishop alone consecrating (*concelebratio ceremonialis*). The former practice survives in ordination Masses of the present day; the latter in our solemnized Mass. What we now call a Low Mass was celebrated as early as the seventh century, but we know that the Low Mass was not ordinary at this early date.

Our present-day liturgical books furnish us with all the prayers and readings for particular services. Originally, liturgical books filled the need, not of a service, but of individual participants, that is, the celebrant, the lectors, the singers.[68] The celebrant's book, the *sacramentary,* contained only the prayers proper to him in his sacerdotal function; it did not contain, as our missal does, the parts intended to be sung by others. The *lectionary,* or book for the lectors or readers, contained the readings. The chants for the choir were contained in books which bore titles suggesting the type of song found therein: *Antiphonale, Graduale,* or *Liber responsalis, psalterium,* and later, *hymnarium, troper, sequentialis,* and so on.

67 Douglas, *op. cit.,* p. 55.

68 Note that these books were written by hand, and were thus called "manuscripts."

In the early *Antiphonale,* there was only the text without its accompanying music. As we have noted, the choir had to memorize the melodies; as they sang these melodies, they followed the hand gestures (chironomy) of the choir leader.

There was no such thing as a Kyriale as we know it. The congregation sang very simple melodies for the *Kyrie, Sanctus,* and *Agnus Dei*—probably the ones of Mass XVIII in the present-day Kyriale. An early *Gloria* melody is supposed to be the one given in Mass XV, and an early *Credo,* our present Credo I.

From its earliest beginnings, the Christian liturgy was offered, not only *for* the people, but *with* the people. Father Ellard summarizes the development of *lay participation* in the liturgy up to the seventh century.[69] This participation, personal and corporate, was expressed in song and action. (1) *Sung participation.* With the exception of the Gradual, there was lay participation in each new choral element as it was added to the liturgy. (2) *Personal participation.* By personally presenting a gift, symbolic of the gift of themselves, the faithful participated more fully in the sacrificial rite. (3) *Participation in action.* Group movement united the people corporeally and tended to develop and strengthen a spiritual unity. There were processions to the church for Mass, to the altar as they gave their gifts at the Offertory, to the altar as they received from God the Gift-of-Gifts in Holy Communion. Singing accompanied all these processions.[70]

REVIEW QUESTIONS

1. Under four points summarize shortly the historical setting of this period.
2. Our text lists several documentary sources of our knowledge of the Roman Rite of this period. What are they?
3. Why did some Councils forbid the singing of those hymns in the liturgy which used texts not scriptural in origin? What was the effect of this ban?

[69] Gerald Ellard, S.J., *Dialog Mass* (New York: Longmans, Green and Company, 1942), p. 18.

[70] In these pages are included pictures of some present-day personal and corporate participation expressed through song and action. Other present-day expressions could also have been pictured. Noteworthy among these latter is that with which, thank God, we are familiar, namely, the procession to, and the reception of, Holy Communion.

4. Explain the origin of the Temporal Cycle.
5. Explain the origin of the Sanctoral Cycle.
6. What is the purpose of the Liturgical Year?
7. What are the Hours of the Divine Office?
8. Can you trace the origin of each Hour?
9. When did *saying* the Office receive the sanction of the Church? How was it prayed before that?
10. Of what prayers is most of the Office composed?
11. List three "further liturgical developments of the fifth and sixth centuries" as given in this text.
12. Select three Church Fathers, not including St. Ambrose and St. Gregory, and give a proof that each was interested in the sung liturgy.
13. What is a *jubilus?*
14. List two contributions to the sung liturgy made by St. Ambrose.
15. Summarize under at least five points St. Gregory's work for the liturgy.
16. Describe the stational observance.
17. Discuss shortly the formation of the Schola Cantorum.
18. What are the titles of the books compiled for use in the liturgy of this (and the next) period of the chant?
19. Did the people — the congregation — have a book? How did they know what to sing?
20. Summarize under three headings the participation of the laity in the liturgy of this period.

SECOND PERIOD — PERIOD OF DIFFUSION AND PERFECTION — 600–1300

A. The Golden Age of Gregorian Chant — 600–1000

THE EARLY MIDDLE AGES — HISTORICAL SETTING

The fifth, sixth, and seventh centuries have been called the "Dark Ages" because there was no flowering of the arts during these years. A certain amount of peace and tranquillity, coupled with a general sense of refinement of taste, is a necessity if the arts are to be developed among the people. The troubled conditions of these years were not conducive to artistic expression.

The *West* was the source of the most confusion. Italy was divided between invading Lombards and occupying Goths, with native Romans caught helplessly between them, and the Papacy apparently doomed until rescued by the Franks (about 754). From then on, the Papal States, given to the Pope by Pepin the Short, King of the

Franks, dominated Italy, although much of Italy was subject to the Franks.

The Franks, under the successors of Clovis, increased their power and holdings. (1) Charles Martel (714–741), Mayor of the Palace under a Merovingian, defeated the Moors (732) at Tours. (2) Pepin the Short (751–768) founded the Carolingian Dynasty, conquered the Lombards, and bestowed the Papal States on the Pope. These included Rome and Ravenna and the strip between them. (3) Charlemagne, the greatest medieval ruler, achieved unity for the West. (*a*) He was crowned by Pope St. Leo as Emperor of the Holy Roman Empire in St. Peter's on Christmas Day in the year 800; (*b*) he enlarged the Frankish realm into one Romano-Teutonic state, which replaced the old Empire and which supported Christianity; (*c*) he Christianized Gaul and its neighbors; (*d*) he spread culture and learning by establishing schools and importing scholars — such as Alcuin and St. Paulinus of Aquileia — from England, Ireland, and Italy; (*e*) he defended the Papacy; and (*f*) he reorganized civil society.

In England, Alfred the Great, after restoring military supremacy by defeating the Danes, restored Anglo-Saxon rule, built up towns and monasteries, and restored Christianity and learning. Ireland, the "land of saints and scholars," was a lighted lamp during these "Dark Ages." The monasticism and culture which flourished there was an influential source of Christianity and general knowledge for England, Scotland, and Wales, as well as for the more northern isles and the continent itself.

The *East* also saw disorder amounting to chaos with but one glimmer of light. Constantinople was allowing its brilliant culture to crystallize.

Mohammedanism began and developed. Mohammed left Mecca in 622 — the Hegira. Islam took such a hold of the people that it formed a crescent around the Mediterranean Sea. Alone it produced a distinctive culture and rule; in some places this culture was influenced by Christianity. The Moslems, defeated at Tours, remained a constant threat to Christianity, especially in the East.

B. The Period of Preservation and Transition of the Chant — 1000–1300

THE LATE MIDDLE AGES — HISTORICAL SETTING

This was an Era of Christian Unity. It was characterized by the close union of Church and State in a Feudal Society. In its *military aspects,* the age produced, on the one hand, the institution of chivalry, and on the other, the interducal wars and eventually the Truce of God. In its *social aspects,* it resulted in a stratified society. *Politically,* the people were conscious of their unity in the Church, and, under the Holy Roman Empire, the influence of the Church pervaded political and military affairs.

In this era the fine arts flourished. Evidences were (1) the flowering of Gothic art; (2) the rise of great universities such as that of Paris and that of Bologne; (3) the beginning of a vernacular (national) literature; and (4) Scholasticism (St. Thomas Aquinas, St. Bonaventure, etc.).

The political and social picture was colorful and varied. Most of Christendom was bound together in the "Holy Roman Empire of the German Nations," which brought Rome and the Papacy into close relationship to the civil government. Otto the Great was the first leader of the new Empire. Under him were countless princes and dukes. Some relatively large cities — called "City-States" — governed themselves and the territory around them. Many formed powerful leagues, such as the Lombard and the Hanseatic Leagues. Within these city-states the guilds developed high social and religious values.

Outside the Empire there were only two Christian governments of any size. There was *France* which the strong Capetian kings were wielding into a proud and Catholic nation under an absolute monarch. Her most glorious king was St. Louis IX; her most devastating heresy, the Albigensian heresy. Then there was *England* where circumstances were shaping a people with representative forms of government. As the result of the Norman conquest of 1066, the

Norman-French fused with the Anglo-Saxon and brought the English Church closer to Rome.

These were the centuries of the Crusades, that glorious pageant of clergy, nobles, and common people who surged eastward to wrest the Holy Lands from the bloodstained hands of the Mohammedans. Knightly orders grew up to make permanent the achievements of the Crusades. Despite the magnificent display of enthusiasm for the faith, these same centuries saw hideous abuses flourishing in the Church's administration — simony, lay investiture, nicolaitism, and nepotism. Popes outstanding in zeal and holiness battled to retain or regain the purity of Church discipline and her freedom from secular domination. Gregory VII and Innocent III are most famous for their fearless defense of the Mystical Body. These popes were greatly aided by the reforms of Cluny and by the rise of the mendicant orders. These centuries, like our own, were remarkably good and at the same time remarkably evil.

THE LITURGY AND ITS MUSIC — INTRODUCTION

As we note in the historical setting, this second period has really two aspects which we must keep in mind. The times, influencing the life and expression of the people, also influenced the "human elements" of the liturgy. Many elements, however, flowering in the years 1000–1300, found their beginnings in the preceding years. Therefore we shall develop the liturgical aspects of the years 600–1300 as one unit. But at the same time we will remember that politically, socially, and culturally this period is not one unit.

I. DIFFUSION OF THE LITURGY

Uniformity of Rite. The East held the principle that the Patriarchal Rite was to be imitated by the suffragan Churches. This was not true of the West. No one denied that the Bishop of Rome was the Patriarch of the West, yet the Western Churches did not all follow his rite.

During these years there was not the ideal of exact uniformity of rite that there is now. The reforms made by Gregory I were intended for the liturgy as celebrated at Rome. In fact, the liturgy celebrated there had to be somewhat adapted to fit the situation elsewhere. Comparatively difficult means of communication between countries, absence of uniform laws, development of local usages, and, as regards the music, a lack of universally understood notation, contributed to nonessential modifications of the human elements of the rite celebrated at Rome.

In the West there was another rite, non-Roman in origin, which was also very popular. This rite was the Gallican Rite. Some authorities group under the term "Gallican" all the Western non-Roman rites.[71] Thus we may consider the Milanese and Mozarabic Rites as Gallican if we so wish. Strictly, of course, the Gallican Rite is the rite used in Gaul. The origin of the Gallican Rite is not a matter of great importance to us here. Some believe it to be a form of the very early Roman Rite; some, a development of the Eastern Rite (either early or late). At any rate it certainly differs from the Roman Rite and it does show Eastern influences.

England. During the time of Pope St. Gregory the Great, that is, in 597, missionaries under St. Augustine of Canterbury were sent to England. St. Gregory cautioned Augustine not to force the Roman Rite on England, but to choose the Roman or Gallican elements he thought best.[72] Nevertheless, St. Augustine brought with him a copy of the Gregorian Antiphonary, and he and his companions, as they approached King Ethelbert of Kent, sang a Roman processional hymn, *"Deprecamur te."*[73] Thus the Roman Rite made entrance and began to supplant the former rites of the country.

"Every monastery founded in the savage forests of Germany, Gaul, or Britain became at once a singing school, and day and night the holy strains went up in unison with the melodies of the far distant city."[74] A *Schola Cantorum* was established at Canterbury; one was also established at York under James, the Deacon

[71] Fortescue, *op. cit.*, p. 98.

[72] *Ibid.*, p. 179.

[73] Aigrain, *op. cit.*, p. 41.

[74] Edward Dickinson, *Music in the History of the Western Church* (New York: Charles Scribner's Sons, 1902), p. 118.

of York, in the seventh century. In 680, John, the Archicantor of St. Peter's, came from Rome to Wearmouth, where he stayed a year instructing in the Roman Chant. England did not easily yield to the change in its liturgical practices, but union with Rome was affirmed frequently. Finally, although in some places there were still slight additions, by the eighth century all the churches followed the Roman Rite. The Celtic Rite lingered on in Ireland and Scotland until the eleventh or twelfth century.

Gaul (France and Germany). The Roman style of singing was introduced into Gaul at an early date. We cannot say definitely when the Roman Rite was first introduced, but it must have been at least by the seventh century, for, as we noted previously, the seventh- or eighth-century manuscript of the Gelasian Sacramentary is a Roman book Gallicanized.

Pope Stephen II in 754 visited the court of Pepin the Short. The differences between the rite of the Romans and that of the Franks were thus made apparent, and Pepin resolved to introduce the Roman practices. The instruction of the Franks in the Roman style of liturgy and chant was begun immediately. These lessons were not according to the desire of some of the Frankish clergy, as we can easily understand. Bishop Chrodegang of Metz, however, supported the decrees of Pepin by introducing Roman ceremonies in his own cathedral and throughout his diocese. A Roman Antiphonal and Responsorial were sent with a teacher from the Roman Schola Cantorum to the Schola of Metz. Later, monks went from Metz to Rome, and on returning home became the teachers of their own people. The Song School at Metz attained great fame even during the lifetime of Pepin. It was considered as excellent as that in Rome and was attended even by the English. It was said that Sigulf learned liturgical usages in Rome but church singing in Metz.[75] The work of Pepin "represents also the beginnings of a political idea of a united empire built on a uniform liturgy and ritualistic music."[76]

Charlemagne completed the work begun by his father. He de-

[75] Wagner, *op. cit.*, p. 207.
[76] Lang, *op. cit.*, p. 67.

manded submission to numerous decrees and ordinances concerning the liturgy. In this work he was, of course, assisted by some clergy in his realm and resisted by others. To Charlemagne is attributed the phrase which Pius X made his own: "Let us return to the pure fount of Gregory." By the time of the death of Charlemagne the Roman liturgy and the Gregorian Chant had officially replaced the Gallican liturgy and chant throughout his empire.

The fact that the Gallican Rite was not quickly supplanted by the Roman deserves more explanation than that of unwillingness to change. As we have seen, the liturgical customs of Rome were devised for Rome and needed adapting before they were practicable in Gaul. Various bishops had tried to do this in various ways.[77] Their commendable action did not lead to uniformity. Charlemagne entrusted the work of uniform adaptation to Alcuin whom he had brought from England to be his liturgical adviser and to lead in the education of his people. Later, a pupil of Alcuin, Amalarius of Metz, attempted to bring some of the chants of the Office into more perfect agreement with the Roman originals. To his amazement, he found the Office at Metz in a more pure form than that in use at Rome at the time. Eventually the compilation of Amalarius influenced the form of some of the Office chants (for example, the Responsory) in the Roman Office and became the foundation of the Roman-Gallic form.

"The centers of Carolingian-Ottonian musical culture, including secular music, were the monasteries. (We must, of course, remember the unique position held by the royal court.) Following the inspired leadership of Alcuin at the Abbey of Tours, the culture of the Middle Ages was concentrated in them. In this intellectual culture music occupied an important position. The reformatory activities of Charlemagne caused a sudden development of monastic schools and learning both in France and in Germany. The old Benedictine Monasteries found a happy and harmonious middle way between the sacred and the secular [learning]."[78]

[77] Wagner, *op. cit.*, p. 209.
[78] Lang, *op. cit.*, p. 68.

Frankish Song Schools flourished everywhere in the ninth, tenth, and eleventh centuries. Especially famous were those of Metz, St. Gall, Paris, Dijon, Cambrai, Chartres, Nevers, and Toul. St. Gall, which became a regular Benedictine monastery about the middle of the eighth century, is particularly important in the liturgical and cultural life of the West. St. Gall and Reichenau continued the work begun among German-speaking peoples by St. Boniface.

Spain. The people of Spain also had a liturgy and a chant of their own — the Mozarabic — which they were not anxious to give up. Near the close of the eighth century there began a movement toward the Roman Rite. But it was not until the eleventh century, under Gregory VII and King Alfonso VI, that the Mozarabic Rite was displaced and even then not everywhere. It still survives in some churches in Toledo — a truly venerable rite and perfectly approved by the Holy See.

Dom Mocquereau, a monk of Solesmes, had the theory that the four Western chants, the Mozarabic, the Gallican, the Milanese, and the Gregorian, were but four dialects of the same musical language. We may still have positive proof that this is so. Although much has been ascertained in late years, the origin of the Mozarabic Chant, and as a matter of fact, the origin of the various Western liturgies and their chants, still offers matter for interesting research.

Italy. Southern Italy had received copies of the Gregorian Antiphonale even during Gregory's time. Yet even in Italy its acceptance was not universal. It is reported that a monastery quite close to Rome had to be commanded, in 850, to give up its pre-Gregorian chant and embrace the Gregorian (Roman) practice.[79] In *Milan* particularly, there was energetic opposition to the introduction of the Roman liturgy and chant. The people of Milan could claim for their liturgy — the Milanese or Ambrosian — a continuity from the time of Ambrose. Charlemagne attempted to force its displacement, but did not succeed. Later attempts by others were also ineffectual. Finally, Alexander VI, in 1497, granted the Milanese the right of the use of their own liturgy. Outside of the places influ-

[79] Aigrain, *op. cit.,* p. 41.

enced by the Milanese Rite, the Roman Rite held sway in Italy. Many places imitated the establishment of the Roman Schola Cantorum. Outstanding are those of Naples, Arezzo, and Monte Cassino.

II. THE SCHOLA CANTORUM

We cannot avoid noticing the influence of the Roman Schola Cantorum during the years we are here considering. The most important source of the diffusion of the Gregorian liturgy and chant was the Schola Cantorum. Peter Wagner declares: "The *Schola Cantorum* in a short time acquired an unforeseen importance. In every country it proved itself to be the powerful promoter of all efforts toward the introduction of the Roman liturgy."[80]

Winfred Douglas, speaking of the Roman Schola Cantorum and its imitators elsewhere (especially at Metz and St. Gall and in other parts of Charlemagne's dominion) says: "This wide-spread diffusion of its musical ideas and of its practical plan of organization for putting them into practice was of immense service to the Christian world. As a result, liturgic choral music became an integral part of the devotional and intellectual life of all Europe, having been ineffaceably stamped upon it during the formative period when the mediaeval world was being slowly molded throughout the so-called Dark Ages. In all that welter of migration, war, political turmoil, and social-transformation, the Song Schools of many a monastery and cathedral, faithful children of a great mother, preserved the ideals and advanced the practice of purely religious music."[81]

III. ROMANO-GALLICAN LITURGY[82]

The Roman liturgy may have supplanted liturgies followed elsewhere in the West but in the end it was influenced by them, particularly by the Gallican liturgy. All non-Roman influences on the Roman Rite are generally referred to as the Gallican influence.

80 Wagner, *op. cit.*, p. 191.

81 Douglas, *op. cit.*, pp. 55–56.

82 Various available works summarize this point interestingly and well: see Fortescue's *The Mass*, pp. 182–184; Dom Fernand Cabrol, *The Mass of the Western Rites* (St. Louis: B. Herder), Chap. IX; Joseph A. Jungmann, S.J., *The Mass of the Roman Rite*, Vol. I (New York: Benziger Brothers), pp. 74–103; Theodor Klauser, "A Brief History of the Liturgy in the West," *Orate Fratres*, Vol. XXIII, No. 2, pp. 64–67.

Most of this Gallican influence came from the countries north of the Alps; some of this influence may have come from the East although through these northern countries.

> . . . in the franco-germanic territory . . . from the eighth to the tenth century, there was distinct vitality and creative activity. It was formerly supposed that the solemn anointings in the ordinations of the clergy, the imposing rite for the consecration of churches with its rich symbolism, the splendid and dramatic liturgy of Palm Sunday and Holy Week, were in the main originally features of the old Roman Liturgy. This opinion has been shown to be quite erroneous. We know now that of the sacramental rites only that of baptism has the major part of its rich ritual from early Christian origin. The ritual structure of all the other sacraments and the sacramentals as we have them today is the result of franco-germanic creative activity, although indeed based upon very ancient sources including eastern ones. The same is true . . . of the liturgy of Palm Sunday and of Holy Week. . . .
>
> The old Roman liturgy was in general almost puritanic in its simplicity and brevity. Greater depth of emotion, greater wealth of language and symbolism, and a certain amplitude of treatment — all this, except in the case of baptism, was contributed by the germanic and celtic clergy of the carolingian empire."[83]

In the chapter outlining the liturgy of the Mass, we note late additions to the Mass prayers. These additions came from the North; they are the prayers at the foot of the altar, the inclusion of the Gloria and Credo in the Mass, the Offertory prayers, the Lavabo, the three prayers before Holy Communion, the prayer before the last blessing, the blessing itself, and the Last Gospel. Fortescue comments: "If one may venture a criticism of these additions from an aesthetic point of view, it is that they are exceedingly happy. The old Roman rite, in spite of its dignity and archaic simplicity, had the disadvantage of being dull. The Eastern and Gallican rites are too florid for our taste and too long. The few non-Roman elements in our Mass take nothing from its dignity and yet give it enough variety and reticent emotion to make it most beautiful."[84]

Two influences which came into the Roman liturgy from north-

[83] Theodor Klauser, *op. cit.,* No. 2, p. 66.
[84] *Op. cit.,* p. 184.

ern lands had far-reaching effects which surely were not intended. (1) One was a new version of "the discipline of the secret." In the early days of the Church only the faithful were allowed to stay for the Eucharist, that part of the Mass which we call "the Mass of the faithful." But in these years, in Gaul, there arose a new idea of saying the Canon in a low voice out of reverence and accentuating the truth that there is a difference in the offerers of the Sacrifice—the celebrating *priest* and the *laity*. But the implication that the laity do not participate in the offering of Christ made present in the Consecration is erroneous. The priest alone, in the name of Christ and through the words of Consecration, effects the unbloody immolation of Christ. "It is because the priest places the divine victim upon the altar that he offers it to God the Father as an oblation for the glory of the Blessed Trinity and for the good of the whole Church. Now the faithful participate in the oblation, understood in this limited sense, after their own fashion and in a twofold manner, namely, because they not only offer the sacrifice by the hands of the priest, but also, to a certain extent, in union with him."[85] Thus speaks Pius XII.

The symbolic and allegorical explanations given to the laity from the ninth century on, "explaining" the parts of the Mass, seem to imply that the Mass was at least beginning to be less a *doing* by the people than a *watching*. It is at this time, also, that the style of architecture fitting the form of the early rite, was changed to our form in which the laity are no longer standing around (*circumstantes*) the altar, but are separated from it by railings. The altar itself had originally stood away from the wall, and the bishop's throne, from the people's point of view, behind it; now the altar was against the wall and the throne to the side. The Mass, which had formally been offered by the celebrant facing the people, had begun, about the year 1000, to be offered by the priest with his back to the people.

(2) As we have seen, probably for centuries both leavened and unleavened bread were used in the Mass, although we suppose that

[85] Pius XII, *Mediator Dei* (New York: America Press, 1948), No. 92. For a further discussion, see Nos. 92–104.

the bread was generally leavened. Our Lord, in all probability, had used unleavened bread in His (first) Consecration; this thought influenced the type of bread used in the rite north of the Alps. The use of unleavened bread, common in the North after the eighth century, was established as a custom in the West by the eleventh century.[86] The change from leavened to unleavened bread was probably a minor but contributing point in the forces which led to the discontinuance of the offering of bread at the Offertory and in the eventual dropping of the Offertory procession.

Other Rites

During the Middle Ages other rites came into existence, all derived from the Roman Rite and not differing greatly from it. These are the rites of certain orders, such as the Dominican Rite, the Carthusian Rite, the Cistercian Rite, and the Benedictine Rite; and the local variations of the Roman Rite in such cities as Paris, Lyons, Salisbury, and York. As we shall see, the Roman Rite was made uniform and obligatory for the West by the Missal of St. Pius V in 1570; however, rites which could claim existence for more than 200 years were allowed to continue.

IV. LOW MASS[87]

We might think that the common mode of offering the liturgy was the Low Mass and that the High Mass (*Missa solemnis*) was the more ceremonious but exceptional offering. Such was not the case. The Mass is essentially Christ's sacrifice and ours, offered by the whole Church. This was originally expressed even in the exterior celebration of this central act of our liturgy. We have seen that from the early days of the Church until about the year 1000 the laity took an active part in any Mass at which they were present, a part which they expressed in word and action. The prayers were offered in common: some prayers (sung) by all the laity, some by a select group of singers (the choir), some by the celebrant or the

[86] Fortescue, *op. cit.*, p. 302.

[87] Read "The Priest Supplies the Other Roles," Chapter VII in *Mass of the Future* by Gerald Ellard, S.J. (Milwaukee: The Bruce Publishing Company, 1948).

deacon or the subdeacon alone. It was the rule, even in the days of persecution, that Masses offered in prison were solemnized.

From at least the sixth century, however, there were Masses offered which did not allow for such solemnity; such was the private Mass. In our time practically all the days of the year are liturgical days, that is, days on which Mass is offered officially, but in the early days of the liturgy this was not so. On the days not liturgical, private Masses could be, and often were, offered with only one or two assisting the celebrant.

In the eighth century, pacts between monasteries promising to offer Masses for the deceased monks, gave impetus to the private Mass. Then, with the increased desire of the people for a Mass of petition or thanksgiving offered to God through Christ, but honoring in a special way our Lord, our Lady, or some saint, *votive Masses* became popular. Through these and other contributing circumstances, private Masses became so popular that a celebrant occasionally offered as many as eight or nine Masses a day, while the offering of three Masses was common enough. (A large number of private Masses contributed to the change in Church architecture which provided numbers of altars.) In the twelfth century[88] one Mass a day for each priest became the rule, but three or four Masses a day were allowed. Since the thirteenth century the number of Masses permitted to each priest has been limited. The general rule in our Western Rite now allows three Masses on Christmas and All Souls' Day, and two or even three on Sundays and some other days, if there is a real necessity.

But, as we have seen, the early Mass books contained the sung prayers of the *persons* participating and not prayers for a *service*. With the increasingly common private Masses, there came into being, first of all, books which contained a few complete Masses in honor of our Lord under some special title, of our Lady, or of some saint; then we have (around the tenth century) the *Missale plenarum;* and finally, still later (1570), the *Roman Missal*. The *Missale plenarum* and the *Roman Missal* will be discussed later.

[88] Fortescue, *op. cit.*, p. 188.

In the private Masses, the celebrant *said* not only the prayers he would sing at a Solemn Mass but the prayers that would be sung by others. It had also become the practice for the celebrant to *say* private and personal prayers at Solemn Mass during the Introit, sung at the beginning of Mass, and during the Offertory procession. Both these practices have entered the now uniform Western Rite and are part not only of the Low Mass but also of the Solemn Mass.

V. CHANT NOTATION

1. Notation of Melody

Notation in some form must have existed even at the time of Gregory, but just what it was we cannot say. Although there are extant fragments written in the eighth century, the first complete manuscript, containing neums, dates from the ninth century.[89] There had been, before the ninth century, various attempts toward a musical notation, but the neumatic notation is the only type of notation which survived.

The modern neums grew out of the grammatical accents of the words. We have said elsewhere that the melodies originally followed the natural rise and fall of the voice when declaiming the prayers. Thus the acute accent, on which the voice rose, and the grave accent, on which the voice fell, led to:

a *podatus* ✓ — grave + acute;
a *clivis* ∧ — acute + grave;
a *torculus* ✓ˆ — grave + acute + grave;
a *porrectus* ⩘/ — acute + grave + acute;
a *scandicus* ⦤ — grave + grave + acute;
a *climacus* /· — acute + grave + grave;

and so on. (The quilisma does not seem to have its origin in the grammar.) This type of neumatic notation — called "oratorical" or "cheironomic" notation — did not give the intervals between the tones. The neums were written in an "open field" (*campo aperto*) above the text.[90] The melodies had to be memorized, and this nota-

[89] Gustave Reese, *Music in the Middle Ages* (New York: W. W. Norton, 1940), p. 133.
[90] *Ibid.* Read pp. 130–148.

tion only recalled what had been learned. We are told that the members of the Schola Cantorum needed nine years to memorize the entire required repertoire.[91]

By the tenth century, the neums were grouped around a line — first an imaginary and then a real line — in such a way as to signify, by their height, the intervals to be sung. This was the beginning of the intervallic or "diastematic" notation. Near the beginning of the eleventh century, a red line to represent **F** was introduced; later a line, either yellow or green, was added for **C**. It was easy to pass from the use of these lines to the idea of the four-line staff.[92]

The invention of the staff is often credited to Guido, a monk of Arezzo (995–1050). What he really did do was to perfect its use and to introduce the **F** and **C** clefs. He also introduced the idea of the *sol-fa* system for the scale. He noticed that in the Church's hymn honoring St. John the Baptist, the first word syllable of each line of the stanzas began one tone higher than the first tone of the preceding line. In the first stanza these first syllables were, as they still are in the liturgical books: *ut, re, mi, fa, sol, la.* With the later change of *do* for the *ut,* and the addition of the one remaining tone, called *si* from *S*ancte *I*oannes (or Joannes), we have the *sol-fa* syllables for all the tones of the scale.

The early forms of the neums differed a good deal in appearance. Thus we read of the notation of St. Gall, Metz, Aquitania, Chartres, Nonantola, and so on. By the twelfth or thirteenth centuries, neums became square or quadratic as we have them now.

Accustomed to the swift communication of ideas, we may be surprised to realize how slowly the perfected staff made its accepted appearance in various countries. Reese tells us[93] that by the twelfth century it had spread to Italian, French, English, and Spanish monasteries, but that in some German monasteries it was not used until the fifteenth century.

Every new invention, every form of advance, contributes to growth, but it also has within it seeds that must be watched so that

[91] Aigrain, *op. cit.,* p. 38.
[92] And later to the five-line staff and finally to the grand staff.
[93] Reese, *op. cit.,* p. 138.

only good may come to fruition. This is true even of the invention of notation. From then on it became much easier for the singers to learn the melodies, and a great impetus was given the music in new and original compositions. As notation became more habitually used, less practice in the singing was demanded and probably less perfection attained. New compositions gradually took the liturgy more and more from the people and finally, in a later period, destroyed the beauty and expressiveness of the chant itself.

2. Notation of Rhythm

In some manuscripts two kinds of rhythmical signs were inserted above the neums. One was the short line, the episema, added to the neums themselves, and the other sign was found in the accompanying letters over the neums. The episema is present in manuscripts of many schools. The letters, called Romanian letters, are found particularly in the manuscripts of St. Gall and, to a lesser degree, in those of Metz and Chartres. Romanus was the name of the legendary singer who was supposed to have introduced the chant at St. Gall. Some of these letters are: **t** — *tenere* (to hold), **c** — *celeriter* (quickly), **x** — *expectare* (to retard), and so on. Naturally, the following of the direction of these letters influenced the expression of the chant.

With regard to the plainsong rhythm as it was in the Middle Ages, there has been in our present day much controversy. There are three main schools of thought: the accentualists, the mensuralists, and the Solesmes school. Each school holds a different explanation of the rhythm of the chant in its "Golden Age" and consequently a different explanation of the Romanian letters. We may briefly summarize their theories.

The *accentualists* believe that the chant, brought to formation around the fifth century, adopted the equal time values of the word syllables in the Greek and Latin of the day. But they hold that the accent was then expressed by stress. Dom Pothier (of Solesmes) is supposed to have been the head of this school. It is interesting to note that some authors deny that stress, as we understand it, was the rhythmic element at the time of the formation of the chant and especially deny that Dom Pothier believed this stress to be a necessary element of plainsong.[94]

The *mensuralists* do not even agree among themselves. In general we may say that they believe that the accent is to be stressed, but that the time values of the notes were not equal. Thus their views are absolutely contrary to the views of Solesmes.

The *Solesmes School* claims Dom Mocquereau as its head. This school teaches that the time values of the notes were equal and that the accent of the word was given prominence by other means than stress — by a higher melodic tone, or by the shortness of the melody sung on the accent. (We must note that the accent of the word is often given only one tone even in quite florid chants.)

There are historical justifications for all of these views. And indeed, it may have been that practice varied somewhat in different monasteries. However, we must have a common interpretation if we are to have a uniform rendition.[95] We know the Solesmes theory results in an artistic expression; therefore we follow it. Moreover, we are using the edition of the liturgical books printed with the rhythmical signs of Solesmes, and thus we may more easily unify our performance.

VI. TROPES AND SEQUENCES

We cannot state for certain the origin of the *trope*. Wagner[96] believes that it is of Greek origin. It is generally attributed to Tutilo, a monk of the Abbey of St. Gall, who died about 915.

The trope was a verbal interpolation (or farce) of the liturgical text. It developed into three forms: (1) the liturgical text plus the interpolation; (2) the interpolation and then the liturgical text; or (3) the combination of the two preceding forms. Here we are speaking of the words only. We will see that there were also three forms in the music to which the tropes were sung. (1) One type

94 Dom Joseph Gajard, *The Rhythm of Plainsong* (Liverpool: Rushworth and Dreaper, 1943), pp. 45–46.

95 We will study the nature of rhythm in a later chapter. See page 148 in Reese for a sample of three different rhythmical interpretations of the same piece.

96 *Op. cit.*, pp. 243–244.

of trope broke the groups of neums of the original melody into single tones and set a syllabic text to them. (2) Another type composed a new melody and a new text, and placed them either before or after the original plainsong composition as it was. (3) Some tropes combined the two preceding types of melodic and textual interpolation. The type most frequently used was the first here explained.

The following "Ite missa est" contains an example of a trope. The verbal interpolation is italicized.

> "Ite *nunc in pace, spiritus sanctus super vos sit, iam* missa est.
> Deo *semper laudes agite in corde gloriam et* gratias."[97]

The interpolated words were sung to the individual tones of the neums in the florid melody of the It*e* and De*o*.

Although tropes to the Credo were very rare, every part of the sung liturgy, with the exception of the Gradual and the Tract, were troped. Kyrie tropes were particularly popular. The Gregorian Masses in the Kyriale are published with accompanying titles. These titles survive from the previous tropes. Thus the trope to Kyrie IV begins "Cunctipotens genitor Deus," the trope to Kyrie XI begins "Orbis factor," the trope to Kyrie II begins "Fons bonitatis," and so on.[98] The trope was at its height in the tenth century.

The *sequence* is often considered a type of trope; this was true in some aspects but not in all. It was a type of interpolation which finally grew into an independent form, and this by the tenth century. It may have originated in northern France;[99] it may have been of Greek origin.[100] But its adoption by Notker Balbulus, a monk of St. Gall, who died in 912, gave it an impetus which led to developments of which he never dreamed. Originally the sequence was an addition, or trope, to the Alleluia melody which had been sung in the liturgy for years. Later, as the sequence tended more

97 Karl Young, *The Drama of the Medieval Church* (Oxford: Clarendon Press, 1933), Vol. I, p. 178.

98 The full trope "Kyrie, fons bonitatis" may be found in *Cantus ad Processiones et Benedictiones SSmi Sacramenti* (New York: J. Fischer, 1927), pp. 51–52.

99 Reese, *op. cit.*, p. 188.

100 Wagner, *op. cit.*, p. 223.

and more to become an independent piece, it had no connection with these Alleluia melodies at all. The sequence became exceedingly popular and its form was most varied. It tended to be a syllabic chant with its text in strophic form repeated. Adam of St. Victor (died about 1192) brought the sequence-form to its highest point of perfection. The sequence is often called "sequentia" or "sequentia cum prosa" or simply "prosa" or "prose."

As we have said, the sequence was a most popular form of composition, and its number was truly countless. (Some say there were as many as 5000.) We are not surprised to find that these sequences became incorporated in the liturgy, although they were not originally so intended. Officially they were not recognized as liturgical. Of the vast number, all except four were later banned from use in the sung liturgy by the Council of Trent:

1. The *Victimae Paschali laudes*—the sequence for Easter, attributed to Wipo of Burgundy who died about 1048.

2. The *Veni Sancte Spiritus*—the sequence for Pentecost, attributed to various people, among them Pope Innocent II who died about 1216.

3. The *Dies Irae*—the sequence of the Mass for the Dead, supposed to have been composed by Thomas of Celano (1220–1249). (This sequence grew out of a rhymed trope to the responsory, *Libera me.*)

4. The *Lauda Sion*—the sequence for Corpus Christi, composed by St. Thomas Aquinas (1227–1274). (Its form and melody are evidently based on Adam of St. Victor's Sequence of the Holy Cross.)[101] Later, in 1727, the Church admitted the use of one other for the Mass of the Sorrowful Mother and thus we now have

5. The *Stabat Mater*—the sequence of Our Lady of Sorrows, attributed by some to Innocent and by others to Jacopone da Todi who died about 1306.

The sequences were much loved even outside the liturgy. They were translated into the vernacular and gave impulse to the ecclesiastical folk song. Part of the *Victimae Paschali laudes* was

[101] *Ibid.*, p. 240.

transformed into the German choral *Christ ist erstanden.*[102] *Christ lag in Todesbanden* practically incorporates the third stanza of the *Victimae Paschali laudes.* This Easter melody was later used as a motif by Bach in his Easter cantata, *Cantata No. 4.*

VII. THE ECCLESIASTICAL DRAMA

The *ecclesiastical drama* is often called the *liturgical drama,* but as it was never part of the official prayer of the Church, the first title is more exact. That this subject lends itself to a study that is great, intensive, and extremely interesting is proved by the fact that Karl Young has brought forth, as the result of his efforts, an authoritative two-volume work, *The Drama of the Medieval Church.*

The church drama grew directly out of troping. "The tropes, or literary embellishments, from which the first dramatic representations arose, were inserted into the liturgy for the serious purpose of adornment and exposition, and they were eventually dramatized in a manifest desire to convey edifying instruction."[103]

> To illustrate what I have been saying with a few examples, let me quote as an example of an interpolated trope-melody with words . . . a text which is sung as Introit and Communion on the Feast of St. Peter's liberation from the prison at Jerusalem. . . . The words of the Introit are as follows . . . Now I know in very deed that the Lord hath sent his angel; and hath delivered me out of the hand of Herod and from all the expectation of the people of the Jews.
>
> This Introit text, taken from the Bible, was preceded by way of introductory trope by the following paraphrase on the Scriptural context.
>
> "A damsel came to Peter, who was knocking at the door, and asked him saying: 'Who art thou, Lord, that knockest so hard at our door?' 'It is I,' answered Peter, 'I, who for the Christian faith was thrown into the dungeon. Open the door, Roda!'
>
> "And she who had wept, knowing his voice opened not the door for joy but ran and announced it to the brethren, Alleluia, Alleluia. And they who had wept so hard, when they saw Peter were all overwhelmed with joy and Peter said: 'Now I know in very deed . . .' etc. (as above).
>
> As can be seen, this introduction to the Introit is already an approach to the liturgical drama; Peter and Roda both appear in a speaking part and with the narrator as the third character one can see in the dramatic

[102] Young, *op. cit.,* Vol. I, p. 176.
[103] *Ibid.,* Vol. II, p. 410.

presentation of such texts the origin of the mediaeval play or musical drama.[104]

The "Quem quaeritis" trope — for which we have the "stage directions" of the tenth century[105] — was also used as a preface to the Easter Introit. In this short study we can only sketch the development of the church drama.[106] We can easily see that it led to the miracle and mystery plays. In fact, it was the ancestor of the various forms of the sung and spoken drama. It was never really liturgical, in our meaning of that word, although it was not formally condemned for use in the liturgy until the Council of Trent.

We will outline, simply for our better understanding, the summary of the development of the early drama as given by Karl Young.[107]

1. *In the Church:* It was an edifying, dramatic performance, essentially international — catholic.	It had the following forms: *a*) Dramatized liturgy, *b*) Dramatized additions to the liturgy in Latin, and *c*) Dramatized additions to the liturgy in Latin with a further addition in the vernacular.
2. Transferred to *Secular Auspices:* It retained common sources in Scripture, in the teachings of the Church, and in legend.	It gave greater scope for development in *a*) A vernacular text, *b*) The person of the actors, *c*) The use of the comic element, and *d*) Many national differences.

VIII. SECULAR SONGS

This subject, while not part of our work, is so closely connected that it may as well be touched upon here. The term "secular songs" applies to all nonliturgical forms of song (except the trope) whether

[104] Jos. Smits Van Waesberghe, *Gregorian Chant and Its Place in the Catholic Liturgy* (Stockholm: Continental Book Company, n.d.), pp. 47–49.

[105] See Reese, p. 194, and also Karl Young.

[106] Lang's *Music in Western Civilization,* pp. 89–96, gives a rather complete but simply styled discussion.

[107] *Op. cit.,* Vol. II, pp. 421–426.

the subject is religious or not. Naturally, such songs existed, but since the means of notation was what it was, and since there was no *Schola* to preserve these melodies, we cannot restore the earliest ones with any exactness.

Chapters VII and VIII of *Music in the Middle Ages,* by the eminent musicologist, Gustave Reese, are devoted to the subject of secular monody, that is, secular unison songs. The performer of the secular songs of this period is familiar to us under the names of Jongleur, Troubadour, Trouvère, Minstrel, Minnesinger, and Meistersinger. All of the songs of this time are more or less influenced by the melodies and forms of the liturgical pieces.[108]

IX. THEORISTS

The establishment of schools to study music led naturally to the need of a theory to teach. Thus arose the theorists of this period — some of whom contribute much, and others little, to our real knowledge. In most cases, practice preceded theory. Therefore we can understand why it is that the theory does not seem to explain everything — for instance, on the subject of Modality. It is not of great importance to us to know who these theorists were. Nevertheless we will mention Boethius, Cassiodorus, and Isidore of Seville, who lived in the fifth and sixth centuries and whose theories were studied in the schools of this period. There was also Alcuin (753–804), Hrabanus Maurus (died 856), Hucbald (840–930), Odo of Cluny (died 942), Guido d'Arezzo (about 995–1050), Hermanus Contractus (1013–1054), John Cotton (about 1100), Johannes de Garlandia (1195–1272?), Philippe de Vitri (1291–1361), Franco of Cologne (who flourished after 1280), and others.

X. EARLY FORMS OF PART SINGING

Part singing made its appearance as early as the ninth century in the form of *organum.* This type of singing used a Gregorian melody as a theme for the principal voice (*vox principalis*) and du-

108 Lang, *Music in Western Civilization,* p. 99. A very accessible book, *Seven Centuries of Solo-Song,* Vol. I, edited by James Woodside and published by G. Schirmer gives us some of the early forms of these solo-songs.

plicated the melody (or, later, sang another) at the interval of a fourth below or a fifth above. The duplicated voice was called the *vox organalis*. The theory and practice in regard to organum varied considerably through the succeeding centuries. For example, Guido d'Arezzo (eleventh century) allowed more than one note of the vox principalis to one of the vox organalis (and also contrary motion and the crossing of parts). John Cotton allowed more than one note of the vox organalis to one of the vox principalis.[109] This sanctions a practice opposite to Guido's. Organum was either strict or free; the distinction between them need not be made here.

To get the "flavor" of organum, take a Gregorian melody as a vox principalis and build a melody, a vox organalis, note for note against it. Two plans for so doing are given here. (1) Organize the complete melody in strict fourths (below). (2) Start the melody with both voices in unison, but keep the lower voice on the same pitch until both voices are a fourth or fifth apart; then continue, this fourth or fifth apart. Do not permit the lower voice to go below the modal final in any case; only the upper voice sings the original Gregorian melody in its complete form. End in unison. The melody of the Gregorian *Adoro te devote,* so treated, will give a good idea of the effect. Note that the Gregorian melody retains its own character even with this treatment.

From now on we will call the vox principalis, or principal voice, by the other names it acquired: the *cantus firmus* or *tenor*. It was called *tenor* from the fact that it held (*tenere*) to the principal melody.

The English developed a form peculiar to themselves — the *Gimel*. The cantus firmus was accompanied by another voice, not in fourths, but in thirds, upper or lower, and sometimes in sixths. The beginning and the end was always either in unison or at the octaves. Out of this form developed the *Faux-Bourdon*.

In organum both voices remained in the free rhythm of the plainsong. In *descant,* however, florid figures above the cantus firmus or tenor were admitted. In descant, therefore, the plainsong

[109] Read pp. 259–261 of Reese, *Music in the Middle Ages*.

melody, used in long notes as a cantus firmus, lost its originality.

The *conductus* was originally a form of the trope. Later (twelfth century) it became a type of composition which used entirely original melodies in all parts. These parts moved in practically the same rhythm and used one set of texts.

The *motetus* is considered by some to be a type of descant. The motet became the leading form of the thirteenth century. In general, a motet — which is not to be confused with the present-day use of the word — is characterized by the use of a different text for the accompanying voice or voices than for the principal voice. This different text was originally in Latin. Eventually, a vernacular *paraphrase* of the principal text was sung by the other voices; finally, even a vernacular text using absolutely *nonrelated* thoughts was used. We can see why this development of the motet had no place in the liturgy.

With the introduction of the *hotchet,* which interrupted the melody and introduced a form of sobbing or sighing, and the introduction in some places of the *cantilena,* which was essentially secular, we can understand that there was a need for Church authorities to rise up in protest at their use in the liturgical services.

These forms of composition became the vogue the last few years of this period and began to be introduced, to a greater or lesser degree, into liturgical services. We can easily see the result of this. We can also easily see what the use of a Gregorian melody as a long-noted cantus firmus did to the melody. In losing its characteristic rhythm, plainsong lost much of itself.

XI. INTRODUCTION OF TIME

When we speak of melodic figures above a cantus firmus, we must realize that notes of equal time value, characteristic of our use of the plainchant, were surely not retained in these part compositions. In the course of the years 1150–1300 occurred the development of the use of *uneven time values.* Theoretical or practical exponents of the idea of uneven values were called mensuralists and the system using notes of uneven values was called the mensural system. Since one of the very important treatises on this subject was written by Franco of Cologne, this period is often called the Franconian period. Explanation of the development of measure can easily be found in music histories.[110] In the mensural system, a short note was represented by the punctum of plainsong notation; a long note was represented by the virga. Later, either idea was represented by the puntum or the virga. Such a theory applied to chant notation would certainly affect the singing of the chant itself.

XII. ACTIVE PARTICIPATION OF THE LAITY

When the active participation of the laity is under consideration, we may consider these years as two periods: from about the year 600 to about 1000, and from 1000 to 1300. For, speaking in general terms, we may say that lay participation in (sung) word and in act, continued to the late ninth and early tenth centuries, and from then on began to decline.

By the ninth century, or even earlier, the common people in the Northern lands rarely understood Latin. But, as we have said, Latin was the literary language and the international language of all the educated. Added to this was the great esteem for all things Roman. Therefore the language of the Romano-Gallican liturgy, even in the North, remained Latin. The language was, of course, a barrier in the understanding of many of the prayers. However, the people were still expected to sing their parts of the liturgy, as the people of earlier ages had sung their parts.

It is generally agreed that up to the ninth and tenth centuries it was still the custom of the people to sing the Ordinary parts of the Mass together in simple unison chant. Yet during these years the chant itself became more and more florid. "The 9th, 10th and 11th centuries were the best period of the liturgy and the chant. The churches vied with one another in the splendor and embellishment of their services, and the faithful flocked in numbers to the liturgical gatherings."[111]

[110] See Theodore M. Finney, *A History of Music* (New York: Harcourt, Brace and Company, 1935), pp. 91–94.

[111] Wagner, *op. cit.*, p. 218.

We cannot say when the choir began to sing the Ordinary with more florid chant melodies. The Kyriale tells us that these melodies are found in manuscripts of such and such centuries; that is, the manuscripts may be of the eleventh century, but the melody itself may have been sung previous to the eleventh century. The more florid melodies for the Ordinary may have appeared at first in monasteries, where all the singers were trained, and where florid melodies would not cause a change in participation. But in the regular churches, their appearance and more continued use by the choir gradually paved the way for "the silent congregation."[112]

A very important force toward the discontinuance of lay participation was, as we have said above, "the transition to a silent recitation of the sacrificial prayers," which Theodor Klauser says "was an event of great moment. The bond uniting priest and people was severed at a point which is the very heart of the liturgy. The capital portion of the sacrificial service thus became the exclusive concern of the bishop or priest, and the people were reduced to the role of passive spectators; and if they might be excluded in this way from the central part of the holy Sacrifice, why not also restrict or omit their active cooperation in other parts of the liturgy, for it often dragged and tended to retard the course of the service? Thus, evidently, a beginning was made which would lead to grave consequences."[113]

The use in the Mass of a bread which the people did not have in their homes, the developing custom of a pre-Mass offering (which we call a Mass stipend), and perhaps other considerations, led to the people no longer joining in procession at the Offertory to offer gifts which had been "regarded and intended as symbolic expression of all the faithful in the offering of the holy Sacrifice, while at the same time they served to ground the virtue of fraternal charity in this central act of worship."[114]

[112] Read "Disruptive Singing in the Choir Loft" in *Mass of the Future* by Gerald Ellard, S.J. (Milwaukee: The Bruce Publishing Company, 1948), Chap. 8.

[113] Theodor Klauser, "A Brief History of the Liturgy in the West," *Orate Fratres,* Vol. XXIII, No. 3, p. 117.

[114] *Ibid.,* p. 119.

But more important still is the point which we have brought out, that it was at this time that "the holy Sacrifice itself had come to be regarded as more or less the exclusive action of the priest. . . . For when once the understanding of the Mass as the united action of all was no longer well grasped, when the Mass was regarded as the action of the priest alone, the offertory procession had lost the very reason in which it was founded."[115] This one misunderstanding of the Mass could cause all lay participation to cease.

The change in participation was so gradual that its future results probably were not at all foreseen. It never was the intent of the Church that any of her children should take the part of an "audience." In her plan for the corporate worship of God, we each have our part. Let us ask God that we may return to its realization.

XIII. SUMMARY

As we said in the beginning of the discussion of this period, the years 600 to 1300 present quite different aspects. Moreover, the evaluation of this period will vary according to the criteria of judging it.

The musical historian sees in the years 1000 to 1300 a source of advancement for secular music — and he is right. The contribution made by the musicians of these 300 years — especially during the last hundred — becomes more apparent in the succeeding centuries. Viewed from the standpoint of active lay participation in the liturgy, however, we find in the musical development of the 300 years a source of decline. This decline also becomes more apparent in the succeeding centuries.

Most of the pure melodies of the chant were composed before the year 1000. From 1000 to 1300, as notation became more systematized, these melodies were written down. The chant melodies during the last 300 years were in part inferior to those of the preceding years. Characterized by a straining for novelty, they were inferior in "simplicity, naturalness and warmth of feeling."[116]

115 *Ibid.*

116 Dom Dominic Johner, O.S.B., *A New School of Gregorian Chant,* 2 English ed., p. 192.

We know now to what the last years of this period were leading. Nevertheless, at the time there was still a united Christian family, sacrificing and praying together as one before God, still singing their prayers as one, in the official musical language of the Church, the Gregorian Chant.

REVIEW QUESTIONS

1. Summarize the historical setting for the years 600 to 1000. What was happening in the West — in Italy, in France and Germany, in England, in Ireland? What was happening in the East?
2. Summarize briefly the historical setting for the years 1000 to 1300.
3. Why do we consider two units in the historical setting and only one unit in the liturgy and liturgical music?
4. Give four reasons why uniformity within the Roman Rite was retarded.
5. Discuss briefly the progress of the Roman Rite in England; in Gaul; in Spain; in Italy.
6. Of what importance was the Schola Cantorum during this period?
7. What is meant by the Gallican influence on the liturgy?
8. Specify some additions to the Roman liturgy which are Gallican in origin.
9. What is the fundamental distinction between the priest's and the laity's offering of the Sacrifice?
10. What is unleavened bread?
11. Name some medieval rites derived from the Roman Rite. Do they differ greatly from the Roman Rite? Are they still in use?
12. Did the High Mass develop from the Low Mass, or is the Low Mass an abbreviated High Mass? Explain.
13. Summarize shortly the development of the Low Mass.
14. Discuss the gradual development of the music staff.
15. Explain the origin of the *sol-fa* syllables.
16. Modern musical notation gives us both the melody and the rhythm of the melody. Was this true of early notation? Discuss.
17. Name three modern schools of thought concerning the rhythm of the chant. Which school do we follow? What does this school tell us of the rhythm of the chant?
18. What was the trope? Give examples.
19. Why is Mass XI called the "Orbis Factor" Mass?
20. Name five sequences in present use in the liturgy. Can you name their authors and tell when they are to be sung?
21. What do you mean by the church drama? What was its origin? To what modern art did it lead?
22. Name some of the forms of part singing which came into being at this time.

23. Discuss active lay participation in the liturgy as it was up to the ninth century.
24. Discuss active lay participation from the tenth to the fourteenth century.
25. Criticize the musical development of the last years of this age (1) from the standpoint of the secular musician, (2) from the standpoint of the church musician, and (3) from the standpoint of the liturgy and lay participation in the liturgy.

THIRD PERIOD — PERIOD OF DECADENCE OF THE CHANT — 1300–1517

HISTORICAL SETTING

Three movements or influences of this time set the stage for the tragedy that was to be the Protestant Revolt — (1) the Avignon Papacy and its sequel, the Great Western Schism, (2) the gradual weakening of the power of the Empire, and (3) the Renaissance.

Christian unity in the West suffered a severe shock in the Western Schism and in the new forms of heresy which infected the spiritual life of the people. Yet, although the Schism had split the Christian world into three "obediences," the people, as a whole, were at least nominally attached to the Church. The Christians of Spain were slowly driving out the Moors; the Christians of Hungary and the Balkans were doing battle with the Turks, even though with but partial success. At the same time, the Inquisition, founded over a century and a half before, was in operation, especially against the Hussites and the Lollards.

Though the foundation of the national states is of the next era, the old political and social order was crumbling. While the Hapsburgs furnished the Empire with its last great emperors, the French were wresting their soil back from England in the Hundred Years' War. England had seen the growth of parliament in power, the Wars of the Roses, and the founding of the Tudor Dynasty. The Black Death, a disaster which swept away vast numbers, contributed its share to the decline of feudalism.

Finally, in 1453 Constantinople fell to the Ottoman Turks. At the death of the emperor, Constantine XI, the Eastern Empire came to an end. Many Greek scholars fled from the East to Italy, bringing with them precious early manuscripts.

A new vital force, expressing itself in the Renaissance, completed the ruin of the old social structure. The substitution of worldly values for other-worldliness, the stress on individual power as against corporate right, the Machiavellian divorce of morality from government, the very practical inventions of gunpowder, printing, and the astrolabe, the consequent widening scope of European activity through exploration and discoveries — all combined to produce an age dissatisfied with the present order, eager for a new.

Had the Renaissance come at a time when the Church was vigorous, it might have brought about a millennium. Even though weakened by heresy, schism, and worldliness, the Church met the challenge of the times, though tardily, and with incomplete success; for the tremendous losses to the Church in the ensuing years, in England, Germany, and Scandinavia, have never been truly recovered.

LITURGY AND MUSIC

By the close of the thirteenth century, the effect of the developments of the preceding years was beginning to appear. There was as yet no definite break with the past — that was for the sixteenth century — but the break was being prepared, even though many who saw it coming strove against its causes.

I. THE BULL OF POPE JOHN XXII

Even by 1322 the musical novelty had taken such a hold on musicians that the clergy needed to be warned. The Decree of Pope John XXII attacks the introduction of the novelties into the liturgy. After declaring the purpose of music in the liturgy and commending the practice of preceding centuries in the Church, he says:

> But certain followers of a new school, giving great attention to the laws of measured time, are intent upon composing their own melodies according to a new system of notes, and these they prefer to the ancient music. The ecclesiastical melodies are sung in *semibreves* and *minimae,*

and are struck with gracenotes; moreover, they break up the melodies by *hoqueti,* they rob them of their virility by *discantus,* sometimes they mix in *tripla* and *moteti* in the vernacular. . . . Indeed, these men run without pausing, they intoxicate the ear without satisfying it, what they sing they imitate by gestures; and thus the desired devotion is completely ignored, and a forbidden frivolousness is introduced.[117]

Then, after threatening the suspension of those who would be guilty of offense against this decree which would forbid such "frivolousness," he goes on:

By this, however, we do not intend to prohibit that occasionally especially on festive days, during solemn Mass and the above-mentioned divine offices, certain consonant intervals be added to the simple ecclesiastical chant, provided these intervals are in accord with the melodies themselves, as, for instance, the consonance of the octave, the fifth, the fourth, and the like; but on the condition that the chant itself remain intact in its integrity, and that no change in the chant be made from music having the proper rhythm.[118]

Most music historians, Catholic or non-Catholic, understand the action of the Pope in this regard. For it is not music as such that is the object of his solicitude but "the offices of divine praises" expressed by the faithful, as he declares in his opening sentences. The edict "may have acted as a partial check, if not as a complete one, thus diverting the flow of musical creation into secular channels."[119]

II. THREE FORCES AT WORK

There were three forces in the world which affected the lives of the people and in turn served as an expression of their spirit. These forces were (1) humanism, (2) nationalism, and (3) the spirit of discovery.

Humanism. With Petrarch (1304–1374) there began in Italy the "new learning" which devoted itself to the study of the Greek and Latin classics. It received a new impetus with the arrival of the Greek refugees after the fall of Constantinople. From Italy it

[117] Pope John XXII, cited by Dom Thuis, *Gregorian Chant A Barometer of Religious Fervor,* p. 28.
[118] *Ibid.,* p. 29.
[119] Reese, *Music in the Middle Ages,* p. 357.

spread throughout the Western World. With the "new learning" was to be associated, besides (1) the love of the classics and (2) a desire to possess their early manuscripts, also (3) a scorn for all that was characteristic of the years since Cicero, (4) a return not only to the study of what was called the humanities but to the mode of life of the pagans, and (5) the beginnings of individualism which is still so apparent in the world. Those who led the way in the "new learning" were called humanists. Humanists were not necessarily to be condemned. Indeed we have outstanding Christians among them, for example, Erasmus and Sir Thomas More.[120] But we may be sure that many others, especially those who imitated the manner of life of the pagans, deserve the title "pagan humanists."

Nationalism. National states, which before were unknown, were gradually coming into being in the Western World. Temporal sovereigns, in order to unify those under their dominion, accented natural individual differences between peoples. This in itself is not an evil, but we, who live in an age of exaggerated nationalism, can see what its undisciplined growth has done to the members of Christ's Mystical Body.

Spirit of Discovery. This was the age of discovery. The finding of other lands and people gave to temporal rulers new subjects, new sources of income; it gave to the Church new souls to bring into union with Christ. We need not think that the spirit of discovery expressed itself only in fields of exploration. "Experimentation was the vogue."[121] We shall see its effect on the music of the times.

III. EFFECTS OF THE THREE FORCES ON THE CHANT

Humanism which looked upon the contribution of the Middle Ages as barbaric and unenlightened, naturally pronounced the simplicity of the chant as barbaric also. *Nationalism* gave rise to schools of music which developed their own type of national musical expression. This was unobjectionable in itself, but the spirit which was here expressed was detrimental to the spirit of universality as

120 Read pp. 101–110 of Carlton Hayes, *A Political and Cultural History of Modern Europe,* Vol. I (New York: Macmillan Company, 1932).

121 Finney, *A History of Music,* p. 107.

expressed in the universal music of the Church, the chant. *The spirit of discovery* experimented with the Gregorian melodies and while so doing deprived them of their rhythm which is their life.

IV. MUSICAL DEVELOPMENTS OF THE FOURTEENTH CENTURY

This was the age of the *Ars Nova* — the "New Art." It is especially noted for the rhythmical procedure which it introduced.[122] It also broadened the use of *musica ficta,* which practically allowed every chromatic tone one desired to use, explaining the chromatic theoretically, and which introduced changes in the current rules of counterpoint. The term *counterpoint* was applied to that type of music which placed a punctum in a new melody against a punctum in a cantus firmus, point-against-point.

During this century there were composed many secular forms of counterpoint. Of these forms, probably the most familiar to us are the madrigal and the canon.

Canonic imitation became very popular in the later polyphonic liturgical compositions. A polyphonic composition is simply one in which there are many melodies ("voices") moving together (*polyphonus*) but all moving as melodies. The melodies of a canon are bound by certain rules (or canons); therefore the composition itself is called a canon. In one type of canon, the first voice begins and the other voices come in later, one by one, singing the same melody. (Our "Three Blind Mice" is sung in strict canon.) "Sumer is icumen in" was, and is, a very popular four-voiced canon of the thirteenth century.[123]

Guillaume de Machault (about 1300–1377) wrote canons as he wrote nearly every other kind of secular music. He wrote little religious music. However, his is the first individually composed polyphonic setting of the complete Ordinary of the Mass.

V. MUSICAL DEVELOPMENTS OF THE FIFTEENTH CENTURY

"The musical development of the fifteenth century was so rich

122 Read *ibid.,* pp. 110–111.

123 Father Ellard has a note on the use of this melody in the liturgy (!). See *Mass of the Future,* p. 80.

and profuse in comparison to that of the preceding centuries that it can best be approached in terms of underlying cause and effect. These may be tabulated as follows:

"1. Founding of royal chapels, and the consequent impetus given to musical activity.

"2. The rise of nationalism, and the consequent musical differentiation on a geographical basis.

"3. The rapid accumulation of musical resources, and the consequent greater scope for men of genius."[124]

Composers of this and the next few centuries are connected with the "national schools" now coming into existence. John Dunstable (died about 1453) was the leader of the early English school. The early Netherlands school was represented by Dufay (1400–1474), by Dufay's pupil, Okeghem (about 1430–1496), and by Okeghem's pupil, Josquin des Pres (1450–1521). The compositions of Des Pres are really great music. Let us listen to the recording of one of his famous motets: *Ave Vera Virginitas;* better yet, let us sing it ourselves.[125] Note the beauty of the melodies expressive of and perfectly fitting the text. Let us also listen to his *Missa "Ave Maris Stella."* When we sing a polyphonic work we realize the independence and completeness of our own melody. When listening to one, we may realize this independence and completeness to an even greater extent. In fact, unless we select a melody which we follow in its course, we may find that the composition is only a maze of moving sound of which we comprehend little.

Josquin des Pres was the foremost composer not only of his time but also for some years to come. His works are still among the musical monuments of all time.

VI. MANUSCRIPTS

With the invention of printing in the fifteenth century — applied everywhere to music in the sixteenth — it became possible to transmit one's musical ideas. For the years 1300–1500 we are still greatly

[124] Finney, *op. cit.,* p. 121.

[125] The music and the recording of this motet and the *Missa "Ave Maris Stella"* may be procured from the Gregorian Institute of America, Toledo, Ohio.

dependent on manuscript copies. We are not surprised to find, in chant manuscripts, some influences of polyphonic writing inserted at will or through ignorance, by copyists. However, as Weinmann points out[126] there are sufficient reliable manuscripts of this period to prove that chant and polyphony were not, and are not, essentially hostile to each other. The use of each art in the liturgy is possible and is, in fact, encouraged by ecclesiastical authority.[127]

VII. ACTIVE PARTICIPATION OF THE LAITY

In his summary of the years 1073 to 1545, Theodor Klauser says:[128] "Notable in the history of the liturgy in this period is the fact that Communion was no longer administered under both species; that the understanding of the Eucharistic Sacrifice and of the intimate relationship of Sacrifice and Communion gradually grew less; that devotion tended to center upon the sacred Humanity of our Lord and that religious individualism sought more and more to satisfy its devotional needs in practices outside the liturgy."

With the continued use of part singing in the choir, and especially with the use of the Ordinary of the Mass sung in polyphonic style (in which the congregation would be unable to join), we must expect that the people would gradually have less and less of an active part in their sung prayer. Again, this decline in the use of the chant was a gradual but, because of the influences of the age, almost an inevitable evil. For it was an evil. At that time, the chant, and no other music in use, permitted the laity their share in the sung prayer of the Church. If we agree with Dom Thuis that the use of the chant can be considered a barometer of religious fervor, we will believe that discontinuing its use may have contributed its share to the preparation for the Protestant Revolt of the next centuries. The Church had her heresies in the past, but never before had so many left the fold of Christ's Church. In the loss of active participation by the people, was there not also somewhat

126 Karl Weinmann, *History of Church Music* (Boston: McLaughlin and Reilly, n.d.), p. 42.

127 See the *Motu Proprio* (on Sacred Music) by St. Pius X and the *Mediator Dei* (on the Liturgy) by Pius XII.

128 *Orate Fratres,* Vol. XXIII, No. 3, p. 116.

of a loss of the true Christian spirit of which active participation in the liturgy is the primary and most indispensable source?

REVIEW QUESTIONS

1. What three influences of the time set the stage for the Protestant Revolt?
2. Discuss briefly the Decree of Pope John XXII.
3. What three forces were especially at work in the world of this period?
4. What was the effect of these three forces on the chant?
5. What is meant by counterpoint?
6. What is meant by a polyphonic composition?
7. Name four polyphonic composers of this period.
8. Discuss the active participation of the laity during this period.

FOURTH PERIOD — PERIOD OF LOSS OF THE GREGORIAN CHANT — 1517–1850

HISTORICAL SETTING

From the Break-Up of Religious Unity to Our Own Times

The archheretics, Luther, Calvin, etc., separated large sections of the Christian world from the Church. At the same time powerful petty rulers rose up against the Empire, and in the ensuing wars — so-called "Religious Wars" — political and religious issues became confused, and much devastation was wrought in the name of God's truth. The Thirty Years' War in Germany was the best example of this condition. This war ended with the Peace of Westphalia, which confirmed the Peace of Augsburg in its principle *"Cujus regio, illius religio."* The true reform of the Church was effected in the same years as the Revolt — chiefly by (1) the Council of Trent (1545–1563); (2) the founding of teaching religious orders, such as the Jesuits; and (3) the efforts of individuals, such as Cardinal Ximenes in Spain.

From the unwillingness to accept infallible doctrine came the attitude that dogma is unimportant but moral rectitude all-important; then developed, thanks to the "Enlightenment" of the eighteenth century, a neglect of faith and an exaltation of reason.

With the power and prestige (and restraint) of the Papacy removed from world affairs, individual rulers could, and often did, rule despotically; and while the great and small national states sprang into prominence, the spirit of national pride grew among all peoples and with it a hatred for neighboring groups. Thus we find, between 1600 and 1800, the rise and flowering of autocracies: Hapsburgs, Bourbons, Tudors and Stuarts, Hohenzollerns and Romanovs, and the so-called "Benevolent Despots." The House of Bourbon held the most splendid of courts; it endured as well the most tragic decline. In 1789 France gave itself over to the Revolution, probably its greatest catastrophe, during which, in the name of liberty, equality, and fraternity, the terrorists executed Louis XVI and his queen. Other peoples than the French caught the radical fever, so that until the middle of the nineteenth century there were intermittent revolutions all over Europe. When Napoleon's fall was completed by the Congress of Vienna in 1815, the thrones of the world had already begun to totter.

These centuries saw (1) the expansion of Europe to the New World and eventually into Asia and Africa; (2) the growth of the "scientific spirit," (3) the dominance of commercialism, (4) the foundation of capitalism, (5) the beginnings of the Industrial Revolution, and (6) the triumph of representative government.

MUSIC AND THE LITURGY

I. INTRODUCTION

In 1517, with Martin Luther there began a revolt from which the Christian world is still suffering. There is no denying that there was a great need of reform in the ideals and lives of many members of the Catholic Church. But true reform must come from within. One cannot reform an organization of any kind simply by leaving it; such is the practice of the revolutionist. The movement initiated by Luther is better called the Protestant Revolt.

Many of the results of the Revolt have already been mentioned in the "Historical Setting." The foundational cause must be especially stressed — the development of *Individualism.* Individualism has been defined as the exaltation of the "I" at the expense of the

"We."[129] It manifested itself in contempt for all authority, secular as well as religious, in the private interpretation of Scripture, and in many other ways. In fact, individualism was affecting all expressions of society — religion, politics, literature, art, music.

II. INSTRUMENTAL MUSIC

There had always been music for such instruments as there were, but with the perfecting of instruments in the fifteenth, sixteenth, and seventeenth centuries, instrumental music took its place in the artistic field. The extended use of instruments led to the rise and development of ensemble and solo instrumental music. The larger forms of composition, developing in the eighteenth century particularly, were the suite, the fugue, the overture, the sonata, the concerto, and the symphony. Instruments were even habitually introduced into the services of the Church. The compositions of Giovanni Gabrielli, composed for liturgical services in St. Mark's Cathedral in Venice, sound very strange to us as "liturgical music" because of the instruments used.

The one instrument which under all circumstances is validly used in the liturgy is the organ.[130] It may have been introduced years before Charlemagne or at his time, but with its later gradually perfected mechanism, it attracted the attention of many well-trained musicians. Since the fifteenth century, but especially since the sixteenth century, it has been the vehicle of much religious musical expression.

III. THE RISE OF OPERA AND ORATORIO

Opera came into being as a result of the efforts of a small group of Florentine musicians to rediscover the use of music in the Greek drama. This was around 1600. We realize from personal experience how this style of drama took hold and developed. The operatic style of music even invaded the liturgy and there desecrated the sung worship by "liturgical arias" and thoroughly "operatic Masses." Naturally, the use in the liturgy of this style of music,

[129] Thuis, *Gregorian Chant A Barometer of Religious Fervor*, p. 30.
[130] See the *Motu Proprio*, Nos. 15–21.

and of the later Masses in the Viennese and concert style, is to be condemned.

The performance of a "spiritual opera" in 1600, in the Oratory of St. Philip Neri, developed into a form of dramatic performance called the *Oratorio*. There have been masterly compositions among the oratorios. Yet, although they are religious in subject, and may even be masterpieces, they are not fitting for use in the liturgy.

IV. POLYPHONIC DEVELOPMENTS

During the sixteenth century, classical polyphony reached its highest peak. There are many names which could be chosen from a long list of those who contributed much to this musical art and whose compositions have been found to possess attributes of true liturgical music. We shall select only the outstanding composers of each national school of polyphony. The Flemish, or Netherlands, School is represented by Orlandus Lassus (1532–1594); the Italian School, by Pierluigi da Palestrina (about 1524–1594); the Spanish School, by Tomas Luis da Vittoria (about 1540–1613); and the English School, by William Byrd (1543–1623). Of these, Palestrina is considered the peer. The German School, founded by Heinrich Isaac (1450–1517) of the Netherlands School, never attained to the polyphonic heights of the other national schools. There are, of course, among the Germans, polyphonic writers of note, as there are many others elsewhere.

Modern harmony was born in the sixteenth century. Some polyphonic works may sound more harmonic than polyphonic because of their chordal development, yet harmony and polyphony are fundamentally different in conception. In a harmonic piece, the composer thinks vertically; in a polyphonic piece, the composer thinks horizontally; that is, the melody of each part is complete without the sound of the other parts.

One sometimes hears criticisms of present-day choirs which seem to specialize in polyphonic singing. According to the principle on which it is based, this criticism may or may not be just. (1) The Church admits to her liturgy any type of music which possesses the necessary qualities of holiness, beauty, and universality. St. Pius X stated that while the chant necessarily possesses these qualities, they are also possessed by Classic Polyphony and may be by other music as well. So, looked at from the standpoint of the music, this criticism is unjust. (2) Considering polyphonic singing from the standpoint of active participation of the laity, we may find more foundation for such a criticism. For we know well that rarely is a congregation sufficiently trained to be able to sing the Ordinary of the Mass in a polyphonic setting; if it were, there should be no complaint at all. We know that it is the desire of the Church that the congregation sing its part of the prayers, that is, the Ordinary of the Mass and the Responses. However, as long as the choir continues to usurp the privilege of the congregation in this matter, we cannot object even if it sings a complete polyphonic Mass. (It would be more to the point to object to the fact that the choir is singing what belongs by right to the congregation.)

V. THE MISSAL

We noted previously that a Low Mass was not originally the rule. Circumstances brought about its introduction even while the High Mass was still the ideal and practice. Where it was necessary for only one priest to "fulfill in his own person the offices of deacon, sub-deacon and the other ministers,"[131] and finally even the office of the choir, all the sacramentary, lectionary, and antiphonale was included in one book, the *plenary missal,* or, as we call it, the *Missal.*

The *Missale plenarium,* or full Missal, began with the tenth century; from the thirteenth century it became very common.[132] The Council of Trent (1545–1563), seeking uniformity in the Roman Rite, entrusted the care of examining, revising, and restoring the Missal to a commission under Pius IV.[133] Thus additions which might have been the result of the restless, subjective, and individualistic spirit of the age were examined (and for the future forestalled),

131 Dom Fernand Cabrol, *The Books of the Latin Liturgy* (London: Sands and Company, 1932), p. 113.

132 Fortescue, *op. cit.,* p. 190.

133 *Ibid.,* p. 206.

and the Roman liturgy was restored to an earlier purity of form. The work of the commission, the *Missale Romanum,* completed under St. Pius V and published in 1570, was henceforth to be used by all in the Western Church. Exceptions were allowed only to those rites which had been in existence for at least two hundred years. Finally, uniformity within the Roman Rite was made obligatory by Church authority.

In January, 1588, Pope Sixtus V founded what is called the *Congregation of Rites*. Its special duties are to see to all that concerns the liturgy of the Church, that is, to enforce regulations, to grant dispensations, to settle questions, to provide Propers for new feasts, etc.

VI. ATTEMPTS WITHIN THE CHURCH TO SAVE THE CHANT

All along there had been attempts within the Church to save the chant and with it active participation in the liturgy. Protestant "reformers," who took whole towns to their Revolt by means of a sung participation in "the divine service," were using the musical knowledge they had gained when they were members of the Church and were misusing the original plan of her *corporate worship.*

At the Council of Trent (1545–1563) ". . . grave complaints were aired about the state of church music. Humanists and churchmen alike complained of the neglect of the text, the bad enunciation and irreverent attitude of singers, the presence of a secular spirit in the music and the overabundance of instruments in the services."[134] There was so little thought of abandoning the use of the chant in the liturgy that there was a strong movement among the members of the Council to prohibit the use of all music except the chant. Nevertheless, the polyphonic style did receive sanction. The Council recommended the supervision of the music of the liturgy to the vigilance and care of the bishops of the various dioceses.

As a result of the Council of Trent, there was a new official edition of the Breviary (1568) and of the Missal (1570). This brought renewed attention to the chant and an intended reform of it began.

[134] Lang, *Music in Western Civilization,* p. 228.

This reform finally led to the *Medicean Graduale* (1614–1615), the work of Suriano and Anerio, and the private undertaking of Raimondi who was head of the Medicean printing house. The *Graduale* was brought out within a year and was full of mistakes. However, this edition was able to secure a commendation by the Pope and later editions were often based on it. At no time was it declared official in the sense that it was obligatory, but it fell just short of that.

"This book," that is, the *Medicean Graduale,* "has considerable importance, because in the second half of the nineteenth century, the Congregation of Rites, believing it to contain the true chant of St. Gregory, had it republished as official chant book of the Church, which position it held from 1870 to 1904. During the seventeenth and eighteenth centuries various other attempts were made to reform the Gregorian chant. They were well-intentioned, no doubt, but only emphasized the downward course things were taking. The practice of singing became worse and worse, and what had been the glory of centuries fell into general contempt."[135]

Thus we see that the reform of the chant attempted by the *Medicean Graduale* did not contribute to a renewed or a widespread use of plainchant in the liturgy. "Other unfavorable circumstances supervened. In *Italy* the triumphal progress of secular, instrumental and operatic music destroyed the last hold which Plain Chant may still have had on the minds of artists and lovers of music. In *Germany,* the Thirty Years' War interrupted the regular observance of the Liturgy and liturgical music. Several pieces began to be omitted or were supplanted by German hymns,[136] a tendency which, in the Rationalistic epoch, found upholders even among the dignitaries of the Church. In *France* the fate of liturgic music was bound up with the liturgic innovation introduced by Gallicanism and Jansenism. In Cathedral, Parish, and Conventual churches 'up-to-date' books ousted the old chant-books which were still faithful to tradition. Nor was there any dearth of original compositions in

[35] H. Bewerunge, "Plain Chant," *Catholic Encyclopedia* (New York: The Encyclopedia Press, 1913), XII: 146. Copyright held by the Gilmary Society, New York.

[136] See Jungmann, *Mass of the Roman Rite,* pp. 147, 154–164.

the sentimental, empty style of the period. Still Plain Chant was at least sung in France, whilst up to the first half of the 19th century it was completely supplanted in many German districts by hymns in the vernacular. Where it was cultivated, its rendition became inartistic. The only gleam of light in this era is the fact that the ecclesiastical authorities constantly insisted that the Plain Chant was the true liturgical musical form."[137] Thus Weinmann summarizes the status of the chant.

We are not intending to imply that the chant is the only true liturgical music. However, the music characteristic of these years was foreign in spirit to the liturgy itself and consequently could not easily express the spirit of the liturgy. In later years, St. Pius X was to condemn the use in the liturgy not of modern music but of all modern music which shows its secular origin; he was also to remind us that we should consider the chant as our model and that the more music conforms to the movement, inspiration, and spirit of the chant, the more liturgical it is.[138]

VII. ACTIVE PARTICIPATION OF THE LAITY

We might have expected that while the Council of Trent was regulating other matters which had to do with the liturgy,[139] it would have attempted to restore a greater voiced participation of the laity; yet the spiritual conditions of the time made such a restoration impossible. The growth of *individualism* and the desire for this individualistic self to be expressed had caused solo-singing to become very popular. Solos had always been a part of the liturgy, but in the sung prayer of the Church, the soloist merely represents the whole people, and then only shortly. In the type and style of solo-singing which developed in this period, we find the expression of an isolated individual; this is completely foreign to the spirit of a prayer which is the prayer of many, one in Christ. The spirit of the times was far removed from the age when "the faithful must have been keenly alive to the fact that their entire lives belong

[137] Weinmann, *History of Church Music,* pp. 45–46. Italics ours.

[138] Pius X, *Motu Proprio,* Nos. 5, 6, and 3.

[139] See Ellard, *Mass of the Future,* Chapter 12, for a summary of the work of Trent.

to God and that they were all one in the Sacrifice of Christ."[140]

Gregorian Chant, which with the advent of measured music had begun little by little to be used as the basis of other compositions, was by this time almost completely misunderstood. The chant books themselves, "corrected" through the influence of the humanists, no longer gave a true picture of the ancient glory of the sung liturgy.

"The new music which now invaded the churches deprived the people of the last vestige of active participation in the sacred rites of the Church, a participation that had been their heritage for centuries — in fact, from the very rise of the Church's Liturgy. The congregation was reduced to the rank of mere onlookers not unlike their role in the theater.[141] With the introduction of female voices into the choir, which now necessitated the rear choir loft (women were not permitted to sing in the sanctuary), the atmosphere of the theater in the church became still more marked; and only too often was the attention of the faithful drawn rather to the rear gallery instead of to the sacred mysteries being celebrated in the sanctuary."[142]

Neither the music used in the liturgy nor the idea of a Sacrifice offered by the priest alone could be an aid toward any restoration of lay participation. Some, notably the Fathers of the French Oratory, attempted to bring the people to a closer realization of their position in the Sacrifice. But their teachings did not have a widespread effect at this time.

A Missal admitting a vernacular translation for the use of the people was still forbidden out of reverence, but more especially because of a fear of heretical (Jansenistic) influences in the translations which had been made (without permission). Thus it became the practice to give the people prayer books of devotion and, finally, books which contained prayers in the vernacular, more or less fitting the various parts of the Mass. Commonly, Mass became a time for

[140] J. A. Jungmann, "The Pastoral Effects of the Liturgy," *Orate Fratres,* 23:489.

[141] Read Chapter 13 of *The Mass of the Roman Rite* by Father Jungmann. On page 149, Jungmann says: "The development in the field of music made it really possible to 'hear' the Mass." (Reprinted with permission of Benziger Brothers.)

[142] Thuis, *Gregorian Chant A Barometer of Religious Fervor,* p. 33.

the congregation to meditate on the Passion of Christ or to say the Rosary (either aloud or privately).[143] We, in our day, have much for which to thank God who acted through St. Pius X. Among the many means this Pope took "to restore all things in Christ" is his encouragement of the use of the Missal by the laity.[144]

In Germany, hymns in the vernacular had been very popular from the late Middle Ages. During the period we are considering, *Mass hymns,* sung by the people in German, replaced first the Proper and then the Ordinary of the Mass. This practice was in absolute good faith, and, with the permission of the Holy See, even now continues in its own form in some dioceses of Germany. It was not until the late nineteenth century that it was generally forbidden to mix the Latin and the vernacular at a sung Mass.[145]

REVIEW QUESTIONS

1. Summarize briefly the historical setting of this period.
2. How would you characterize the spirit of this age?
3. How did it manifest itself in religion?
4. How did it manifest itself in politics?
5. Define individualism. How did it manifest itself in the music of the liturgy?
6. Which instrument is validly admitted to the liturgy?
7. Name one sixteenth-century composer from each national school of polyphony.
8. What have you to say of those choirs who sing only polyphonic music?
9. Explain the origin of the Missal.
10. What is the origin of the *Medicean Graduale?* Why was it natural that it would be full of mistakes?
11. Discuss the position of the chant in Italy, in Germany, and in France during this period.
12. Discuss in brief lay participation in the liturgy of this period.

143 Needless to say, we are not condemning this practice which received the recommendation of Leo XIII. We note, nevertheless, that the Holy See in nowise leads us to the opinion that it believes that a Rosary said aloud is the best form of vocal prayer during the Mass.

144 See also *Mediator Dei,* No. 105.

145 Pius X, *Motu Proprio,* No. 7. Disciplinary laws are made by the Church as the glory of God and the good of souls require. For the same reason the Holy See may in future years modify or change its disciplinary laws. In all events we will correspond and co-operate with the will of God as He guides and directs us through His established authority in His Church.

FIFTH PERIOD — PERIOD OF RESTORATION OF THE CHANT — 1850–

HISTORICAL SETTING

The past century has seen a great deal of progress in the sciences, especially in medicine, chemistry, and physics. It has also seen a further breaking down of Christian ideas and ideals in the conduct of individuals and of nations: witness the hostile relations between labor and management, the near success of the Nazi and Fascist movements, the emergence of the Communist bloc, and two World Wars. Witness, further, the League of Nations and the United Nations failing to work out a peace based on law and love, and see again the clouds of war hovering over the world. During this same period, especially in the latter half, there has been a revival of the religious spirit, although its force has not been sufficiently widespread to crush the antireligious spirit at war against it. Throughout this century, however, the Church has been singularly blessed with outstanding vicars.

LITURGY AND MUSIC

I. INTRODUCTION

By the middle of the nineteenth century there had been evidences of a reawakening of the religious spirit. All the "isms," the false philosophies which had followed in the wake of the Protestant Revolt, had failed to satisfy man. Many sought satisfaction in further "isms," but in others there stirred a desire to return to God who alone can satisfy man's restless yearnings.

During these same years, the seed of the liturgical revival was sown and took root. In Germany, the groundwork was begun by Kasper Ett (1788–1847), and especially by Karl Proske (1794–1861) in Ratisbon. Franz Witt (1834–1888), with evident zeal, devoted himself to the reform of Church music. He is responsible for the establishment of the Cecilian Society in 1869. This Society has for its object the promotion of true Catholic Church music. The fact that true Catholic Church music was not at first considered from the standpoint of the singing congregation is perhaps to be expected.

Some other individuals also worked for the reform of Church music and contributed their time and talents to the awakening liturgical movement. But the bulk of the work was accomplished by a group.

II. THE WORK OF THE SOLESMES MONKS[146]

What no individual could ever accomplish, a group of religious, bound by rule to the "Opus Dei," made competent by all their training, and united under one obedience, could quite effectively bring about. When *Dom Gueranger* secured the priory of Solesmes in 1832 and there re-established the Benedictine life in 1836–1837, he was determined to inspire his community with a complete devotion to the Church and to the Holy Father, and to reintroduce the Roman liturgy where Gallicanism had prevailed. It is a little difficult to summarize the Solesmes contributions to the Roman liturgy. Dom Gueranger himself began to publish, in 1841, the volumes of *The Liturgical Year*. This work aims to familiarize the faithful with the liturgy itself.

Dom Jausions and *Dom Pothier* (1835–1923), at the command of Dom Gueranger, began to examine various codices in order to compile a Graduale for the monastery of Solesmes. This was in 1860. Dom Jausions died in 1870, but Dom Pothier continued the work. Their *Les Melodies Gregoriennes* was published in 1883; the Graduale, *Liber Gradualis*, in 1883. *Dom Mocquereau* (1849–1930), a pupil of Dom Pothier, aimed particularly to restore the rhythm of the chant. The school of research which he established at Solesmes has given to the world its monumental achievements in the *Paleographie Musicale*. This work contains photographic reproductions of the principal plainchant manuscripts and scientific treatises on the subject of the chant itself. The first volume was produced by Dom Mocquereau in 1889. It "demonstrated by the reproduction

[146] A more developed summary of this point may be found in *The Fundamentals of Gregorian Chant* by Lura F. Heckenlively (Tournai: Desclée and Co.), pp. 277–295.

Pope Pius XII

With permission of Rev. Fabbrica di S. Pietro in Vaticano.

St. Pius X

St. Gregory the Great

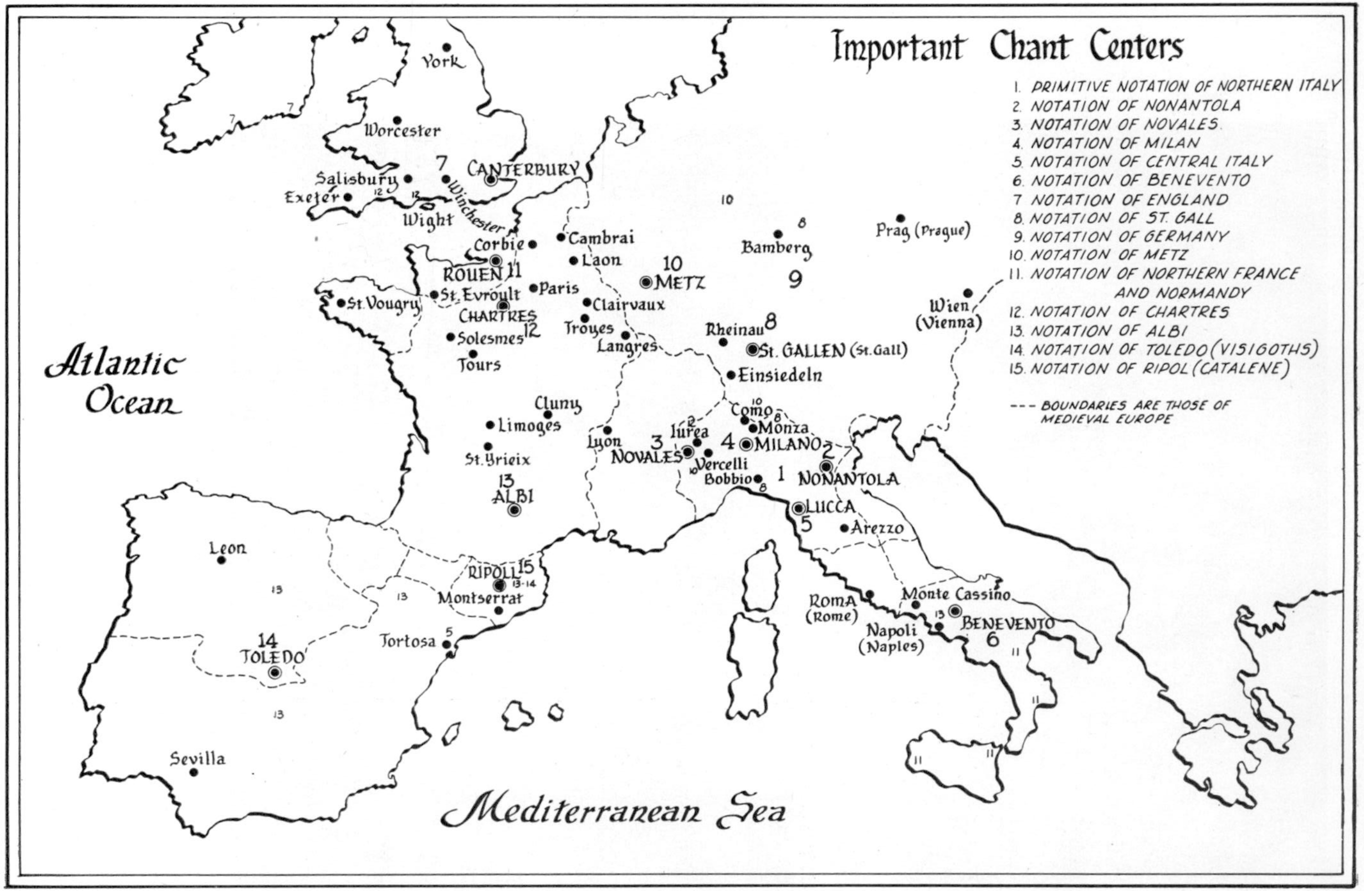
Important Chant Centers
1. PRIMITIVE NOTATION OF NORTHERN ITALY
2. NOTATION OF NONANTOLA
3. NOTATION OF NOVALES
4. NOTATION OF MILAN
5. NOTATION OF CENTRAL ITALY
6. NOTATION OF BENEVENTO
7 NOTATION OF ENGLAND
8. NOTATION OF ST. GALL
9. NOTATION OF GERMANY
10. NOTATION OF METZ
11. NOTATION OF NORTHERN FRANCE AND NORMANDY
12. NOTATION OF CHARTRES
13. NOTATION OF ALBI
14. NOTATION OF TOLEDO (VISIGOTHS)
15. NOTATION OF RIPOL (CATALENE)
--- BOUNDARIES ARE THOSE OF MEDIEVAL EUROPE
Atlantic Ocean
Mediterranean Sea
York
Worcester
Salisbury
Exeter
CANTERBURY
Winchester
Wight
Corbie
ROUEN
St. Evroult
St. Vougry
CHARTRES
Solesmes
Tours
Cambrai
Laon
Paris
Clairvaux
Troyes
Langres
METZ
Bamberg
Prag (Prague)
Wien (Vienna)
Rheinau
St. GALLEN (St. Gall)
Einsiedeln
Cluny
Limoges
St. Yrieix
ALBI
Lyon
NOVALES
Ivrea
Vercelli
Bobbio
Como
Monza
MILANO
NONANTOLA
LUCCA
Arezzo
Roma (Rome)
Monte Cassino
BENEVENTO
Napoli (Naples)
Leon
TOLEDO
Sevilla
RIPOLL
Montserrat
Tortosa

Important Chant Centers

of more than two hundred manuscripts of the Responsory *Justus ut palma,* the possibility of recovering with certainty the melodic tradition."[147] New volumes still appear as the result of the continuous labors of the monks under *Dom Gajard,* the present choir director at Solesmes.

Many other Benedictines, at Solesmes and elsewhere, as well as diocesan priests and religious of other orders and communities, and many lay people, have devoted themselves to the service of the Church in the Gregorian restoration and the spread of the liturgical movement.

III. PAPAL LEADERSHIP

The Popes of these past 100 years have given their sanction to the various efforts made to revive the use of the chant and have themselves led in the revival of the sung liturgy.

1. Pope Pius IX

During his troubled reign, Pius IX (1846–1878) contributed to the restoration. On December 16, 1870, he recognized the efforts of the Cecilian Society in a papal brief. The *schola cantorum* was renewed at the Lateran in 1868, and "institutions for the study and teaching of church music were founded in Milan, Rome, and Venice, the latter by the Patriarch Sarto, the future Pope Pius X."[148] The *Medicean Graduale* had been reprinted in 1868 with a thirty years' monopoly granted by the Holy See. Thinking it to be authoritative, Pius IX, in 1873, declared it the official edition.

2. Pope Leo XIII

In 1878, Leo XIII reaffirmed this choice. Both Popes recommended the use of the book but neither made its reception a matter of obligation. Before its thirty-year license was up, the errors in that edition of the chant were well known. Though the Vatican did not recall the privileges granted to this book, Leo XIII openly encouraged the research of the Solesmes monks in his brief of May 17, 1901.

[147] Aigrain, *Religious Music,* p. 97.
[148] Lang, *Music in Western Civilization,* p. 1009.

3. Pope Pius X

Ever on the alert for whatever would promote the piety of the faithful, Joseph Sarto, as a young priest in Tombolo, established a night school for adults who could neither read nor write. So that there might be congregational singing in the parish church, he included in the curriculum of the school the teaching of the chant along with a study of the catechism. As pastor of Salzano and canon and chancellor of Treviso, he demonstrated his solicitude for the sung liturgy. This solicitude was even more apparent when he was bishop of Mantua. Here he established a choir of clerics which he taught personally. His diocesan music regulations were so binding that anyone who had nonapproved books in his choir was *ipso facto* suspended.

As patriarch of Venice, Cardinal Sarto reformed the music at the Basilica of St. Mark's and issued (in 1895) a pastoral letter which regulated the music of the diocese. At this time he became a personal friend of Ravanello, later the choirmaster at Padua, and of Perosi, whom Leo XIII appointed to the Sistine Choir. Pius X made Perosi the "Perpetual Maestro of the Sistine Choir."

It was in his work as Pope Pius X, that Joseph Sarto brought his efforts to culmination. When he was made pope, he took as his motto: "To restore all things in Christ." A few weeks later, in one of his first official acts, he began his attempt at restoration in *The Instruction on Sacred Music,* which we speak of as the *Motu Proprio*. Only by studying the *Motu Proprio* can we appreciate his concern for the sung liturgy and his care that "the faithful may again take more active part in ecclesiastical offices."[149] Later official acts, especially the decrees concerning the early Communion of children, and Its frequent and even daily reception, continue to have as their object the restoration of all in Christ.

St. Pius X realized the need of a reliable official edition of the chant. For this reason he established a commission, in 1904, to prepare a Vatican edition. This commission was under the presidency of Dom Pothier. The Solesmes monks presented to Pius X the

[149] *Motu Proprio,* No. 3.

results of their many years of labor. The *Kyriale Vaticanum,* which we know as the *Kyriale,* appeared and was declared authentic by the Congregation of Rites on August 14, 1905. In August, 1907, a decree of the Sacred Congregation prohibited the use of any other edition than the *Vatican Edition of the Gradual* which appeared in 1908. In April, 1911, the same Congregation officially permitted the use of editions of the *Vatican Edition* with the rhythmical signs of the monks of Solesmes. The *Antiphonale,* which contains the chants for the Divine Office, appeared in 1912. A school of Sacred Music, established at Rome in 1910 by Father de Santi, was given the title of "Pontifical School" by Pius X.

4. Pope Pius XI

Through Pius XI the Holy Spirit continued to guide the Church in its strivings for a closer union with Christ. The celebration of the official prayer of the Church, both in its externals and in its inner spirit of social worship, was therefore the object of his solicitude also. The fiftieth anniversary of his priestly ordination nearly coincided with the silver jubilee of the *Motu Proprio.* The papal document often referred to as *The Apostolic Constitution,* December 20, 1928, celebrated both anniversaries. Its title is *Divini Cultus Sanctitatem.* In this document Pius XI declares the sacredness of the liturgy — the "close relationship between dogma and sacred liturgy, as likewise between Christian worship and the sanctification of souls."[150] He commends those who have obeyed the past regulations concerning the music of the liturgy and, reaffirming these regulations in even stronger language than Pius X had used, he suggests "practical ways and means" to insure that these recommendations be observed. We note that the practical ways and means include the injunction: "In order that the faithful may take a more active part in divine worship, let that portion of the chant which pertains to the congregation be restored to popular use."[151]

Pius XI established the feast of Christ the King in 1925, and authorized a fitting Mass. Ten years later, in an encyclical letter, he

[150] *Apostolic Constitution,* Introduction.
[151] *Ibid.,* No. IX.

defined the character of the Christian priesthood and instituted a special *Mass of Our Lord Jesus Christ the Eternal High Priest.*

5. Pope Pius XII

We can easily imagine that Pius XII might have instituted these two Masses if Pius XI had not already done so. His own encyclicals, *The Mystical Body of Christ* (June 29, 1943) and *Mediator Dei* (November 20, 1947), stress the unity of the faithful with and in Christ, the kingly Head of the Body and priestly Mediator between God and man.

Pius XII, following his predecessors Pius X and Pius XI, concerns himself with the fuller corporate worship of Christ's Church. One could never adequately summarize the *Mediator Dei.* If it is read in faith, it cannot but bring one to a greater realization of the grace given us in being members of the mystical Christ. As Pius XII himself says:

"Let the faithful, therefore, consider to what a high dignity they are raised by the sacrament of baptism. They should not think it enough to participate in the Eucharistic sacrifice with that general intention which befits members of Christ and children of the Church, but let them further, in keeping with the spirit of the sacred liturgy, be most closely united with the High Priest and His earthly minister, at the time the consecration of the divine Victim is enacted, and at that time especially when those solemn words are pronounced, 'By Him and with Him and in Him, is to Thee, God the Father almighty, in the unity of the Holy Ghost, all honor and glory for ever and ever'; to these words in fact the people answer 'Amen.' Nor should Christians forget to offer themselves, their cares, their sorrows, their distress and their necessities in union with the divine Saviour upon the cross."[152] Surely this offering of themselves is true participation in the liturgy. The encyclical continues:

"Therefore, they are to be praised who, with the idea of getting the Christian people to take part more easily and more fruitfully

[152] *Mediator Dei,* No. 104.

in the Mass, strive to make them familiar with the 'Roman Missal,' so that the faithful, united with the priest, may pray together in the words and sentiments of the Church. They also are to be commended who strive to make the liturgy even in an external way a sacred act in which all who are present may share. This can be done in more than one way when, for instance, the whole congregation, in accordance with the rules of the liturgy, either answer the Mass in an orderly and fitting manner, or sing hymns suitable to the different parts of the Mass, or do both, or finally in High Mass when they answer the prayers of the minister of Jesus Christ and also sing the liturgical chant."[153]

In the next paragraph, Pius XII observes that a dialogue Mass cannot replace the High Mass "which, as a matter of fact, though it should be offered with only the sacred ministers present, possesses its own special dignity due to the impressive character of its ritual and the magnificence of its ceremonies."[154] He warns those who, even through zeal, may misapply the express desire of the Church that all actively participate in the liturgy:

"Many of the faithful are unable to use the Roman missal even though it is written in the vernacular; nor are all capable of understanding the liturgical rites and formulas. So varied and diverse are men's talents and characters that it is impossible for all to be moved and attracted to the same extent by community prayers, hymns and liturgical services. Moreover, the needs and inclinations of all are not the same, nor are they always constant in the same individual."[155]

"But however much variety and disparity there may be in the exterior manner and circumstances in which the Christian laity participate in the Mass and other liturgical functions, constant and earnest effort must be made to unite the congregation in spirit as much as possible with the divine Redeemer, so that their lives may be daily enriched with more abundant sanctity, and greater glory be given to the heavenly Father."[156]

[153] *Ibid.*, No. 105.
[154] *Ibid.*, No. 106.
[155] *Ibid.*, No. 108.
[156] *Ibid.*, No. 111.

In the same encyclical, Pius XII exhorts the bishops of the various dioceses to "supervise and regulate the manner and method in which the people take part in the liturgy."[157] We must co-operate to the utmost of our ability with the leadership in our diocese in this as in every other respect.

IV. CONCLUSION

"The reader who has read and considered this present survey of the history of the Roman liturgy will doubtless be struck by the thought that even a very small alteration or innovation in the sphere of the liturgy may be like the start of an avalanche; the beginning may be quite imperceptible, but the consequences may be widespread and far-reaching. How many occurrences in the slipping and sliding process have come about since the time when the Canon began to be recited silently! Indeed, one may say that this seemingly slight divergence from the ancient tradition has in natural consequence determined the entire course of development in Christian piety in subsequent centuries, and has brought about all those features which many now regret.

"From the above it is evident, too, how great is the responsibility of anyone who would undertake a decisive step in such matters. Great patience and restraint is required in all questions presented by the liturgical revival of our times. Decades of years, of intensive study and reflection and planning, are not too much when there is question of assuring the right future development of an organic liturgy, the life and the life-work of which is to continue for hundreds and thousands of years."[158]

We may be inclined to wonder, since Pius X asked the Catholic world in 1903 to return to an *active* participation in the liturgy, why after all these years we have not yet completely responded. We cannot explain away a disregard of the wishes of the Holy See, but we can explain, somewhat, why regard for its wishes may not be too evident. For it takes more than a spirit of obedience to put the *Motu Proprio* into effect. It requires knowledge and deep under-

157 *Ibid.*, No. 109.
158 Klauser, *op. cit.*, No. 4, p. 160.

standing, and it requires available music material which is according to the spirit of the liturgy. Not all have the same training and equipment. "Unto whomsoever much is given, of him much shall be required" (Lk. 12:48). Let each, individually, be sure that his spirit is one with the Church, with Christ in His authority in the Church. Let each, individually, feel a responsibility to co-operate with his pastoral heads as they lead toward a fuller participation in the liturgy.

Civilization draws individuals closer to each other, their interdependence is intensified. Yet no one denies that this emancipates them. So, also, is it true that if we lived as members of the Mystical Body, we would find our individuality, not lost, but sublimated. We should be free with the freedom of the children of God: "by the freedom wherewith Christ has made us free" (Gal. 4:31).

The same would be true of nations in the Mystical Body. We will never have the unity for which we long until we are, at least in spirit, one in Christ. We say "the family that prays together, stays together" — the same is true of parishes, of cities, of countries, even of international groups.

The true Christian spirit is sadly needed in the world today. But while we appreciate this fact, we should also realize that the world includes the smaller world in which we live. Do we ourselves have this true Christian spirit? What are we doing to acquire it? Are we truly seeking it, as far as circumstances allow, where St. Pius X tells us it is to be found? His Holiness, Pope Pius XII, reminds us that "the most pressing duty of Christians is to live the liturgical life, and increase and cherish its supernatural spirit."[159] Through participation in the liturgy may we bring its spirit into our lives.

Participation in any of the liturgy should gradually bring about in us a transformation in Christ. This is especially true of participation in the Sacrifice of Calvary, through the rite whose divine elements were established by the God-Man Himself, through the rite which He offered for and with us as He prayed:

"Holy Father, keep them in thy name whom thou hast given me;

[159] *Mediator Dei,* No. 197.

that they may be one, as we also are. . . . I pray . . . that they all may be one, as thou, Father, in me, and I in thee; that they also may be one in us; that the world may believe that thou hast sent me. . . . I in them, and thou in me; that they may be made perfect in one: and the world may know that thou hast sent me, and hast loved them, as thou hast also loved me" (Jn. 17:11, 20, 21, 23).

REVIEW QUESTIONS

1. Name three persons who contributed to the liturgical revival in Germany.
2. Name four outstanding monks of the Abbey of Solesmes who contributed greatly to the liturgical movement.
3. Cite contributions of each of these monks.
4. Cite two acts of Pius IX which showed his interest in the sung liturgy.
5. Cite two acts of Leo XIII which showed his interest in the sung liturgy.
6. Summarize briefly the work of Pius X for the sung liturgy (1) before he was pope and (2) after he was pope.
7. How did Pius XI show his interest in the liturgy?
8. Give the titles of two encyclicals of Pius XII which stress our unity in Christ.
9. To whom did Pius XII entrust the supervision and regulation of active participation of the laity in the liturgy?
10. "Great patience and restraint is required in all questions presented by the liturgical revival of our times." Discuss.
11. Comment on the apparently slow response to the existing regulations of the Church as regards the sung liturgy.
12. What is the importance of the individual in the Mystical Body of Christ?
13. How can individuals, cities, countries, and even nations, assure themselves of peace?
14. What should I do to ensure the growth of the true Christian spirit in the world?

The Mass M

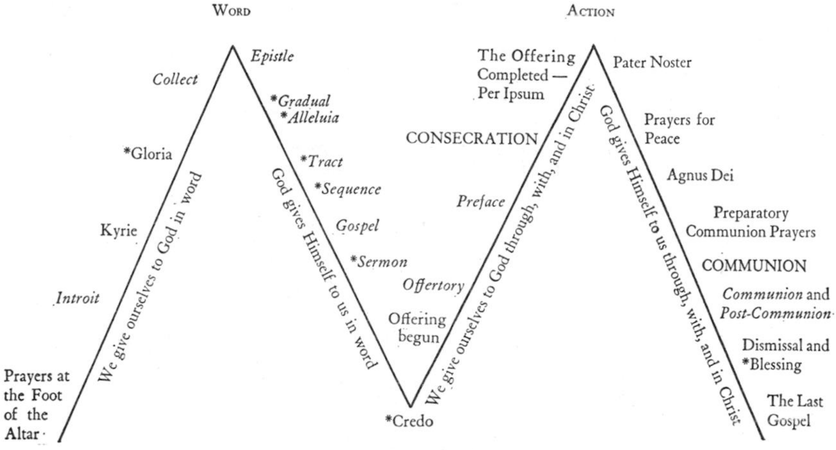

EXPLANATION

I. The Fore-Mass — Word

1. We give ourselves to God in words expressive of our relationship to Him.
2. God gives Himself to us in the inspired words of the Old and New Testaments, in His direct words in the Gospel, and in His authoritative presence in the Church speaking through the sermon.

II. The Mass of Sacrifice — Action

1. Under the exterior sign of bread and wine we give ourselves to God. In the Consecration Christ changes the substance of this bread and wine into Himself. Thus the offering of the Consecrated Bread and Wine is both the sign of our offering and the offering of Christ Himself which He makes with and for us and which we make through, with, and in Him.
2. God gives Himself to us in the Body, Blood, Soul, and Divinity of Christ present under the exterior appearances of bread and wine.

* * *

The prayers italicized are Proper, therefore variable, in each Mass.

The prayers asterisked are sometimes omitted.

CHAPTER VI

OUTLINE OF THE LITURGY OF THE (HIGH) MASS[1]

THE MASS OF THE CATECHUMENS — FORE-MASS

THE WORD PART OF THE MASS

A. Man Talks to God — The Service of Prayer

I. THE "ASPERGES ME" AND PSALM 50 (THE "MISERERE")

Sung by the priest and people during the sprinkling of holy water.

1. The blessing with holy water — with its accompanying Antiphon, Psalm, versicle, and Oration — arose from the desire of the Church that souls be purified before offering the Mass.
   a) Holy water is the symbol of the water of Baptism by which we were cleansed from sin and made children of God.
   b) We should bow or kneel and make the sign of the cross when we are blessed with holy water.
2. The *Asperges Me* and the *Miserere* are replaced by the *Vidi Aquam* and *Psalm 117* during the Paschal season.

II. THE "PREPARATORY PRAYERS" AT THE BEGINNING OF THE MASS

These prayers are expressive of contrition and of hope. Originally the celebrant, on arriving at the altar, said private prayers as a final preparation for the sacred rite about to begin; a number of sug-

[1] This chapter will not discuss every detail of the liturgy of the Mass, as that would be beyond the scope of the present work. Moreover, many excellent books on the Mass are easily available. Besides the authors quoted in this chapter, we would like to recommend *The Breaking of Bread* by John Coventry, S.J., published by Sheed and Ward, 1950.

gested prayers for this purpose are found in early Mass books. The present form of these, the latest additions to the Mass, was fixed by the Missal of Pius V (1570).[2] They are said by the celebrant and the ministers around the altar during the singing of the *Introit* and *Kyrie* by the choir and congregation.

1. *The Sign of the Cross, the Sign of Redemption*
   - *a*) This sign is fittingly placed at the beginning of the Mass which is the renewal of the Sacrifice of Calvary.
   - *b*) We also make the sign of the cross at the first words of the Introit, or entrance psalm, originally the formal beginning of the Mass.

2. *Antiphon and Psalm 42*
   - *a*) "I will go unto the altar of God. To God, who giveth joy to my youth." Participation in the life of God is the fruit of the altar of Calvary. The soul participating in this life is in eternal youth.
   - *b*) The Psalm, but not its Antiphon, is omitted during Passiontide and at Masses for the Dead.

3. *The "Confiteor"*
   - *a*) This is a public confession of sinfulness and is followed by an Absolution.
   - *b*) Begun probably in the silent prayer of the celebrant as early as the seventh century, the present form, in use by the thirteenth or the fourteenth century, was prescribed for the Western Rite by the Missal of Pius V.

4. *Versicles and Responses, and the Oration "Aufer a nobis"*
   - *a*) The versicles are a transition from the *Confiteor* to the Oration which ends the preparatory prayers.
   - *b*) The *Aufer a nobis* is an old Roman prayer.[3]

[2] Adrian Fortescue, *The Mass* (New York: Longmans, Green and Company, ninth impression, 1950), p. 225.

[3] *Ibid.*, p. 226.

5. *The Kissing and the Incensing of the Altar*

a) In the seventh century there was "a greeting for the coliturgists and also for the two objects most intimately connected with the liturgy, objects which represented Christ, the Gospel book and the altar. Of these only the kissing of the altar has been retained in the universal Mass rite."[4] The ceremony of kissing the altar is of ancient origin. It was introduced into the Mass at an early date, but its accompanying prayer is of the eleventh century. Through the kiss, the altar, Christ Himself, and the saints are honored.

b) Incense, used in both Jewish and pagan sacrifices, entered the Christian ceremonies early. The transition from carrying incense before persons to be honored to actually incensing them, was soon followed by the custom of thus honoring sacred objects, especially the altar which typifies Christ, and the Gospel book which contains His words.

III. THE INTROIT – PART OF THE PROPER

1. *History*

a) When the celebrant and the rest of the clergy came into the church in real procession[5] it was natural that their entrance should be accompanied by song.[6] Most of the texts of these songs, as well as the majority of the other Proper chants, are taken from the Book of Psalms. The verses of the psalm were originally sung antiphonally by two divisions of the choir although the Antiphon itself was sung by the whole choir.

b) The Introit is still sung by the choir.

c) The *Gloria Patri* was added to the psalms at least as early as the fifth century. Since the psalms were for the most part sung from memory, we are not surprised that the con-

[4] Jungmann, *The Mass of the Roman Rite,* Vol. I, p. 311. Quoted with permission of Benziger Brothers, Inc., publishers and copyright owners.

[5] See Chapter V for a description of the Station Procession.

[6] Fortescue, *op. cit.*, p. 217.

gregation did not ordinarily join in the singing. However, we note that in the Carolingian reform, the people were urged to join in the *Gloria Patri* at the end.[7] We should bow reverently whenever the *Gloria Patri* is sung.

d) The processional chants — the Introit, Offertory, and Communion chants — were sung during the time of the movement (1) into the church for Mass, (2) to the altar to offer the sacrificial gifts, (3) to the altar to receive the Return-Gift of God. The processional chants had the same general purpose (to assist the people to remain recollected during the movement) and the same general form.

e) The most important part of the Introit, both musically and textually, is the Antiphon. This does not imply that the psalm is unimportant. As the procession became shorter and the Antiphons became more florid, the psalm verses were lessened, and sometimes the thought was, by the same stroke, made less apparent.

f) Originally, during the course of the Introit, the celebrant and his ministers entered the church, said preparatory prayers kneeling before the altar, then rose and greeted the altar with a kiss. The celebrant did not then recite the Introit as he does now.

g) As we noted above, we still make the sign of the cross at the first words of the Introit.

h) Masses take their name from the first words of the Introit, for example, *Laetare*-Sunday, the *Requiem* Mass, etc.

i) In the Middle Ages the Introit was commonly troped.[8]

2. *Form*

a) The Past Form

(1) Antiphon, first verse of the psalm, Antiphon, second verse, Antiphon, third verse, etc., until, at a signal from the celebrant, the psalm verses were discontinued and

[7] Jungmann, *op. cit.*, p. 325.

[8] See Chapter V, p. 114 f., for an explanation of the tropes.

the Introit was concluded with the Antiphon, *Gloria Patri,* and Antiphon.

(2) Antiphon (sung by the choir), verse (sung by a soloist or cantors), Antiphon (by the choir), *Gloria Patri* (by cantor or cantors), and Antiphon (by the choir).

These two forms were at times varied in rendition.

b) The Present Form

Antiphon, verse, *Gloria Patri,* and Antiphon.

3. *Significance*

The Introit announces the mood in which we come to the service of God. It is ". . . the overture to the drama of the Mass that is to follow. Just as in an overture the principal theme is heard so in the Introit the mystery of the feast or its mood finds expression."[9]

IV. THE "KYRIE ELEISON" — PART OF THE ORDINARY, SUNG BY THE PEOPLE

1. *History*

a) There are several theories concerning the origin of the *Kyrie eleison* in the Mass. Some say that it is a remnant of the litanies which were sung at the beginning of the Mass in imitation of the Greek litanies, and others, that it is a relic of the station procession. In any case, this acclamation, which has come to us from Holy Scripture, was used in the Eastern liturgy at least as early as the fourth century,[10] and in the West, as early as the sixth century.

b) Pope St. Gregory I declared that the *Christe eleison* was in use at his time.[11]

c) Originally the clerics began the *Kyrie* and the people responded. Gradually the special singers (the *schola cantorum*) took an outstanding part in it and finally assumed

[9] Pius Parsch, *The Liturgy of the Mass,* translated by Frederic C. Eckhoff (St. Louis: B. Herder, 1940), p. 85. This book from which we often quote is a popular but authoritative book on all aspects of the Mass.

[10] Fortescue, *The Mass,* p. 232; Parsch, *op. cit.,* p. 96.

[11] Parsch, *op. cit.,* p. 96.

its performance completely. However, the Church still wishes it to be a congregational song.

d) It was very popularly troped.[12] The titles given to the plainsong melodies of the congregational songs in the Ordinary of the Mass are the first words of the old *Kyrie* tropes.

2. *Form*

The number of invocations was unlimited until at least the seventh century. Originally they were continued until the celebrant gave a sign. By the ninth century their number was fixed at nine.[13]

3. *Significance*

The terseness and brevity of the *Kyrie* makes it a very fitting congregational cry of petition. It must be sung with a realization of our insignificance, spiritual poverty, unworthiness, and need of redemption. "We cannot hope to receive from God a gift or grace unless the desire has first been awakened in us. The knowledge of our needs must be accompanied by a spirit of humility."[14]

4. *Ceremonies*

In the absence of particular diocesan regulations, at this time and throughout the Mass, the congregation should, as far as possible, follow the clergy in the sanctuary with regard to kneeling, standing, and sitting.[15]

V. THE "GLORIA IN EXCELSIS DEO" — PART OF THE ORDINARY, SUNG BY THE PEOPLE

1. *History*

a) This is a very early Christian hymn of praise. St. Athanasius, in the fourth century, recommends it as a morning hymn.[16]

12 See Chapter V, p. 115.

13 Fortescue, *op. cit.*, p. 237.

14 Parsch, *op. cit.*, p. 97.

15 Laurence J. O'Connell, *The Book of Ceremonies* (Milwaukee: The Bruce Publishing Company, 1943), p. 179, footnote.

16 Parsch, *op. cit.*, p. 99.

b) We are not sure when it was first introduced into the Mass, but we find it in the Roman Mass of the sixth century. Originally the rubrics permitted its use only at a bishop's Mass, at a priest's Easter Mass, and at the Mass of ordination. Since the twelfth century it is sung at all Masses of a festive character.

c) The *Gloria* was intoned by the celebrant and continued by the choir of clergy about the altar.[17] Its first melodies were practically a syllabic recitation.[18]

2. *Form and Content* (*According to Parsch*)[19]

a) Introduction. This section "contains the program of our Lord's life and of our redemption by Him," that is, glory to God and peace to men of good will (to "men that are God's friends" as Monsignor Knox says[20]).

b) Praise and thanks to the Father. "We give thee thanks for thy great glory."

c) Praise and prayer to the Son for salvation. "Thou alone art most High." "Lamb of God . . . receive our prayers."

d) Praise of the Holy Ghost in union with the Father and the Son.

3. *Significance*

a) "The 'Gloria,' the angelic hymn, was born when the King of angels was born. Composed by the Holy Spirit, sung by the angels, completed by the Church! It is the Church's morning hymn to the Father, Son and Holy Ghost."[21]

b) "The Gloria is the joyful response to the pleading of the Kyrie; it is the jubilant anthem of redemption of the children of God. Having made known in the Kyrie our need

[17] Such statements are to be understood as noting the general custom. We must realize that liturgical practices were not made uniform until 1570.

[18] Peter Wagner, *Introduction to the Gregorian Melodies,* translated by Agnes Orme and E. G. P. Wyatt, Vol. I (London: Plainsong and Medieval Society, 1901), p. 69.

[19] *The Liturgy of the Mass,* pp. 102–106.

[20] Lk. 2:14. From *The New Testament* in the translation of Msgr. Ronald A. Knox, copyright, Sheed and Ward, Inc., New York, 1944.

[21] Martin B. Hellriegel, *The Holy Sacrifice of the Mass* (St. Louis: Pio Decimo Press, 1944), p. 26.

for salvation, now in the Gloria we express with gratitude and joy our confidence in the knowledge of our redemption: I have been redeemed by Christ, I am a child of God, an heir of heaven; therefore I am jubilant."[22]

4. *Ceremonies*

We bow at the following words: *Deo, Adoramus te, Gratias agimus tibi, Jesu Christe, suscipe deprecationem nostram.*

VI. DOMINUS VOBISCUM

1. This greeting is found in Old Testament formulas. It is both a wish and a statement of the truth. The priest kisses the altar — ("the Altar is Christ") — ". . . kisses Him, Christ, and through Him the Father and receives from the Father through Christ the kiss of friendship, of sonship, of life and of love."[23] Then the priest turns to the people and with outstretched hands transmits these same graces to them in this greeting. During the Mass we stand when this greeting is sung.
2. The *Dominus vobiscum* is used eight times in the Mass. It is an invitation to take an active part in the Mass, particularly in that part which follows immediately.[24]
3. "The Lord be (or *is*) with you." We answer in gratitude and with fervor: "And with thy spirit."
4. If there has been a *Gloria,* a bishop sings *Pax vobis* in place of the *Dominus vobiscum* here.

VII. THE COLLECT — PART OF THE PROPER, SUNG BY THE CELEBRANT

1. *History*

a) The Collect was the conclusion of the entrance rite. It followed the Litanies (the *Kyrie* now) and the hymn (the *Gloria* now).[25] It is still the conclusion of this part of the Mass.

22 Parsch, *op. cit.,* p. 105.
23 Hellriegel, *op. cit.,* p. 24.
24 Parsch, *op. cit.,* p. 111.
25 Fortescue, *op. cit.,* p. 245.

b) Formerly there was only one Collect. In the very early days of the Church it was an extemporaneous prayer.

c) During the days of stational observance, both in the church of the assembly and in the stational Mass, the celebrant in a Collect prayed for, and in the name of, the people.

d) The oldest Collects of the liturgy are noted for the brevity of their expression.

e) At the end of the first and last Collect, we sing "Amen," a Hebrew word meaning "So be it." "By this word the congregation gives its assent to the prayer, and declares itself to be one with the priest."[26]

2. *Form*

There are four parts to a Collect: (1) the introduction, (2) the statement of the reason for our petition, (3) the petition itself, and (4) the conclusion.

3. *Significance*

a) We address this and all our other prayers to God "through Christ our Lord,"[27] our Mediator with the Father. "Amen, amen I say to you, if you ask the Father anything in my name, he will give it you" (Jn. 16:23).

b) The Collect of the day is sung at Mass and also at Lauds, Terce, Sext, None, and Vespers. It "unites beautifully the Mass and the Divine Office. . . . What a glorious picture! Three hundred and seventy-five thousand priests saying daily *one time* plus *five times* the official solemn prayer of the Church, presenting their own intentions and those of three hundred and sixty million faithful by this prayer 'through Jesus Christ our Lord, God's Son' to the Father in heaven!"[28]

4. *Ceremonies*

a) We bow as we are called to prayer by the word *Oremus;*

[26] Parsch, *op. cit.,* p. 118.

[27] Read Karl Adam, *Christ Our Brother* (New York: Macmillan Company, 1931), "Through Christ Our Lord," Chap. III.

[28] Hellriegel, *op. cit.,* p. 27.

we should bow likewise when the Holy Name of Jesus occurs.

b) In a festal Mass we stand as the Collect is sung; in a Requiem Mass we kneel after the word *Oremus*.

B. God Talks to Man — The Service of Reading

Now it is God's turn to speak. Three messages He sends us, the Epistle, the Gospel and the Sermon. Not in vain did we ring three times at the merciful heart of our God: "Kyrie, Christe, Kyrie." From each Person of the Blessed Trinity we receive an answer. The *Father* speaks, not personally, but through an ambassador, either of the Old or of the New Testament. The *Son* Himself speaks in the Gospel. The *Holy Ghost* speaks through His anointed mouthpiece, the priest.[29]

I. THE LESSONS — PART OF THE PROPER

1. *The Early Readings*

a) The Jewish Synagogue service consisted of (1) two scriptural readings, one from the Law, the other from the Prophets; (2) the singing of psalms; (3) common prayer; and (4) a discourse or sermon. As we have seen,[30] this service influenced the early form of our Fore-Mass.

b) Readings, the singing of psalms, and a sermon are still evident in this concluding part of the "Mass of the Catechumens." The number and order of the readings varied from place to place, but there is evidence that from early times there were in the Mass three, and perhaps even more, scriptural readings, the last always from the Gospels. The homily following the Gospel reading was an explanation and application of the Word of God read from Scripture.

2. *The Present-Day Readings*

a) The Lesson or Epistle

(1) The subdeacon chants this reading to a simple melody, then kneels before the celebrant to receive his blessing

[29] *Ibid., p.* 31.
[30] See Chapter V, pp. 72 and 74.

and to kiss his hand placed on the Epistle book. "This concluding rite expresses the return of the Book of the Epistles to the celebrant, who commissioned the subdeacon to read; and the celebrant, by placing his hand on the book, receives the book again."[31]

(2) We sit during the chanting of the Epistle.

(3) "Deo gratias" — "Thanks be to God!"

b) The Gospel

(1) Since the eleventh century, the Gospel has been preceded by the prayer *Munda cor meum* in which the priest prays for grace to worthily proclaim the Gospel.

(2) The Gospel is sung by the deacon who first lays the Gospel book on the altar, prays and is blessed, receives the book, and then, preceded by incense and lights, carries it in procession to the ambo. "The singing of the Gospel begins. We behold a beautiful scene: the subdeacon holds the book, unless it is placed on the ambo; it is surrounded by lighted candles and enveloped in clouds of incense. These are honors paid to God and to Christ alone; the liturgy, we know, sees here the presence of Christ."[32] It is Christ who speaks to us in the Gospel and whom we honor in it.

(3) "God be with you" — "And with thy spirit."
"The continuation of the holy Gospel according to —."
"Glory be to thee, O Lord." We make a small sign of the cross on our forehead, on our lips, and over our heart. After the Gospel, "Praise be to thee, O Christ!" is said.

(4) ". . . the Gospel is the climax of the Mass of the Catechumens, it is the first approach to the mystery of the Eucharist, forming the transition to the holy sacrifice, for it is the same Christ speaking to us in the Gospel, who later appears to us in the Holy Sacrament and, in

[31] Parsch, *op. cit.*, p. 126.
[32] *Ibid.*, p. 129.

the sacrificial banquet, bestows on us the graces of salvation that were announced in figure and parable in the Gospel."[33]

(5) The principal thought of the day is found in the Gospel.

(6) During the reading of the Gospel, out of reverence we stand erect and still.

(7) After the Gospel has been sung, the celebrant kisses the open book; at a Solemn Mass he is then incensed.

c) The Sermon

From the very beginning the sermon was considered an integral part of the liturgy. Originally it was given from the cathedra (the throne); then finally from the highest step of the ambo or pulpit.

". . . the central point of the Mass of the Catechumens is the cathedra, the symbol of the Church's office of teaching; around it the entire Mass of the Catechumens takes place. In the Mass of Sacrifice the altar becomes the central point, the symbol of the death of Christ on the cross."[34]

II. THE CHANTS BETWEEN THE LESSONS — PART OF THE PROPER

This is a very old part of the liturgy, coming, as we have said, from the Synagogue service. The original Christian use was probably: reading, psalm, reading, psalm, reading; the present order generally is: reading (Epistle), psalm (Gradual), psalm (Alleluia), reading (Gospel). The chants between the lessons have not the same purpose as the processional chants; these are an integral part of the liturgy. Originally all action at the altar was suspended as they were sung, and everyone listened. Present-day practice directs the congregation to sit (and meditate) during the singing of these psalms.

[33] *Ibid.*, p. 131.
[34] *Ibid.*, p. 44.

1. *Gradual*

   a) History

   (1) This, the most ancient of all the chants of the Mass,[35] is called the Gradual because it was originally sung from the lower step or *gradus* of the ambo. It is also called *Responsorium,* because it was sung responsorially. The psalm verses were sung as a solo, each verse alternating with a refrain, or responsory, sung by the congregation. From the standpoint of prayer, the congregational refrain is the most important part of the Gradual.

   (2) The person chosen for the solo verses had to be exemplary in his life. His name was given to the celebrant before the Mass, and after he was approved no one could take his place as soloist without the celebrant's permission.

   (3) Except in Easter week, the Gradual is replaced during the Paschal season by an Alleluia chant.

   b) Form[36]

   (1) The Gradual has had various forms throughout the centuries. Originally it was: responsory sung by the soloist, responsory sung by the people, first psalm verse by the soloist, responsory by the people, second psalm verse by the soloist, responsory by the people, and so on, the soloist alternating verse after verse of the complete psalm with the responsory by the people. Then it became: responsory sung by a cantor (a soloist) or cantors, responsory by the people or the rest of the choir, verse by a cantor or cantors, responsory by all. This last form was often varied.

   (2) Now we generally have the responsory sung once, followed by one psalm verse which the cantors and the

[35] Wagner, *Introduction to the Gregorian Melodies,* p. 72.
[36] *Ibid.,* pp. 72–78.

choir divide between them, but which they finish together.

c) Significance

Often, but particularly on certain feast days, the text of the Gradual looks back to the preceding lesson on which we meditate during the singing.

2. *The Alleluia*

a) History

(1) "This ejaculation, occurring constantly in the psalms, is also inherited from the Synagogue"[37] from which it came into Christian use. According to the testimony of St. Jerome, at Bethlehem as early as the fourth century, a psalm alternating with *Alleluia* was sung at this point in the liturgy. Pope St. Damasus is supposed to have introduced it into the Roman Mass at the instigation of St. Jerome.

(2) Sung at first only on Easter Sunday and then throughout the Easter season, the *Alleluia* was finally permitted by St. Gregory I on all Sundays and festivals except during Lent and on fast days. It is not sung at Requiem Masses.

(3) The *Alleluia* was, and still is, a true responsorial chant.

(4) A soloist sang the first *Alleluia* and the verses of the psalm from the step of the ambo. The cantor of the *Alleluia* (or of the Tract) could not be the Gradual soloist.

(5) The *Alleluia* was one of the first of the Mass melodies to be troped.

b) Present Form

(1) *Alleluia* sung by cantors, *Alleluia* sung by all the choir, a psalm verse sung by the cantors, *Alleluia* sung by all.

(2) The "Greater Alleluia," sung during the Easter season (with the exception of Easter week) has this form:

[37] Fortescue, *op. cit.*, p. 268.

Alleluia, Alleluia, psalm verse, *Alleluia,* psalm verse, *Alleluia.*

c) Significance

(1) In the *Alleluia* and its verse we prepare our souls to receive Christ in the Gospel which is to follow.

(2) "Alleluia" means "Glory be to Him Who Is." "-ia" = "Yahweh." The jubilus or florid melody on the final syllable has been much discussed, but that which seems most conclusive is attributed to St. Augustine: "And for whom is *jubilatio* more fitting than for the ineffable God? He is ineffable, for speech is too poor for Him; and if speech cannot help thee there and thou darest not be silent, what remains but to exult so that thy heart may rejoice without singing words, and the immeasurable breadth of joy may not experience the restriction of syllable."[38]

3. *The Tract*

a) History

(1) This chant replaces the *Alleluia* in the Requiem Mass and on days of penance if the day has a certain solemnity.

(2) The Tract is one of our oldest chants and is sung by the entire choir, probably to our oldest melodies. At one time it may have been, at least partially, a solo.[39]

(3) Various reasons have been given for its title.

b) Form

The Tract is sung continuously verse after verse with no responsories and with no repetition of text. This chant always uses a number of psalm verses, sometimes a complete psalm.

4. *The Sequence*

The Sequence is discussed in Chapter V. Only five sequences are retained in our present liturgy.

[38] St. Augustine, cited by Wagner, *Introduction to the Gregorian Melodies,* p. 33.
[39] Wagner, *op. cit.,* p. 86. See also Fortescue, *The Mass,* p. 271.

C. Conclusion of the Mass of the Catechumens

I. THE "CREDO" — PART OF THE ORDINARY, SUNG BY THE PEOPLE

1. *History*

   a) The *Credo* is an amplified version of the more terse Apostles' Creed, the customary profession of faith at Baptism.

   b) It appears in the liturgy of the Mass at Antioch in the fifth century, and in Spain in the sixth century. Benedict VIII made it an official part of the Roman liturgy in the eleventh century.

   c) Sung at first only on those days to which its own phrases refer, it is now sung on all Sundays and on greater feasts.

   d) Its place in the liturgy varies in the different rites of the Church.

   e) The *Credo* was intoned by the celebrant and then continued by all the faithful.

2. *Form and Content*

   a) I believe in one God:

   (1) The Father Almighty,
   The Creator of heaven and earth.

   (2) The Son,

   (*a*) Who is also God and proceeds from the Father before all ages.

   (*b*) Who became incarnate through the Holy Spirit, was born of Mary ever a virgin, Who lived and died as man for us and for our salvation, Who rose from the dead and ascended into heaven whence He will come in glory to judge the living and the dead.

   (3) The Holy Spirit,

   (*a*) Who is also God and proceeds from the Father and the Son.

   (*b*) Who speaks through His authority on earth.

   (*c*) Who sanctifies and gives life.

(i) The Church, which is His divinely established authority and to which He gives life, is one, holy, catholic, and apostolic. In this Church is one Baptism for the remission of sins.

(ii) Those who live in His life will, after rising from a mortal death, live eternally.

3. *Significance*

a) In the *Credo* we publicly and corporately profess our faith. Note that generally the public prayers of the Church are offered in the plural and therefore they use the term "we." The *Credo* is a personal and individual act of faith, and therefore it uses the term "I."

b) "To engender faith was the purpose of the Mass of the Catechumens; we listened to the readings and to the sermon in order to strengthen and confirm our faith. Faith is the porter standing at the entrance of the sanctuary of the sacrifice; faith is the pre-requisite for those graces that we hope to receive in the sacrifice. The Credo therefore is a fitting transition from the Ante-Mass to the Mass of Sacrifice."[40]

4. *Ceremonies*

a) The *Credo* is sung standing. (We sit if, and when, the celebrant sits, and stand when he stands.)

b) We bow at the words: *Deum, Jesum Christum, Et incarnatus est . . . homo factus est, simul adoratur*. On Christmas and on the feast of the Annunciation all kneel at *Et incarnatus est,* etc. In some places the congregation always kneels at these words.

II. DISMISSAL OF THE CATECHUMENS

History

This dismissal is no longer customary in our liturgy. When it was still the practice, groups of catechumens, excommu-

[40] Parsch, *op. cit.*, p. 150.

nicants, and others whose presence was considered out of place during the sacrifice of the faithful, were dismissed after a special prayer for each. In some places, this dismissal took place before the Gospel, in others before the *Credo,* and in still others after the *Credo.*

THE MASS OF THE FAITHFUL

THE ACTION PART OF THE MASS

A. Man Gives to God — The Sacrificial Offering

THE OFFERTORY

I. "DOMINUS VOBISCUM" AND "OREMUS"

1. *Dominus vobiscum* and *Oremus* generally precede an oration offered in the name of the people, but we do not have an oration at this place in our present liturgy. (1) This greeting and call to prayer may be a relic of the "prayers of the faithful" which were formerly said by all as they began their offering of the sacrifice. (These "prayers of the faithful" were somewhat like the series of orations in our Good Friday liturgy.) (2) It might have been that the Offertory action (prayer-in-action) was considered so important that it was preceded by *Dominus vobiscum* and *Oremus,* the general signal for prayer. (3) Or it might have been that the Secret prayer, coming at the end of the Offertory action, was considered the prayer which followed this *Oremus.*
2. Although the Offertory chant in the Requiem Mass is a direct prayer of petition most Offertory chants are not.

II. THE OFFERTORY

"The faithful of those days (A.D. 300–1100) understood well that they all partook both in the offering of the Mass and in the receiving of the Eucharist, both in sacrifice-oblation and in sacrifice-banquet. The ancient ceremonial brought this out very plainly. The faithful approached the altar at the Offertory and at the Communion first to give and later to receive. The Mass was both their gift to God through Christ and God's gift to them through Christ."[41]

1. *The Offertory Action*
   - *a*) The Offertory action of former days
     - (1) In former days, everyone — pope, clergy, and people — offered gifts which symbolized the offering of themselves to God. The people came in procession to the altar to present their offerings of bread and wine, oil, fruit, gold, silver, etc. The number who were to receive Holy Communion were judged from the number who made offerings, and the necessary amount of bread and wine was set aside to be consecrated. The rest of the offerings were blessed after the Consecration and were kept for the support of the Church, particularly for the support of the clergy and of the poor.
     - (2) The celebrant washed his hands after receiving the offerings.
     - (3) The celebrant said the Secret prayer — "*oratio super oblate secreta*" — over the gifts to be consecrated, asking God to receive them and to take them and their offerers into the sacrifice of Christ.
   - *b*) Although Church synods tried to retain the Offertory procession, it was gradually and generally abandoned during the Middle Ages.[42] It has never been really abolished.[43]
2. *Offertory Chant — Part of the Proper*
   - *a*) History
     - (1) A chant to accompany the offering existed at least by the first half of the fifth century. St. Augustine introduced it into the African Church, adopting probably either the Milanese or the Roman Rite. Since it is not in the Holy Saturday Mass, we know that the Roman Rite did not have it from the beginning.[44]

[41] Father Busch, cited by Hellriegel, *The Holy Sacrifice of the Mass,* p. 41.
[42] See Chapter V, pp. 109 and 123, Nos. III and XII.
[43] See the *Mediator Dei,* Nos. 89–90.
[44] Wagner, *op. cit.,* p. 93.

(2) The chant was inserted to assist the faithful to remain recollected during the Offertory procession. The length of the procession determined the number of psalm verses to be sung. In the Gallican liturgy of St. Germanus only the word *Alleluia* is sung at this time.[45]

b) Form

(1) Originally the psalm here was sung somewhat as the Introit had been at first, that is, with the two halves of the choir alternately singing the psalm verses and joining together in an Antiphon between the verses. By the time of Gregory I this form was modified and the verses were given to a soloist.[46] Thus the chant became more and more responsorial, the Antiphon becoming the responsory. As the chant became more florid and as the Offertory procession became shorter or was omitted, the Offertory song became only an Antiphon.

(2) Our present-day Offertory is generally only an Antiphon. The Requiem Offertory Antiphon is followed by a verse and a repetition of part of the Antiphon.

3. *Significance of the Offertory Procession and Offering*

a) The gift we offer represents the giver. In offering bread and wine we offer a form of food and drink, the sustenance of life. Through this symbolic gift we offer not only our labor and suffering but our very life itself; the act of offering signifies man's surrender to the will of God.

b) There is a corporate union of the offerers. Each comes with his offering which is changed into the one Christ; each comes with his individuality which is merged into the Mystical Body of Christ.

c) "This entrance into the sacrifice of the Lord was beautifully expressed in the offertory procession: the faithful brought to the altar their gifts which symbolized their own selves. Thus they laid themselves upon the altar of sacrifice,

[45] *Ibid.*, p. 94. [46] *Ibid.*, p. 95.

to die with Christ; they ascended the cross to die with Him. We are united with Christ in sacrifice. This indeed is the most profound significance of the Offertory — our entering into the sacrificial death of Christ."[47]

4. *The Present Form of the Offertory*
   a) The layman's offertory was at one time a prayer expressed in action; now for the most part it is a prayer expressed in words.
      Prayers at the offering of the bread and wine date from about the thirteenth century.[48]
   b) The offering of bread
      (1) The bread is called "this spotless host" in anticipation of the Consecration.
      (2) Unleavened bread has been universally used since the eleventh century. Probably both leavened and unleavened bread were used in the early days.
   c) The mixing of the water and wine
      The water has long been understood as symbolizing our human nature. Christ assumed human nature that we might partake of His divine nature.
   d) The offering of the chalice
      "the chalice of salvation" — this phrase also anticipates the Consecration.
   e) *"in spiritu humilitatis"*
      A prayer for a more perfect self-offering. ". . . may our sacrifice so be offered . . . that it may be pleasing to Thee."
   f) Prayer to the Holy Spirit — to sanctify and "bless this sacrifice"
   g) Incensing prayers
      (1) "At the High Mass God's gifts, God's altar, God's priest and God's people are incensed."[49]

[47] Parsch, *op. cit.*, p. 163.
[48] M. Gavin, *The Sacrifice of the Mass* (London: Burns, Oates and Washbourne, Ltd., 1903), p. 97.
[49] Hellriegel, *op. cit.*, p. 46.

(2) "We use incense . . . as prescribed by the Church. . . . It has reference to two things: first, to the reverence due to this sacrament . . . and secondly, it serves to show the effect of grace, wherewith Christ was filled as with a good odour . . . and from Christ it spread to the faithful by the work of His ministers according to 2 Cor. ii, 14: *He manifesteth the odour of his knowledge by us in every place;* and therefore when the altar which represents Christ, has been incensed on every side, then all are incensed in their proper order."[50]

h) *"Lavabo"*

The priest's hands are washed after receiving the offerings and handling the incense. Hand-washing, which was much in use in the Hebrew rite, has been used from the early days of the Church to signify a desire to purify one's intention.

i) Offering to the Trinity

"Receive, O Holy Trinity, this oblation. . . ." This prayer comes from the liturgy of St. Ambrose.[51]

j) *"Orate fratres"*

(1) "Since the Middle Ages, the clergy or the server responds with a prayer, that the sacrifice may be graciously received by God."[52]

(2) "my sacrifice and yours"

k) The Secret prayer

(1) Although this prayer varies in each Mass, it always expresses the thought that the gifts on the altar are symbolic of the offering of ourselves.

(2) This prayer which was originally said aloud began to be said silently at Rome about the eighth century.

(3) The Collect, Secret, and Postcommunion prayers are offered by the celebrant in the name of all. In each

[50] Thomas Aquinas, *Summa Theologica* (London: Burns, Oates and Washbourne; American edition: New York: Benziger Brothers), III, Q. 83, Art. 5, Obj. 2.

[51] Parsch, *op. cit.*, p. 182.

[52] *Ibid.*, p. 183.

Mass there are as many Secret and Postcommunion prayers as there were Collects.

l) *"Per omnia saecula saeculorum. Amen."*
The congregation voices its assent to the prayers of the Offertory through this *Amen.*

5. *Summary*

a) "The essence of the Offertory lies in the offertory procession of the faithful who thus show their active participation in the Mass. With the discontinuance of the offertory procession, the Offertory became a pre-offering of the Eucharistic sacrifice, which follows. It has become since then a sacerdotal liturgy. But the layman should, even now, see in the offertory procession, even though it be performed only spiritually, the essence of the Offertory."[53]

b) The contribution we make to the collection should be made in the spirit of the "gift-offering" for which the collection has been generally substituted.

THE PREFACE TO THE CANON

I. THE PREFACE

The Offertory is over. And yet it is not over. It was only the beginning of an oblation which "through Him and with Him and in Him" will ripen into a perfect Sacrifice, an oblation worthy of the majesty of that great God before whom the angels tremble, the powers stand in awe, the seraphim and cherubim cry out unceasingly: "Holy, Holy, Holy is the Lord of sabaoth." Had we no more to offer than a little bread, a little wine and our own selves we could indeed exclaim with St. Peter: "Lord we have laboured all night . . . all during Mass . . . and have caught nothing."

Thanks be to God, we have *One* who is able to make our oblation truly worthy of God, One who will turn the bread into His sacrificial Body, the wine into His sacrificial Blood and ourselves into Himself. "When I shall be lifted up I will draw all things unto Myself."

The moment of that great change draws nigh. Therefore, "Sursum corda!" Lift up your hearts! "Gratias agamus . . . Domino Deo nostro."

[53] *Ibid.*, p. 184.

The Introit Procession

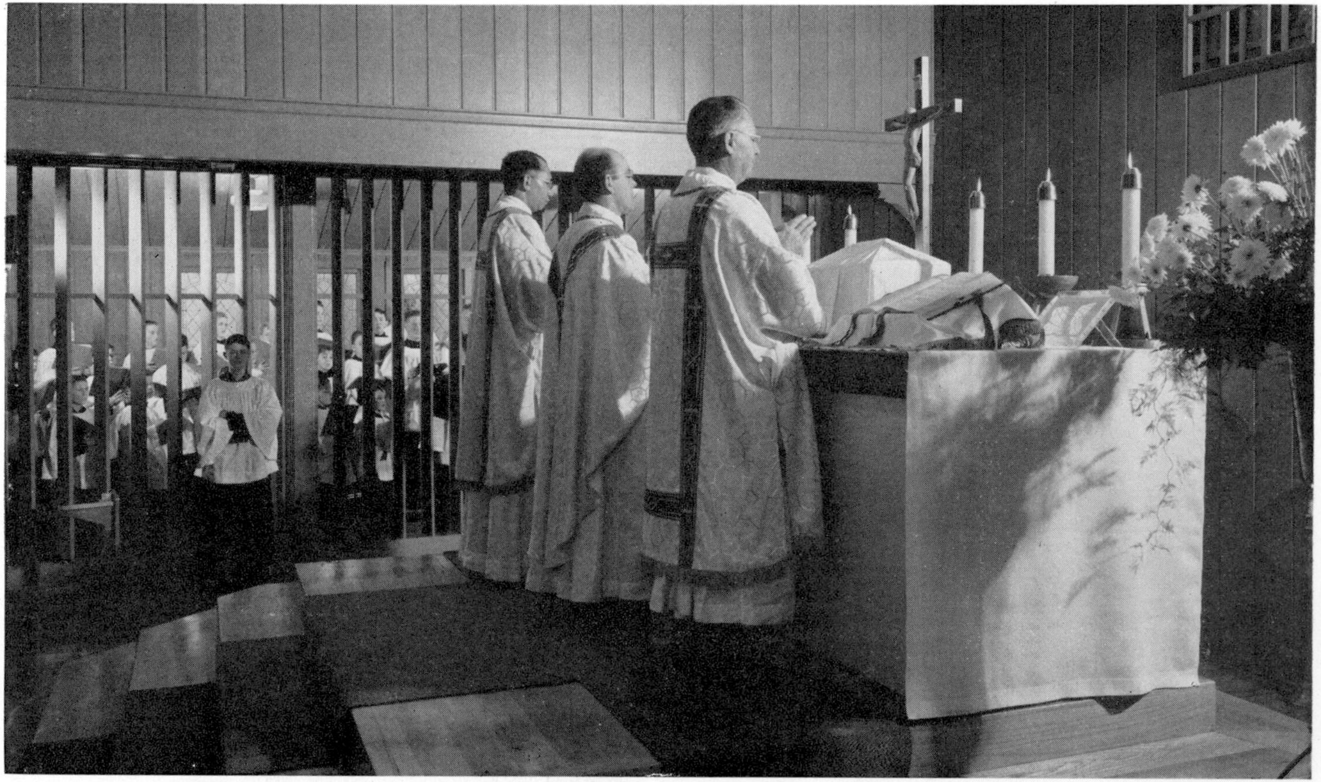

The Choir Alternates With the Congregation Singing the Gloria

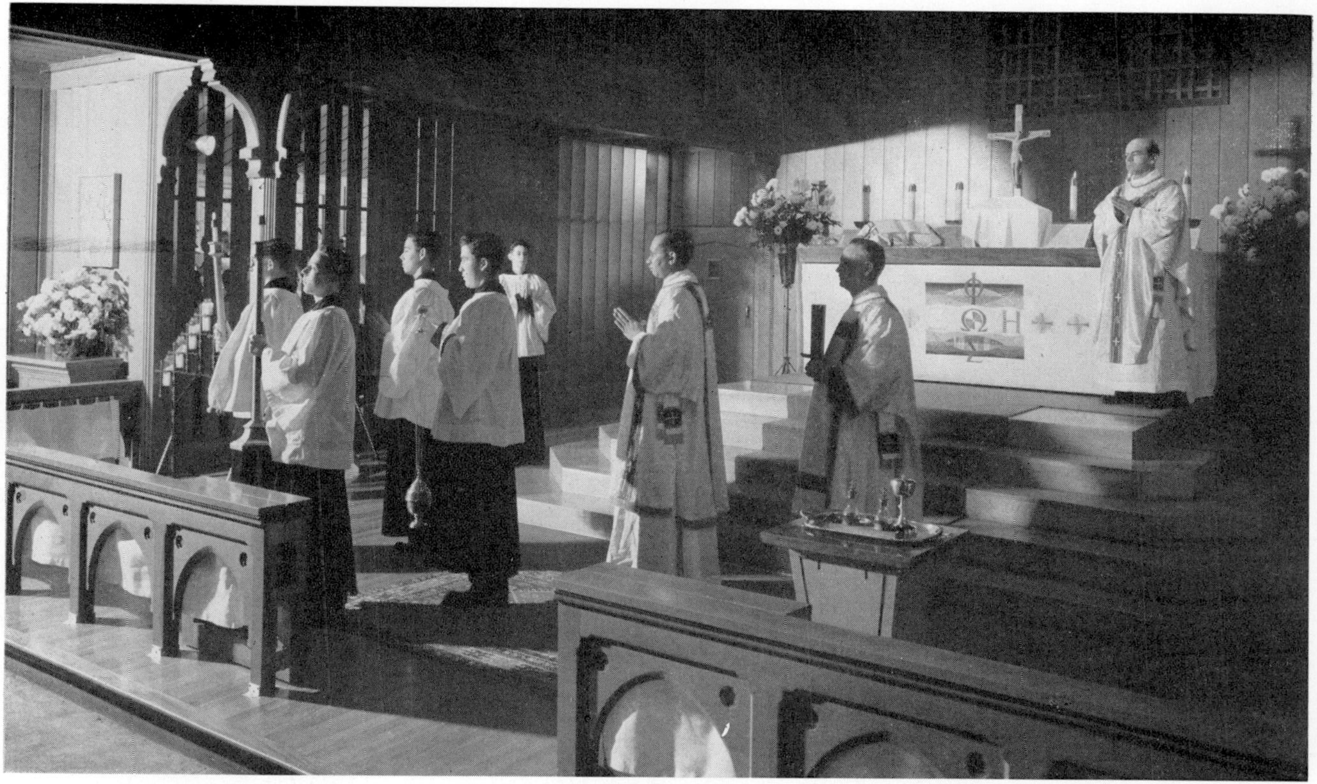

The Gospel Procession

One Form of the Laymen's Offertory

Let us celebrate the Eucharist to the Lord our God! The Preface leads us into the Holy of Holies where we shall give thanks (gratias *agere,* "do" thanks) to God "through Christ our Lord." In union with the heavenly choirs we fall down before the Lord God and exclaim: "Sanctus, sanctus, sanctus," and joining the apostles, disciples and children of the first Palm Sunday, we welcome with palms of love the King of Peace who is about to enter into the city of His eucharistic Jerusalem: "Blessed is He who cometh in the name of the Lord. Hosanna in the highest!"[54]

1. *The Acclamations*
   a) These have been in the Roman liturgy from at least the third century.
   b) "God with you" — "And with thy spirit."
   "Lift up your hearts" — "We have lifted them up to the Lord."
   "Let us give (or *do*) thanks to the Lord our God" — "It is meet and just."
   The Preface continues: "Truly it is meet and just . . ." etc.
2. *The Preface*
   a) This is a prayer of thanksgiving and of praise offered *"per Christum Dominum nostrum."* It is "a poem in free verse."[55]
   b) The Preface praises God first in general terms and then for a particular reason according to the feast being celebrated; we unite our voices and join in the adoration and praise of the heavenly choirs.

II. THE "SANCTUS" — PART OF THE ORDINARY, SUNG BY THE PEOPLE

1. *History*
   a) This chant which concludes the Preface was added to the Roman Mass about A.D. 120 by Pope Sixtus I. Originally it was begun by the celebrant and continued by the whole congregation. In many places, priests were obliged to join in the singing, and the *Te igitur* was not begun until the *Sanctus* was finished.[56]

[54] Hellriegel, *op. cit.,* pp. 49–50.
[55] Parsch, *op. cit.,* p. 214.
[56] Wagner, *op. cit.,* pp. 99–100.

b) The original *Sanctus* melody is said to be that in Mass XVIII and in the Requiem Mass. When the choir usurped the rights of the congregation to sing this chant, richer melodies were composed.

2. The text, almost word for word from the Bible, recalls the visions of Isaias and St. John.

   Hosanna, a Hebrew word, is expressive of triumphant joy, loyalty, and love.

III. THE "BENEDICTUS" — PART OF THE ORDINARY, SUNG BY THE PEOPLE

1. The *Benedictus* is the conclusion of the *Sanctus*. The harmonized Masses so prolonged the *Sanctus* that the *Benedictus* was not sung until after the Elevation. It is evident that it is more liturgically in place where the celebrant recites it. However: "On January 14, 1921, the Sacred Congregation of Rites decided that the Benedictus should be sung after the consecration 'in all sung Masses as well for the living as the dead, no matter whether plain song or any other chant be used.' "[57]
2. "Blessed is He that cometh in the name of the Lord. Hosanna in the Highest."
3. "The Hosanna in excelsis is cognate to the Gloria in excelsis."[58]

THE CANON — THE RITE OF CONSECRATION

When we assist at the holy sacrifice of the Mass, we stand in the midst of the assembled Creation in the presence of this mystical Calvary. Here, the Church, our loved ones, the saints, the poor souls, all created beings are assembled beneath the cross, and in the midst of all these we find ourselves. Truly, the Canon is the universal prayer, embracing the whole world in the genuine spirit of the liturgy. "And I, if I be lifted up from the earth, will draw all things to myself."[59]

I. HISTORY

1. The discussion of the history of the Canon would be long and

[57] Dom P. Gregory Hugle, *The Spotlight on Catholic Church Music* (Boston: McLaughlin and Reilly, 1935), p. 60.

[58] Parsch, *op. cit.,* p. 129.

[59] *Ibid.,* p. 195.

involved and would not be of much advantage for our present purpose. We know from the New Testament accounts that at the Paschal Meal, the Last Supper, our Lord said a prayer of thanksgiving and then changed bread and wine into His Body and Blood. As we have seen in Chapter V, the early prayers of the Church were free, even extemporaneous, agreeing in general outline only; thus in the very early days of the Church, those who followed Christ's command to "Do this for a commemoration of me" probably composed here a prayer of thanks, or used such a prayer as our Lord had used at the Paschal meal, and within the prayer said the words of consecration in our Lord's name. At least by the third century there were set forms of the Eucharistic prayer, or the prayer of thanks; yet even these forms were changed or added to until the pontificate of St. Gregory the Great. "Since the time of Gregory I, no essential change has been made in the Canon, and therefore we may conclude that our present Canon has been in use since about A.D. 600."[60]

2. Until at least the third century the prayers of the Canon were said aloud, but gradually they came to be said silently. Now, except for a slight raising of the voice at the *Nobis quoque peccatoribus,* the celebrant says in silence all the prayers from the *Hosanna in excelsis* to the closing words of the Canon, *per omnia saecula saeculorum.* "The Canon is really the sacrificial prayer, and is intended to be recited by the sacrificing priest alone, who therefore, in the Roman liturgy, recites it silently."[61]
3. Up to the eleventh or twelfth century there was only one elevation in the Mass, that which comes at the end of the Canon and which we now call the little elevation. The greater elevation, just after the Consecration, was begun in the Middle Ages and was established in the Roman Ordo in the fourteenth century.[62] This greater elevation was inserted so that the

60 *Ibid.,* p. 192.
61 *Ibid.,* p. 186.
62 Fortescue, *op. cit.,* p. 338.

faithful might immediately adore Christ made present in the sacred species of bread and wine. The little elevation still concludes the rite of the offering of Christ (and of us with Him) to His eternal Father.

II. FORM OF OUR PRESENT CANON

The Preface is generally not considered part of our present-day Canon, but it still bears its title of Preface. The structure of the Canon creates concentric circles around the Consecration itself.[63] (In this outline the circles will be noted in Numbers 1 and 5 and 2 and 4 under the next heading, No. III.) We have three remembrance prayers and two offering prayers; then the *Consecration* directly preceded by the Last Supper narrative and followed by a remembrance of Christ's Passion, Resurrection, and Ascension; then two offerings and three remembrance prayers again. The Canon closes with a solemn prayer of offering and the little elevation.

III. PRAYERS OF OUR PRESENT-DAY CANON

1. *Three Remembrance Prayers*

a) We offer the sacrifice for the peace, preservation, unity, and governance of the Church, for our Holy Father, and for all bishops, particularly our own.

In the manuscripts of the Middle Ages, the "T" at the beginning of this prayer, the *Te igitur,* was often illuminated. Its form suggested the cross of Christ and led to our present practice of inserting in the Missal a picture of Calvary just before the "Canon Missae."

b) We pray for the living.

(1) Formerly the deacon read from double tablets, or diptychs, the names of those who were to be particularly remembered at Mass. Now the celebrant pauses here and mentally names persons for whom he is especially praying. We should do the same.

[63] See the diagram on page 196 in *The Liturgy of the Mass* by Parsch.

(2) Those "standing around" (*circumstantium*), and their families and friends, are especially remembered. In early times those who participated in the Mass stood around the altar which was in the center of the church.

c) We honor the memory of all the saints, but particularly our Lady, the twelve Apostles, and twelve (male) martyrs, all of whom are mentioned by name.

2. *Two Offering Prayers*

a) We beg God to accept our sacrifice, and we pray for peace, for preservation from hell, and for the reward of heaven.

(1) As the priest says the *Hanc igitur* he extends his hands over the offerings. Through this symbolic gesture which comes to us from the Jewish sacrifices, the priest shows that Christ has become for us a vicarious victim, taking on Himself the guilt of our sins and atoning for them through Calvary which is now being renewed in the Mass.

b) We beg God to make our oblation (in reality *us,* whom it represents) blessed, approved, ratified, reasonable, and acceptable.

3. *The CONSECRATION*

a) Here the priest no longer prays, but within a simple narrative of the events of the Last Supper, he speaks as Christ Himself in the words of consecration: "This is my Body. This is my Blood."

b) A bell rings as the Sacred Host and the Chalice are elevated. An indulgence of seven years each time—and a plenary indulgence once a week if it has been done daily—is granted to those who look upon the Host and say: "My Lord and my God."

The custom of ringing the bell here was introduced about 1200;[64] that of the incensing dates from the fourteenth century.

[64] See Fortescue, *The Mass,* pp. 342–344, for a short and interesting account of the use of bells during the Mass.

c) "A few moments ago only our gifts were there on the altar, the good but poor bread, the good but inexpensive wine; and the gift of our poor selves, which these altar gifts symbolize, was on the altar of our hearts. Not much to give to God. Then came the consecration. Our gifts on the altar become Christ; our heart-altar gifts are united with Him. Now we can give God our Father a gift truly worthy of Him. We can now give God to God — and ourselves in and with and through Him. Now indeed have we given Him an acceptable gift. Here at the Consecration we see the Mystical Body at its height. United together are Christ the great high priest, the human priest His instrument, the royal priesthood of the participating people. Here is the *'Totus Christus,'* the whole Christ, united in the reenacted Calvary that is the Mass."[65]

d) We make a remembrance of Christ's Passion, Death, Resurrection, and Ascension. Our redemption is completed in Christ's death, His resurrection from the dead, and His ascension to His Father. "And if Christ be not risen again, your faith is vain, for you are yet in your sins. Then they also that are fallen asleep in Christ, are perished. . . . But now Christ is risen from the dead, the firstfruits of them that sleep" (1 Cor. 15:17, 18, 20).

4. *Two Offering Prayers*

a) We ask God to accept our offering as He accepted the sacrifices of the sinless Abel, the obedient Abraham, and the royal Melchisedech. These sacrifices of the Old Law, prefiguring the sacrifice of Christ, were pleasing to God in virtue of Christ's sacrifice. Ours, too, are pleasing to God as we offer them with, in, and through Christ.

b) We pray that the Angel may take our sacrifice to the heavenly altar with which we pray to be joined. We look forward to a full participation of the sacrifice in Holy Communion.

[65] Richard L. Rooney, S.J., *Light on the Liturgy* (St. Louis: The Queen's Work, 1945), Part II, p. 28.

5. *Three Remembrance Prayers*

   a) We pray for all the faithful departed who are signed "with the sign of faith," but especially for those whom we name. Formerly these names also were read from diptychs. The "sign of faith" reminds us of the indelible character placed on our souls in Baptism.

   Again we remind ourselves that all our prayers are of worth only "through Christ our Lord."

   b) We pray for ourselves (*nobis quoque peccatoribus*) that, although unworthy, we may be joined with the saints. Then certain saints are named: St. John (thought to mean St. John the Baptist) and fourteen martyrs (seven men and seven women).

   The clergy about the altar used to remain bowed until the celebrant raised his voice at the *nobis quoque peccatoribus.*

   c) We ask a blessing on nature. It was probably here that the offerings not used in the Sacrifice, and other natural objects as well, were blessed.

6. "By Him, and with Him, and in Him, is unto Thee, God the Father almighty, in the unity of the Holy Ghost all honour and glory for ever and ever. Amen."

   a) "This doxology is a presage of a scene that may take place at the end of time. The last of those who are to be saved has been incorporated into the mystical body of Christ. Christ our Lord comes into the presence of His heavenly Father to announce that the work of the redemption has been accomplished: 'My Father, the redemption of the human race has been consummated. The breach between Thee and mankind has been closed. Through Me, and with Me, and in Me, is unto Thee, Father, in the unity of the Holy Ghost, all honor and glory.' Then all those who have been saved will fall down in adoration before God's throne. It will be one of those magnificent liturgical moments, such as St. John pictures in the Apocalypse; it will be the closing scene in the drama of salvation."[66]

b) "The priest finishes the Canon. He takes the Host and the Chalice and lifts them up to heaven. It is now, with the closing prayer of the Canon, that the Victim is offered up to God. 'The lifting up of the victim as an offering to God,' says Bossuet, 'was formerly one of the ceremonies of the sacrifice. The Body and Blood of our Lord are now lifted up in the same spirit, these being really and truly our victim.' "[67]

c) "Amen." In this word the faithful are privileged to unite their voices, closing the solemn prayer of the Canon. In the early Church this was the only *Amen* in the Canon.

IV. "OFFERING" IN THE CANON

We must try to keep in mind that, during Mass and particularly at the Consecration, the primary and essential thing is the offering of the sacrifice; the adoration of the Species is entirely secondary. We should strive to impress ourselves and those committed to our care, with a deep understanding of the sacrificial action. The Mass is not a "devotion," it is not the adoration of the Eucharist; it is the sacrifice offered by Christ, and in this offering we are actually participating since it is also our sacrifice. We come to Mass, we celebrate Mass, not so much to adore Christ in His divinity, as to offer Him, the divine Lamb, to our heavenly Father.[68]

B. God Gives to Man — The Sacrificial Banquet

I. THE PLACE OF A BANQUET IN A SACRIFICE

1. *In Any Sacrifice*

The purpose of sacrifice is to achieve or increase union between the offerer and the one to whom it is offered. In a sacrifice-banquet even pagans saw their offering ratified and accepted and themselves guests of the deity.

66 Parsch, *op. cit.*, p. 254.
67 Dom Gaspar Lefebvre, *Daily Missal* (Bruges: Declée, 1934), p. 66.
68 Parsch, *op. cit.*, p. 237.

2. *In the Sacrifice of the Mass*

a) In the Sacrifice of the Mass we seek, through Christ, union with God. In the Sacrifice-Banquet of Holy Communion God gives us not only the union of friendship but gives us Himself as the food and nourishment of our souls.

b) "The all important thing is Christ's holy sacrifice; and the fruit of that sacrifice is Holy Communion."[69]

c) Our sacrifice-banquet is communal.

(1) As our sacrificial offering was personal and yet communal, so also is our Communion.

(2) We are individually and personally united with Christ and individually transformed in Him, but as we are united to the Godhead because of our union with Christ, so also we are united with His mystical members because of our union with Him.

(3) As we are affected personally by the reception of Holy Communion, so also we should be affected socially.

(4) The effect of Holy Communion is union with the Mystical Body. "The unity of the Mystical Body is the fruit of the true body received" [sacramentally].[70]

(5) "The Church of Jesus Christ needs no other bread than this to satisfy fully our soul's wants and desires, and to unite us in the most intimate union with Jesus Christ, to make us 'one body,' to get us to live together as brothers who, breaking the same bread, sit down to the same heavenly table, to partake of the elixir of immortality."[71]

d) "In the sacrificial meal we receive in return the bread which we offered in the Offertory; but now it has been changed, it has become divine. This transformation of natural bread into divine bread is profoundly symbolic of the Mass. We have said that the gift is the representative of the giver. As the gift was transformed, so, too, is the giver. He, the natural

69 *Ibid.*, p. 260.
70 St. Thomas Aquinas, *Summa Theologica,* III, Q. 82, A. 9. See also Q. 73, A. 3 and 4.
71 Pius XII, *Mediator Dei*, No. 120.

man, comes to the sacrifice; he returns home transformed, participating in the divine nature. This is the salvation which is merited for us in the holy sacrifice of the Mass."[72]

II. PREPARATION OF THE SACRIFICIAL MEAL

1. *The "Pater Noster"*

   a) Although its place may differ, this prayer occurs in every liturgy. We do not know when it was introduced into the Roman Rite. It is found in its present place in the Mass at the time of Gregory I who writes: "It also seemed most inappropriate to me, to recite at the sacrifice a prayer which was composed by some learned person, and to omit the recitation of the prayer which our Saviour Himself had composed, in the sacrifice of His body and blood."[73]

   b) "It is as though we assembled about the holy table, as members of the great religious family, and recited our table prayer. . . . We may say that the fruit of the sacrifice and the effect of Holy Communion are the fulfillment of the petitions of the Our Father."[74]

   c) There are seven petitions of the *Our Father*. This prayer, given us by our Lord Himself, summarizes completely the desires of a true child of God. The first three petitions seek God's glory, the fourth asks for temporal and spiritual sustenance ("our daily bread"), and the last three ask particularly for what pertains to our salvation.

   d) The congregation joins its voice in the last petition and the celebrant says: "Amen."

2. *The Prayer "Libera nos"*

   We pray for deliverance from evil (sin) and, through the intercession of our Lady and the saints, for peace.

3. *The Breaking of Bread*

   a) It is recorded that our Lord broke the bread at the Last

[72] Parsch, *op. cit.*, p. 261.
[73] St. Gregory I, cited by Parsch, *The Liturgy of the Mass*, p. 282.
[74] Parsch, *op. cit.*, pp. 284–285.

Supper. This ceremonial act which was continued in the early days of the Church was also a practical necessity as long as the sacrificial bread was in a loaf form.

b) The practice of mingling a particle of Bread with the sacred Wine[75] has come to us from the times when a piece of the consecrated Bread (*fermentum*) was sent from the Papal Mass to the Masses offered elsewhere in Rome, and when a piece of the consecrated Bread (*sancta*) was reserved from Mass to Mass. Through this practice the unity and continuity of the Mass were shown.

c) A threefold breaking of the sacred Bread was introduced into the ninth-century Roman Rite as observed outside of Rome. There is still a threefold division of the Host; the smallest part is dropped into the chalice and the celebrant receives the remaining two Particles.

4. *The "Agnus Dei" — Part of the Ordinary, Sung by the People*

a) History. Scholars do not agree as to the date of the introduction of the *Agnus Dei,* nor as to the number of repetitions, nor even as to its position in the liturgy.

(1) In the pause of the breaking of the bread, the *Agnus Dei* was sung by priest and people.[76]

(2) It was sung at Rome under Pope Sergius (seventh century), but it may have been in use before his time.

(3) The text of the *Agnus Dei* is from the *Gloria.* By the eleventh or twelfth century, the *dona nobis pacem* was in use. Soon afterward, *dona eis requiem* was used for the Requiem Mass.

(4) At first it was sung by the clergy and the people to a simple melody (probably that in Mass XVIII). Gradually, as it was sung by the schola, the melody became more florid.

[75] See Parsch, *The Liturgy of the Mass,* pp. 287–294, for a discussion of the breaking of the Bread and Its mingling with the sacred Wine.

[76] Fortescue and Parsch say it was sung during the fraction. Wagner says it was sung during the kiss of peace also, *Introduction to the Gregorian Melodies,* p. 102.

b) Form

The number of repetitions of text was not at first precisely defined; probably the number depended on the length of time taken by the fraction and the kiss of peace.[77] The practice of only three repetitions came into use between the ninth and twelfth centuries.

c) Significance

(1) The text, recalling the greeting of Christ by St. John the Baptist, is in place here just preceding Holy Communion.

(2) The fruit of the Sacrifice is "the taking away of sin" and "the granting of peace" to the soul.[78]

5. *The Kiss of Peace*

a) This is a sign of our union with Christ and with each other. The kiss of peace "points out clearly that the holy Eucharist has as one of its chief aims to effect union and true brotherly love among all the members of Christ's Mystical Body."[79]

b) Both the prayer for peace and the kiss of peace are omitted in the Requiem Mass.

6. *The Preparatory Prayers*

a) Prayer of confidence—addressed to Christ as the Son of God.

b) Prayer of humility—also addressed to Christ.

In this prayer only the body of Christ is mentioned. Probably there was once another prayer for the reception of the Precious Blood.[80]

III. THE SACRIFICIAL MEAL

"Lord, I am not worthy that Thou shouldst enter under my roof; say but the word, and my soul shall be healed."

[77] Wagner, *op. cit.*, p. 102.
[78] Parsch, *op. cit.*, p. 296.
[79] Rooney, *Light on the Liturgy*, Part II, p. 41.
[80] Parsch, *op. cit.*, p. 303.

Before the people's Communion, the *Confiteor* is said, the absolution is given, the priest says, "Behold the Lamb of God . . ." and then "Lord, I am not worthy . . ." is repeated.

1. *The Priest's Communion*
   a) "May the Body (May the Blood) of our Lord Jesus Christ preserve my soul to life everlasting. Amen."
   b) In thanksgiving for the reception of the Body of Christ, the priest receives the Blood of Christ. We can properly thank God for His gifts only by a right use of them.[81]

2. *The Communion of the Faithful*

   "As he gives the body of Christ (with its concomitant blood) to each communicant, the priest makes the sign of the cross with the Host and prays: 'May the body of Our Lord Jesus Christ preserve thy soul to life everlasting. Amen.' The sign of the cross reminds us that we have received the fruit of the sacrificial tree of the cross, the body of Christ broken there and pierced, the blood shed thereon reunited now in the glorified Christ. The divine victim is given back to us as God's gift-in-return for our offerings at the offertory and our offering during the canon."[82]

3. *The "Communio" (Communion Chant)—Part of the Proper*
   a) History
      (1) The *Communio,* a processional chant sung during the people's Communion, was at first rendered antiphonally. Its purpose was the same as the other processional chants, that is, to help the recollection of the people during the processional movement. Up to the seventh century, Psalm 33, chosen because of its eighth verse, "Taste and see," was the only psalm used as the Communion chant.

[81] *Ibid.,* p. 306.
[82] Rooney, *op. cit.,* p. 44.

(2) The number of psalm verses depended on the time occupied by the distribution of Holy Communion.

(3) The text of our present-day Communion chant is not always taken from the Psalms. Often the Antiphon refers not to the Communion but to the Sacrifice as a whole.[83]

b) Form

(1) This chant was sung as was the Introit. Here, too, the celebrant gave a sign when it was time for the *Gloria Patri* and Antiphon.

(2) From the fourteenth century onward the psalm verses began to be omitted everywhere. Now only the Antiphon remains (although a verse is still added to the Communion Antiphon in the Requiem Mass).

(3) Psalm verses are permitted to be sung, however, as they were formerly, during the distribution of Holy Communion to the faithful.

c) Significance

"Often it is the *Communio* which calls attention to the mystical action of the Mass. Sometimes it brings the principal verse of the Gospel into relief, as if to say that it has been mystically enacted in the Mass."[84]

IV. CONCLUSION OF THE COMMUNION RITE

1. *Ablution Prayers*

a) The first prayer reminds us that our state of soul affects the graces we receive.

b) The second prayer asks that the fruit of Holy Communion *cleave* to those who have received It.

After this prayer, the celebrant *says* the *Communio.*

2. *Postcommunion Prayers—Part of the Proper, Sung by the Celebrant*

a) "God is with you!"

[83] Parsch, *op. cit.,* p. 318.
[84] *Ibid.,* p. 313.

b) In the Eastern Rite the predominant idea of these prayers is that of thanksgiving for the Sacrament. In the Roman Mass we ask that the graces of the Sacrament may be obtained.[85]

c) Prayer over the people

This old benediction prayer, preceded by *Humiliate capita vestra Deo,* is omitted in most Masses, although it is still present in the weekday Lenten Masses. Parsch believes that this prayer disappeared because of the blessing after the *Ite missa est.*[86]

V. CONCLUSION

1. *Dismissal and Blessing*

a) "Dominus vobiscum" — "Et cum spiritu tuo."
"Ite missa est" — "Deo gratias."

(1) If there has been no *Gloria* in the Mass, *Benedicamus Domino* is sung instead of *Ite missa est. Requiescat in pace — Amen* is sung in the Requiem Mass.

(2) If the Ordinary of one of the Masses from the Kyriale has been used, the melody of the *Ite missa est* is the same as the melody of the *Kyrie eleison.*

b) Before the blessing, the celebrant says a last prayer that the sacrifice which was offered might be acceptable and "through Thy mercy be a propitiation for me, and all those for whom it has been offered. Through Christ Our Lord. Amen."

c) In Requiem Masses there is no blessing of the people.

2. *The Last Gospel*

a) The Prologue of the Gospel of St. John was not included in the early Roman Mass. In the Middle Ages this Gospel was considered a Sacramental[87] and priests often recited it as they left the altar. The Missal of Pius V finally sanc-

85 *Ibid.*, p. 322.
86 *Ibid.*, p. 325.
87 *Ibid.*, p. 330.

tioned its use at the end of the Mass itself. In some Masses a feast or a Sunday is commemorated by reading its Gospel in place of this Gospel of St. John.

b) "We may be very grateful for its introduction. A more beautiful *summary of the whole work of Redemption* which the Mass itself renews, does not exist than those golden words:

The Word was God. . . .
In Him was life,
and the life was the light of men. . . .
The light shineth in darkness,
and the darkness hath not overcome it. . . .
To as many as receive Him
He gave power to become the children of God. . . .

There is no better sentiment in which to come away from the Table of Sacrifice."[88]

3. *"Deo Gratias" — "Thanks be to God!"*

[88] Gerald Ellard, S.J., *Christian Life and Worship* (Milwaukee: The Bruce Publishing Company, 1940), p. 207.

CHAPTER VII

RHYTHM

THERE are three modern schools of thought with regard to the rhythmic interpretation of the chant.[1] If we would have a uniform rendition of the chant melodies, we must adhere to the principles of one, and only one, of these schools.

In 1907, as a result of the labors of the Vatican Commission headed by Dom Pothier of Solesmes, the *Vatican Edition* of the *Graduale* was brought out and declared official. Later, Desclée and Company, official printers to the Holy See, published the *Vatican Edition* with the addition of what is known as "the rhythmical signs of the monks of Solesmes." In 1911, this publication was officially authorized by the Sacred Congregation of Rites for the use of the Western Church. Since this officially accepted edition is now in quite general use, and since by following the Solesmes theory of rhythm we may secure an artistic interpretation of the chant melodies, we join the followers of the Solesmes school.

A. Nature of Rhythm

Before the discussion of the nature of rhythm as such, let us be sure that we understand two fundamental points. (1) Rhythm and time are not synonymous, nor are they as closely bound together as might be imagined. This will be explained more fully later. (2) Accent is not always connected with stress. Stress may accompany the accent but it is not necessary to it. Nor is the accent always to be found on a down-beat. Stress, accent, down-beat — all these may, but do not necessarily, appear together.

[1] See Chapter V, pp. 113–114.

Rhythm has been defined by Plato as "order in movement." "In music, order is established by the differentiation of certain notes, which differentiation may be effected in several ways."[2] A note may be given prominence over its neighbor in four different ways.

1. The first means and the least artistic is by *change of volume,* that is, by force, stress, or intensity.

2. The second means, constantly used in artistic singing, is by *change of quality.* This type of accent is easily demonstrated.

3. The third means is by *change of duration.* Here we either slightly lengthen the note to which we wish to give prominence, or, if we wish to express its vitality or "spring," we shorten it. (Generally, we shorten the up-beat and give a bit more time, relatively, to the down-beat.)

4. The fourth means is by *change of pitch.* To raise or lower the voice immediately sets up a differentiation. Note that in expressive speaking we generally raise the word or syllable to which we wish to give prominence.

Rhythm, or "order in movement," may be expressed through any or all of these means. "Though rhythm is essentially the same in all music, yet it varies in character with different musical systems. In modern music, for example, rhythm depends largely on harmonic considerations, and has been described as entirely a question of the positions of cadences."[3]

In the Solesmes school of chant it must be "thoroughly understood that the rhythmical ictus [or the count of 'one'] does not of itself involve force or stress but takes its colour from the syllable on which it falls. The independence of accent and rhythm goes with treating the accent lightly, and it forms . . . together with the legato which makes it possible, the chief characteristic of the Solesmes style."[4]

[2] Benedictine of Stanbrook, *A Grammar of Plainsong* (Liverpool: Rushworth and Dreaper, 1934), p. 43.

[3] *Ibid.*

[4] Dom Gregory Sunol, *Text Book of Gregorian Chant* (Boston: McLaughlin and Reilly, n.d.), p. 106. It may be well to recall here that the Solesmes rendition of the chant does not permit a divided beat on any note. Every tone is given a full beat or two full beats, but never a half-beat or one-and-a-half-beats, etc. Expressive neums permit a slight lengthening of some of their tones, but they do not permit a division of beat.

"Rhythm is order in movement." To be complete a movement must have two parts — a beginning which is a rise and an end which is a fall. "All the theorists, from Priscian and Aurelian down, speak of a *natural* rhythm produced by the accents: an *arsis* when the voice rises, a *thesis* when, no longer sustained by excitement, it falls. In other words, we have the gently bracing . . . and the relaxation or repose . . ."[5] The two parts of a movement are often referred to as arsis and thesis, energy and repose, or rise and fall. Dom Mocquereau called them "elan" and "repos." We may also call them up-beat and down-beat, if we associate only rest or end with the down-beat.

Bar lines on a Gregorian staff are to the music as punctuation is to a literary composition; the bar lines indicate certain divisions in the music itself. The quarter bar indicates the end of a section or incisa; the half bar, the end of a member; the full bar, the end of a period or phrase. There may be several sections in a member and several members in a period. The following example contains two parts in each division:

Period or Phrase

Member | Member

Incisa (Section) | Incisa (Section) | Incisa (Section) | Incisa (Section)

As we decide the rhythm of a Gregorian piece, that is, as we decide the position of the arses and theses, we must remember that there are three "orders" of rhythm: (1) elementary and simple rhythm, (2) composite rhythm, and (3) greater rhythm. *Elementary* and *simple rhythm* points off the arsis and thesis of one simple movement. *Composite rhythm* points off the relative arsic and thetic quality of the ictic note (that is, the count of "one") in the compound beats in each section or incisa, while expressing at the same time the rise and fall of the incisas in their relation to each

[5] Rene Aigrain, *Religious Music* (London: Sands and Company, n.d.), p. 83.

other. *Greater rhythm* outlines the movement of the period or phrase.

Elementary rhythm is found within composite rhythm and gives way to it. Both are found in and are subservient to the greater rhythm.

B. Elementary and Simple Rhythm

I. ELEMENTARY OR SIMPLE BEAT RHYTHM

We have already learned how to "count" Gregorian music.[6] In "counting" we are pointing off the time rather than the rhythm, although, as we shall see, we are thus numbering the pulses which are parts of the rhythm. (Let us always call the *fall* of the rhythm the count of *one*. This will help to make things clear.)

In plainsong we find a free alternating of time-groups consisting of two or three counts, the binary and ternary groups. In other words, in plainsong we count either "1-2" or "1-2-3." As we count "1-2," we may visualize it in a measure, thus: | 1-2 |. This is time. | 1-2 | 1-2 | 1-2 | 1-2 | makes four time-groups.

The rhythm in these four measures will not be found within the measure as the time is. *Time* is within the measure bar; *rhythm* is astride the measure bar. | 1-2 | is time; 2 | 1 is rhythm.[7] In 2 | 1 we have the two essentials of rhythm — the arsis and thesis, the "elan" and "repos." The count of "two" is the arsis; the count of "one" is the thesis. 2 1 is an elementary rhythm.

This elementary movement or rhythm may be likened to the movement in swinging. We may visualize swinging from one point to another as: 2 1 and think of this as one elementary rhythmic group. The end of the rhythmic group is the count of "one."

II. SIMPLE RHYTHM[8]

Simple rhythm, like elementary rhythm, is an arsis followed by

[6] See Chapter I, p. 9.

[7] The chironomical signs are used with the permission of Desclée and Company, Tournai, the holders of the copyright.

[8] Not all authors use these terms to indicate the same type of rhythm even when they agree on the rhythm itself.

a thesis. But, whereas in elementary rhythm, the simple beats formed the arsis and thesis, in simple rhythm the time-groups, or compound beats, form the arsis and thesis. Thus:

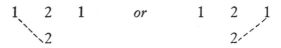

2 1 — elementary rhythm,
1 2 1 2 — simple rhythm.

III. POINTS TO REMEMBER

1. The Preliminary Movement

We may note that we do not just sit in a swing and hope to move. Either we ourselves must furnish the preactivity which takes us to the point of departure (and this preactivity may be likened to a preliminary *felt* movement) or someone must furnish it for us. Thus the point of departure may be the end of a preliminary movement.

1 2 1 *or* 1 2 1
2 2

The dotted line represents the preliminary movement.

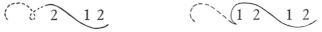

2 1 2 1 2 1 2

To sing rhythmically, it is necessary that we feel the preliminary movement (in the tempo in which we are going to sing). We know from experience that a swinger who is being "pushed" must feel the movement furnished for him if he plans to continue it on his own power. So also, a singer must secure from the musical introduction to a sung piece, not only the tonality, the mood, the meter, and the tempo of the piece, but also its movement — its rhythm. Singers must keep this in mind as they listen to an introduction. (Organists must also bear this in mind. They should mentally sing the introduction and continue this singing throughout the piece.)

2. The Rhythmic Character of the Count of "Two"

When rhythming a piece we must not forget that the note which precedes the count of "one" is *always arsic.* To say that a note is arsic is to say that it must have energy, spring, upward movement, activity — "elan."

If the time-groups are | 1-2-3 | 1-2 | the "two" of the first measure may be either the prolongation of the thesis on the count of "one" or it may be the beginning of the arsis on the next beat. The arsic or thetic character of the count of "two" in a three-count time-group depends on the word of the text and on the music which is accompanying the word of the text. The last measure of an incisa is always counted "1-2" and is always predominantly thetic; a final note before a full bar is always counted "1-2" and is purely thetic.

3. The Rhythming of Syllabic Chant

To rhythm a syllabic chant demands a special study of the principles which must be followed; then each case must be considered individually and the principles applied. All this demands more space than can be given here.[9] It is advisable for singers to refer to a book in which syllabic chants are already rhythmed.

To assist us to understand, however, what is involved in rhythming a syllabic chant, let us consider some fundamental points. The Latin *word* has both a natural rhythm and a natural melody. The natural rhythm of the Latin word demands a coming to rest (or an ictus — a thesis) on the last syllable of the word. The natural melody demands that the highest note be on the tonic accent, that is, on the principal accent of the word. In most cases those who rhythm the chant try to place the ictus on the last syllable of the word; they try to observe the natural rhythm of the word. Sometimes this is not possible. If the last syllable of the word coincides with the ictus in the music, we say that the word is a *rhythmic word,* for its natural rhythm is then observed. If the last syllable is not ictic, we say that the word is a *time word.*

[9] In his book *Gregorian Chant* (Toledo: Gregorian Institute of America, 1945), Father Klarmann furnishes clear rules for rhythming a syllabic chant.

Throughout plainsong there are examples of the word yielding its natural rhythm and melody to the exigencies of the music; also of the music yielding to the exigencies of the words. (In any case, we must always give more or less "spring" to the word accent.) We shall find, however, that although the rhythm and pitch of the music may or may not coincide with the natural rhythm and melody of the individual word, the rhythm and pitch of the musical phrase will correspond, for the most part, with the rhythm and melody of the word phrase.

4. The Relation Between Tempo and Rhythm

As the tempo of the sung piece changes, the plan of the relative arsic and thetic values of the simple beats may have to be modified. In other words, as the counts of "one," the ictic notes in the time-groups, sound closer together because of a faster tempo, their nature according to the greater rhythm must take precedence. (Greater rhythm will be discussed later in this chapter.) The tempo in which we sing influences the expression of the rhythm itself. Therefore, we must not sing so slowly that the smaller rhythms are overly evident; we must not sing so rapidly that they are ignored. Our singing, to be truly artistic, must express all the orders of rhythm according to their relative importance.

C. Composite Rhythm

No music in which we express only elementary rhythm is much of a musical whole. Each elementary rhythm is, in a sense, always present, but it finds itself in a still greater rhythm.

When we were children, we sometimes had a turn in swinging until our feet touched the limb on the next tree; thus all our swinging back and forth had a definite goal. Of course we did not incessantly pump until we reached that limb; sometimes we pumped and sometimes we did not although we were still swinging. But if our friends awaiting their turns demanded that we touch the limb soon, we pumped more often than not. After we had reached our goal we were supposed to "let the old cat die." Sometimes we "died down" straight to the end; sometimes we "died down" for a while, but to prolong the turn we occasionally gave a few extra pumps.

In this swinging, each movement back and forth was still there, but it was part of a much greater whole. Each small movement had its beginning (its arsis) and its end (its thesis), but the end of each small movement was either a new "pump up" (arsis) or a greater "dying down" (thesis) within the continued swinging experience. So in the rhythm of plainsong each elementary rhythm is present but as part of the whole.

Elementary, simple, and composite rhythm may be compared and contrasted under the following three points. (1) One arsis followed by one thesis forms either an elementary or a simple rhythm. A composite rhythm is (*a*) an arsis followed by two or more theses, (*b*) two or more arses followed by one thesis, or (*c*) several arses followed by several theses. (2) In elementary rhythm each note is considered as one beat and is either arsic or thetic. In simple rhythm, time-groups are considered as compound beats, a full time-group being considered only one compound beat; therefore, to be complete, a rhythm must encompass at least two time-groups or compound beats. In composite rhythm, time-groups are also considered as compound beats; however, a composite rhythm must have at least three compound beats. (3) In elementary rhythm each ictic note is counted "one" and is thetic. In composite rhythm the ictic note is also counted "one" but it may be treated either as an arsis or as a thesis.

I. RHYTHM OF THE INCISA

The **incisa,** the smallest section of the music, is from one bar on the staff to the next bar. Since the incisa will always comprise at least three compound beats, its rhythm will always be composite. To determine the composite rhythm of the incisa we must determine the **arsic** or **thetic** character of the **ictic** note (the count of "one") in each compound beat. A great aid in locating these arses and theses are Father Thibault's rules which he says "are neither infallible nor absolute," but which, nevertheless, will be "of great assistance until practice and training can replace them."[10] The following is almost entirely Father Thibault's diagram:

COMPOSITE RHYTHM

Nature of the Compound Beat

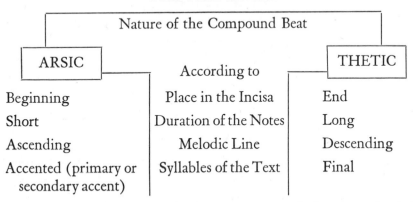

ARSIC	According to	THETIC
Beginning	Place in the Incisa	End
Short	Duration of the Notes	Long
Ascending	Melodic Line	Descending
Accented (primary or secondary accent)	Syllables of the Text	Final

Note that these rules apply to each incisa and that it is the ictic note of each time-group of the incisa that is here under special consideration.

According to the above plan we consider each ictic note from four standpoints. If from any one standpoint the ictic note is not definitely arsic or thetic, its character is considered "a matter of opinion" under that consideration. The majority of the four times we find the ictic note either arsic or thetic determines its character in the composite rhythm.

II. RHYTHM OF THE MEMBER

Several incisas, or sections, together form what is technically called a member. (The member is bound by the half bar.) Composite rhythm embraces not only the rhythm within each incisa, but also the rhythm found in the relationship of the incisas with each other. In other words, composite rhythm embraces both the rhythm of the incisa and the rhythm of the member. Quoting Father Thibault further: "In order to relate the various incisas into

[10] Ethelbert Thibault, "Rhythm and Chironomy," *Catholic Choirmasters Course,* Clifford Bennett, ed. (Toledo: Gregorian Institute of America, 1945), C.L. 79.

a unified flowing movement, a strong center of attraction or aim must influence the separate elements. It is the principal accent . . . which acts as the focus of attraction or aim in the compound rhythm. In this way, all the compound beats which precede the principal accent will lead to it, even though there may be theses among them; likewise those compound beats which follow the principal accent will lead from it, even though there may be some arses among them."[11] So also, in swinging, we "pump" to a point, even though we may "die down" a few times before we reach that point.

How can we locate the principal accent? Father Thibault gives us three rules.[12] (1) "When there is a melody without an accompanying text, the principal accent is the highest compound beat." (2) "When the melody is largely on the same degree, as in a response or recitative, then the text will indicate the principal accent in the form of the phraseological accent." Thus:

"Et cum spiritu tuo."

(3) "The melodic or principal accent corresponds to the phraseological accent of the text. Gregorian composers carefully united their melodies with the words in such a way that their music parallels the words in spirit."

D. Greater Rhythm

As we noted previously, in pointing off composite rhythm we point off the rhythm of the incisa and the rhythm of the member. In greater rhythm we outline the over-all rhythm of the period or complete phrase. (The period is bound by a full bar, single or double.) As in composite rhythm there is a principal accent toward which we move, so also in greater rhythm there is a principal accent in the period which influences our greater movement. (This last principal accent may be likened to the point at which we finally touch the limb when swinging.)

The various incisas and members must be coupled together "ac-

[11] *Catholic Choirmaster Course,* C.L., 80. [12] *Ibid.*

cording to their role and importance"[13] in such a way as to express the thought contained in the verbal and musical sentence. The elements which aid us to express this greater rhythm while we still express the smaller arses and theses of the elementary and of the composite rhythm, are the various *links* found in the music itself. They are the melodic link, the link of proportion, the dynamic link, the rhythmic link, and the link of articulation. These links not only coexist but sometimes coincide in the course of the melodic phrase.

1. *Melodic Link.* Plainchant is so wedded to the text of the liturgy that its music outlines and accentuates the thought of the liturgy itself. Plainchant, as all truly vocal music, is verbal music. The fore-phrase of the musical period has been likened to the antecedent clause of a grammatical period and is called the *protasis;* the after-phrase of the musical period has been likened to the subsequent clause, and called the *apodosis.*

The composer of plainchant has taken great care to link the fore-phrase and after-phrase in a melody which expresses the relativity of thought already existent in the textual period. We, as singers, have only to follow his plan intelligently and artistically. A peak in the melody will be found either in the fore-phrase or in the after-phrase; the greater rhythm will rise to this peak and fall from it. "Sometimes the phrase begins on its melodic summit; the protasis then appears in all its elan from the very first notes."[14]

2. *Link of Proportion.* "The proportional link depends on the number of members in the period, on their length, on their modal qualities, on the climaxes and on the importance of their long notes and rests."[15] This, again, has been established by the chant composer. But we must note the melodic and rhythmic attractions in the phrase if we would express the proportion intended by the composer. "The singer is capable of destroying this relationship of proportion, either by not giving the different pauses their right length, or by exaggerating their length."[16]

[13] Sunol, *op. cit.*, p. 110.

[14] *Ibid.*, p. 111.

[15] Thibault, *Catholic Choirmasters Course,* C.L., 82.

[16] Sunol, *op. cit.*, p. 114.

3. *Dynamic Link.* In the greater rhythm, the principal arsic group coincides with the principal accent of the word phrase and with the highest melodic group. The greater rhythm offers a change in dynamism as a means of linking the parts of the period into an expressive and artistic whole. "To produce the effect of naturalness one must graduate the intensity from one accent to another and from one ictus to another, so as to reach the summit of the melodic line almost imperceptibly: the same must be done coming down, but in reverse order, or decrescendo. The accents and ictuses will thus be stronger or weaker in proportion as they are nearer to or farther away from the general accent of the phrase."[17] However, "a complete alteration of the intensity line already worked out by the compound rhythm should not take place. Only its proportions are modified."[18] For example:

a possible composite rhythm: mp mf mp mp mf mp
a modified greater rhythm: mf f mf mp mf mp

4. *Rhythmic Link.* "This link is called by some authors the agogic or kinetic link."[19] It must be handled very well or the rhythm will be completely spoiled. It invites a singer to feel a more forward movement during the protasis and a more backward movement during the apodosis. "Pump" toward the climax of the fore-phrase, and "die down" (after the accent) but keep "swinging" on the ictus during the after-phrase.

This link may be more easily understood if we liken it to the energy of an automobile in motion. Progressing from one place to another in a car, we find it necessary to regulate or modify our speed of movement for several different reasons. (1) Coming close to a side street we take our foot off the accelerator and prepare to use the brake; no car appears in the street and we again accelerate and resume our speed. So, also, in the movement of a melody we

[17] *Ibid.,* p. 111.
[18] Thibault, *loc. cit.*
[19] *Ibid.*

observe the dotted notes within or at the end of an incisa, relaxing after the principal accent which precedes them but picking up energy as we go from these long notes into the next part of the musical phrase. (2) Approaching a red light we slacken the speed of the car preparing to stop. However, as we come to the corner, if the light turns green, we, instead of stopping, again pick up energy. At the end of a member we often feel the same slacking of energy within us, indicating a contemplated pause, but, not breaking the movement, we gather energy again as we proceed to the next incisa. (3) At an arterial highway or a red light we bring our car to a complete stop, but we do not stop the movement of the engine. At the end of periods, at full bars, we come to a break or silence in the melody, but we keep our energy pulsing within us so that we may begin the next phrase without an hiatus or break in the inner movement. (4) As we observe all these necessary and required changes in energy but do not stop the engine of the car until we reach our destination, so also we should express the varying energies of the rhythmic movement in the melody, which itself expresses the climaxes and cadences of the word phrases. However, we should not break the movement within us until the melody is completed. Furthermore, as a good driver never changes the movement of the car suddenly but meets all the required slacking and picking-up of energy with smooth control, so the good singer directs the energy of his own movement from the beginning to the end of the composition.

5. *Link of Articulation.* The link of articulation is found at the *mora vocis,* the dotted note, at the end of the incisas. "The dotted note before the pause ought never to be produced as if the singer had been distracted and unprepared and then found himself bumping against it. This is the impression received when the voice drops heavily and strongly on the final note. . . . To render the *mora vocis* well . . . it must be borne in mind that the note thereby prolonged fulfills two functions: it ends one member and leads to another. It transmits life from one clause to the next; the life-blood of melody and rhythm pass through it, and it should be affected by this. It

must not therefore be coldly rendered, on the vain plea that it is only a holding-note or prolongation of the voice. In conformity with this first trait, the *mora vocis* must be soft and smooth, so as to give an impression of repose; yet it has hardly alighted, so to speak, when it enters upon its second function of joining the preceding to the following clause, and it must prepare for this transition by adapting itself to the beginning of the new member and take on in advance, as it were, its colour and physiognomy. The end of the *mora vocis* will therefore assume the dynamic value as well as the tone colour of the first note at the beginning of the new clause; it should melt into it and adapt itself to its character. If the new member begins on a strong note, the timbre should end with a light crescendo . . . if, on the other hand, it begins on a weak note, it should adapt itself to this by a delicate decrescendo."[20]

This last link is very important to the singer; it must not be misused nor should it be neglected. The first beat of the long note must be treated according to its place in the incisa; that is, it must be softer. The second beat of this long note (that is, the dot) must anticipate the character and color of the first tones of the next incisa.

REVIEW QUESTIONS

1. Which modern school of thought do we follow in our interpretation of the chant rhythm?
2. What does this school have to say concerning the nature of accent?
3. How did Plato define rhythm? Explain his definition.
4. Cite four means of giving a note prominence over its neighbor. Explain each.
5. What terms are used to refer to the parts of a movement?
6. Explain the meaning of the bar lines on the Gregorian staff.
7. What are the three "orders" of rhythm? Demonstrate or explain each.
8. How does time differ from rhythm?
9. Summarize the discussion of each of the four "points to remember."
10. How does composite rhythm differ from elementary rhythm with regard to (*a*) the order of the arses and theses, (*b*) the nature of the beats, and (*c*) the rhythmic character of the ictic notes?
11. What name is given to the rhythm of the incisa?
12. What four helps does Father Thibault give to locate the arses and theses in the incisa?

[20] Sunol, *op. cit.*, p. 114.

13. Following Father Thibault's plan, rhythm an incisa of plainsong.
14. What name is given to the rhythm of a member?
15. How can we locate the peak in the rhythm of a member?
16. What means do we have to express the rhythm of a member?
17. What name is given to the rhythm of a period?
18. What means do we have to express the rhythm of a period?
19. Explain each kind of link.
20. Select an Ordinary chant from one of the Gregorian Masses. Study its text, and note the composite and greater rhythm of its music. Using the techniques of choral recitation, read the words aloud so that the principal accent of the incisa or member (composite rhythm) and of the period (greater rhythm) are evident and in proper relationship.

E. Summary and Application[21]

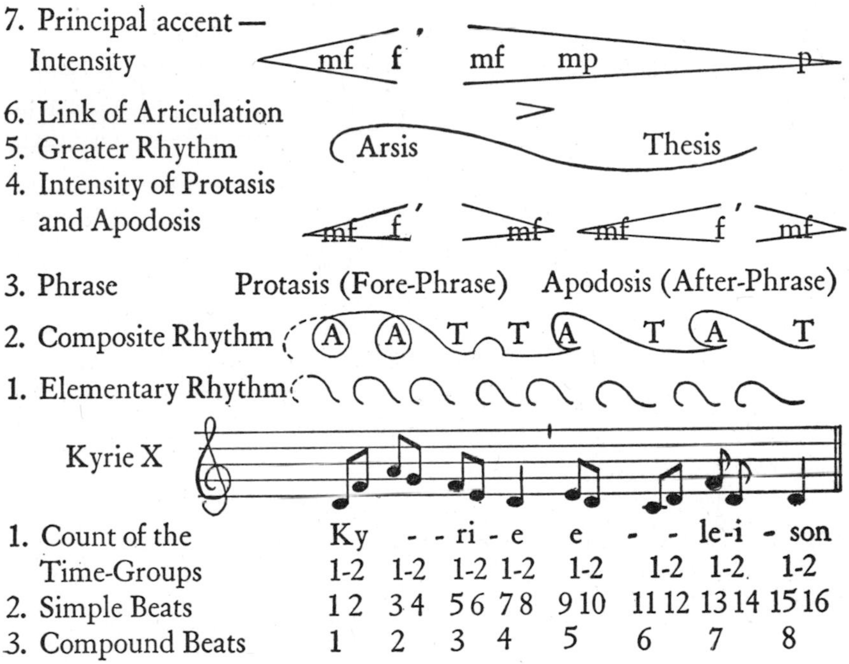

[21] This example contains only two incisas. Therefore the rhythm of the period coincides with the rhythm of the member.

CHAPTER VIII

MODALITY

MODERN musicians are seeking to understand the Gregorian scales and the whole Gregorian tonality in order that they may comprehend the art of music itself; we may study the tonality of the chant for the same reason. We may also study it in order to obtain a greater appreciation of our heritage. With this in mind it is easy to understand why secular musicians are so interested in the rich and varied means of expression which the modal scales afford. But investigation is even more important to us as a means of furthering song in our active participation in the sacred liturgy. For any study which helps us to participate more fully in the sung prayer of the Church is of interest and of value to us.

This chapter follows what is called the *classical theory*. In reality, medieval musicians evolved this classical theory long after the Gregorian melodies were composed; consequently, it may not be the theory followed by the original composers of chant. As a matter of fact, this theory does not answer all the questions aroused by the chant melodies themselves. Therefore, modern theorists, pre-eminently among them Dom Desrocquettes, have worked to establish an explanation which will satisfy both theoretically and practically. These theorists base their explanations on the earlier classical theory which, consequently, will be our guide in this study.

In Chapter I of this text we read that a diatonic scale is a scale of whole and half steps in their natural order and that there are eight diatonic scales in plainsong. These diatonic scales have their whole and half steps arranged in different orders; for example, one scale may be —⌣———⌣—, and another may be ———⌣——⌣.[1] Each diatonic scale has a tone on which a melody in that scale must end; this tone is called the *final*. In each scale there is also a tone which is almost as important as the final; this tone is called the *dominant*. Modal scales differ in (1) the order of their whole and half steps and (2) in the relationship of these whole and half steps to a tonic and a dominant.

Two of the eight plainsong modes are commonly used in modern music; we call them the major and minor modes. We are so familiar with these that we may forget that they are really two of the eight Gregorian modes. Consequently, in modern music, we sometimes mean the other six modes when we say modal scales. In reality all scales are modal.

This chapter discusses some of the modal scales in more or less detail. To understand this discussion we must know the meaning of the following terms.

Mode—a manner of arranging whole and half steps and their relationship to a tonic and a dominant.

Final—the note on which the composition ends.

Dominant—the note which dominates the melody and around which much of the melody is built.

Range—the notes which are generally found in a melody. The range from re to $\overline{\text{re}}$ (2 to $\dot{2}$) means that the melody lies between these tones.

Tetrachord—a series of four tones.

Pentachord—a series of five tones.

Authentic modes—modes I, III, V, and VII.

Plagal modes—modes II, IV, VI, and VIII.

REVIEW QUESTIONS

1. Why do we study modality?
2. Is the classical theory the only theory that can be followed in the study of modality? Explain.

[1] In this chapter, as in preceding chapters, a whole step is signified by — and a half step by ⌣.

3. What is a diatonic scale? How many diatonic scales are used in Gregorian music?
4. How do the modal scales differ?
5. Define the following: mode, final, dominant, range, pentachord, tetrachord.
6. Which modes are the authentic modes? Which are the plagal modes?

Mode I

If we begin on **D** on the piano and play up to the **D** an octave higher, we have played the modal scale of **D** which is Mode I. The *range* of Mode I is from **D** to **D′**; the pattern of the whole and half steps of Mode I is – ◡ – – – – ◡ –.

In all the authentic modes (Modes I, III, V, and VII), the lowest five tones form a *pentachord*. Thus in Mode I the pentachord is **D – E ◡ F – G – A.** The first and lowest note of the pentachord is also the *final* of the mode. This final, which is the last note of many phrases, is always the last note of the concluding phrase of the melody. The fifth and highest note of the pentachord is the *dominant* note. In Mode I, **D** is the final and **A** is the dominant.[2] From the last note of the pentachord, or **A**, there are four tones to the octave **D′**: **A – B ◡ C′ – D′**; this is the tetrachord of Mode I.

The plan of Mode I may thus be summarized:

D – E ◡ F – G – (A) – B ◡ C′ – D′
x

If we can remember that the interval from **E** to **F** and from **B** to **C′** is always a half step and that all the others are whole steps, and if we can easily recognize a skip, for example, of a step and a half or of two whole steps, and know how these skips should sound, we will be able to sing in any mode simply by using the letter names of the notes. However some singers may find this too difficult. Many may prefer to use the *sol-fa* syllables.

In Chapter I we see a plan of the white keys of the piano from **C** to the octave **C′**. When **C** is called "do" or "1," the half steps are sung between **E** and **F**, called *mi* ◡ *fa* or 3 ◡ 4, and between **B** and **C′**, called *ti* ◡ *do* or 7 ◡ $\dot{1}$. If in singing our modal scales we wish

[2] We will mark the final as "x" and the dominant as "( )."

to use the *sol-fa* syllables according to this plan, we may do so. Then we see that:

D − E ⌣ F − G − (A) − B ⌣ C′ − D′ *called*

re − mi ⌣ fa − sol − (la) − ti ⌣ $\overline{\text{do}}$ − $\overline{\text{re}}$ *or*

2 − 3 ⌣ 4 − 5 − (6) − 7 ⌣ $\dot{1}$ − $\dot{2}$

will give us the same melody. When we sing "re" or call **D**, "2," we might think that we are singing the scale of **C** beginning on the second tone; this is not the case. We are singing the scale of **D** and we will find that the final is **D** and not **C.** We call **D** either "re" or "2" merely to help us to find the whole and half steps more easily.

It is possible to sing the chant without knowing the plan of the modal scales. But if we know the plan we shall be able to sing a chant melody more intelligently and to read it more quickly. Let us illustrate. We see that the *Gloria* of the Gregorian Mass XIII is marked as Mode I. Therefore we expect that the melody should lie between **D** and **D′** (or between 2 and $\dot{2}$); that the composition should end *finally* on **D** (or 2); that the note which dominates should be **A** (or 6); and that if the composition is quite regular, there should be skips between **D** and **A** (between 2 and 6) and between **A** and **D′** (between 6 and $\dot{2}$). Let us see if this is so.

Let us prepare to sing the melody of this *Gloria.* First we note that while the melody does not ascend beyond **D′** or $\dot{2}$ at any place, it occasionally touches the one note below the low **D**. Most of the melody lies on the pentachord, **D − E ⌣ F − G − A** or 2 − 3 ⌣ 4 − 5 − 6. This is written **D − E ⌣ F − G − A**, but we should sing a melody at the pitch which is best for our voices and which best expresses the type of piece we are singing. A *Gloria*, a hymn of praise, is sung more expressively at a higher than at a medium pitch. Let us sing the scale of Mode I at various pitch levels and make our selection of key, considering the type of piece we are to sing, our voices, the place in which we will sing, its acoustics, etc., etc.

In preparation for a First Mode composition, we may sing a vocal exercise on the modal scale of **D**, using the *sol-fa* syllables and singing in the key we select as best for us. Following the plan below we will sing first the pentachord and the tetrachord ascending, then the tetrachord and pentachord descending, then skips characteristic of the mode or skips found within the composition for which we are preparing, thus:

23 45 6. — 671̇ 2̇. — 2̇1̇7 6. — 65 43 2.
24 64 2. — 2. 6. — 65 43 2. — 61̇ 2̇.
2̇. 6. — 65 43 2. — 21 2. — 232 2.

This preparation may seem somewhat long, but if we know and can sing the range, final, dominant, pentachord, and tetrachord of each mode, it takes but a few seconds to "prepare our ears" for a plainsong melody.

We have learned that the accidental of **B-flat** is allowed in any mode but that it appears often in the scale of **D** (First Mode). To prepare for a **B-flat** in the melody, let us sing:

23 45 6. — 67̸ 6. — 67̸ 65 6. 2.
65 43 2. — 122 6.7̸ 6.

We may know the *Kyrie* of Mass XI from memory. Let us see if it follows all the regular rules of the First Mode and if we may conclude, therefore, that it is a regular First Mode melody.

REVIEW QUESTIONS

1. Is Mode I an authentic or a plagal mode?
2. What is the range, pentachord, tetrachord, final, and dominant of Mode I?
3. Of what practical use are the *sol-fa* syllables in singing the modal scales?
4. If we call **D** either "re" or "2," does that mean, necessarily, that **D** is the second note of a scale?
5. In what key is music written on the Gregorian staff?
6. How does the use of the **B-flat** change the scale pattern?

Mode II

We said that Mode I is an authentic mode. The plagal mode that is related to Mode I is Mode II. In fact, Mode I and Mode II are so closely related that we find them together in many compositions which are marked as Mode I. Mode II has the same pentachord and final as Mode I.

D – E ⌣ (F) – G – A

2 – 3 ⌣ (4) – 5 – 6

We shall soon see, however, that although they are so much alike, Modes I and II are not truly identical for they do not have the same dominant nor is the position of the tetrachord the same. The dominant of Mode II is found in the center of the pentachord, that is, on **F**, or "fa," or "4." The tetrachord has the same letter names but in Mode I the tetrachord is above the pentachord while in Mode II the tetrachord is below the pentachord.

Ạ – Ḅ ⌣ C – D – E ⌣ (F) – G – A

The ranges of these modes are different also. We see that the range of Mode II is from **Ạ** to **A.**

If we *compare* Modes I and II we find that:

they have the same pentachord: **D – E ⌣ F – G – A** or 2 – 3 ⌣ 4 – 5 – 6

and the same final: **D** or 2

If we *contrast* them we find that:

they have different dominants: Mode I — **A** or 6
Mode II — **F** or 4

and different ranges: Mode I — **D** to **D′** or 2 to 2̇
Mode II — **A,** **to A** or 6̣ to 6

Furthermore we see that the tetrachord of both modes is **A – B ⌣ C – D** or 6 – 7 ⌣ 1 – 2 but in Mode I the *tetrachord* is *higher* than the pentachord and in Mode II the *tetrachord* is *lower* than the pentachord.

The use of the **F** or *fa clef* is characteristic of the Second Mode since the range in letter names is so low. The use of this clef makes it possible to place the notes on the staff. In a Second Mode melody we expect the range of **A,** to **A** ($\underset{\bullet}{6}$ to 6), the dominant of **F** (4), and the final of **D** (2).

Let us see if compositions bear out this theory. Glancing through the *Sanctus* and *Agnus Dei* of Mass XII, we see that the range of these compositions is from **A,** to **A** ($\underset{\bullet}{6}$ to 6) and that **D** (or 2) is the final of practically every phrase. **A** (or 6) may seem to predominate; it surely does appear often as the top note of the pentachord which it is. But we will also find that **F** (or 4) is very important. We will note, also, the use of the low tetrachord.

In preparing to sing this mode, we will begin, as we did before, with the pentachord. Here we sing up and down on the pentachord, and then down and up on the tetrachord, so that we *end* on the *final* of **D** (or 2). Using *sol-fa* syllables, sing:

23 45 6. —65 43 2. —21$\underset{\bullet}{7}$. $\underset{\bullet}{6}$. —$\underset{\bullet}{6}\underset{\bullet}{7}$1 2.
242 12 2. —$\underset{\bullet}{6}$1 23 2. —2$\underset{\bullet}{6}$ 12 2.—24 67 6.
65 43 2.

Modes I and II

Since these related modes are so very much alike, although not identical, they are often used together in one composition. If the melody of a composition includes only the pentachord, it is generally marked as Mode II; an example is found in the third *Gloria* of the "Cantus ad libitum" in the Kyriale. But if the melody of the composition includes the pentachord and both the upper and lower tetrachords, it is marked as Mode I. It is comparatively easy to decide which phrases are in the First Mode and which are in the Second Mode. The *Kyrie* of Mass IX is an example of this type of composition.

REVIEW QUESTIONS

1. Is Mode II an authentic or a plagal mode?
2. To which mode is Mode II related?
3. Give the range, pentachord, tetrachord, final, and dominant of Mode II.
4. Compare and contrast Modes I and II.
5. What clef is often used in the notation of Second Mode melodies? Why?
6. Name a First Mode composition you know.
7. Name a Second Mode composition you know.
8. Name a composition which is in both Modes I and II.

Transposed Modes

Theorists do not agree as to the nature and purpose of a transposed mode. Although we know that not all transposed modes are truly transposed, we may call any mode "transposed" if its final is other than the one we would expect. In Chapter I we saw that the regular finals of the modes are:

Modes I and II	—**D** or 2
Modes III and IV	—**E** or 3
Modes V and VI	—**F** or 4
Modes VII and VIII	—**G** or 5

If **A**, **B**, or **C** are used as finals, we may, for all practical purposes, say that the melody is a transposed mode.[3] Note that the final is the deciding factor. Modes I and II transposed have **A** as a final; Mode III transposed also has **A** as a final; Mode IV transposed may have either **A** or **B** as a final; Modes V and VI transposed have **C** as a final. Modes VII and VIII are not transposed.[4]

It is not at all uncommon to find a transposed Mode II. Whenever Mode II is written on the staff using the **C** or *do clef*, we may expect the transposed Second Mode. Can you tell what the range would then be? What would be its final? its dominant? its pentachord?

[3] Dom Desrocquettes' theory of the three modal groups is clearly set forth in Course Lessons 86 to 95 of the *Catholic Choirmasters Course,* obtainable from the Gregorian Institute of America, Toledo, Ohio.

[4] A transposition of mode must not be confused with a modulation which will be discussed later in this chapter. A transposition apparently repeats the same modal melody at a different pitch. In a modulation the melody enters a different mode.

In the Gradual of the Requiem Mass we find an example of a transposed Second Mode.

REVIEW QUESTIONS

1. How may a transposed mode be recognized?
2. Give the final and dominant of Mode I transposed.
3. Give the final and dominant of Mode II transposed.

Suggested Melodies

Mode I: Kyrie XI, IV, and XIII; Gloria XIII; Agnus Dei XIII and XVI; Credo IV; Victimae Paschali Laudes; Ave Maria; the Responsory: Rorate Coeli; Gloria Laus et Honor; Pueri Hebraeorum; Vexilla Regis; Jesu Dulcis Memoria; the Sequence: Veni Sancte Spiritus: Libera Me Domine

Mode II: Sanctus XI, XII, XV, and XVI; Gloria XI; Agnus Dei XIII; the Offertory of the Requiem Mass; the Antiphon: Ego Sum

Mode II transposed: O Filii et Filiae; the Gradual and the Sanctus of the Requiem Mass

Modes I and II: Kyrie IX and X; the Dies Irae

Mode III

The next group of two modes is built on **E**. The range of Mode III is from **E** to **E′** (or from 3 to $\dot{3}$). The pentachord is **E** ⌣ **F** – **G** – **A** – **B** (or 3 ⌣ 4 – 5 – 6 – 7) and the tetrachord is **B** ⌣ **C′** – **D′** – **E′** (or 7 ⌣ $\dot{1}$ – $\dot{2}$ – $\dot{3}$). **E** (or 3) is the final. The ancient dominant is found, as was the dominant of Mode I, on the last note of the pentachord, that is on **B** (or 7). We say *ancient dominant*, for when it was allowed to flat the **B**, so that sometimes the melodies used **B** and at other times **B-flat**, it was found that **B** lost its dominating quality. Consequently, in plainsong composed after the introduction of the **B-flat**, the **C** above the **B** was used as the dominant. Therefore while we still have an ancient dominant of **B** (or 7), we also have in this mode a *modern dominant* of **C′** (or $\dot{1}$).

If **B** is the dominant in the Mode III composition we are preparing, we may sing as a vocal exercise:

34 56 7. — 712 3. — 321 7. — 76 54 3.
35 76 54 3. — 37 3. — 32 3.

In the *Gloria* of Mass XIV, many phrases use the ancient dominant. We will note, however, that this *Gloria* is by no means a regular composition in the Third Mode with the use of the ancient dominant.

Third Mode compositions using the modern dominant of **C′** (or $\dot{1}$) are quite common. In a vocal exercise preparing for this we would sing:

345 67 $\dot{1}$. — $\dot{1}\dot{2}$ $\dot{3}$. — $\dot{3}\dot{2}$ $\dot{1}$. - $\dot{1}$76 54 3.
35 6$\dot{1}$6 56 3. — 3 325 6$\dot{1}$ $\dot{1}$. — 34 32 3.
36 56 3. — 543 3. — 56 5. 3.

The *Pange Lingua* is an example of a plainsong composition using the modern dominant.

E ⌣ F − G − A − B ⌣ (C′) − D′ − E′
3 ⌣ 4 − 5 − 6 − 7 ⌣ ($\dot{1}$) − $\dot{2}$ − $\dot{3}$

REVIEW QUESTIONS

1. Is Mode III an authentic or a plagal mode?
2. What is the range, pentachord, tetrachord, and final of Mode III?
3. What is the ancient dominant of Mode III? What is the modern dominant?
4. What caused the change of dominants?
5. Name a Third Mode composition you know.

Mode IV

Mode III is an authentic mode. Mode IV is a plagal mode. Mode IV is also built on **E** as the final. The pentachord is **E⌣F−G−A−B** (3⌣4−5−6−7) and the tetrachord is again **B⌣C−D−E** (7⌣1−2−3) except that, as in all plagal modes, the tetrachord is below the pentachord. The range of Mode IV is from **B,** to **B** (or from 7̣ to 7).

The ancient dominant is found, as in the other plagal modes, in the center of the pentachord, that is, on **G** (or 5). However, when a modern dominant was used in Mode III, a modern dominant was also introduced into its plagal Mode IV. As the next tone higher than the ancient dominant was chosen for the modern dominant of Mode III, so in Mode IV the next tone higher than the ancient dominant was chosen as its modern dominant. Thus we now have in Mode IV:

B, ◡ C – D – E ◡ F – G – (A) – B

7̣ ◡ 1 – 2 – 3 ◡ 4 – 5 – (6) – 7

The Fourth Mode is the most irregular of all the modes. We will find that Fourth Mode melodies often suggest melodies of the First Mode, of the Second Mode, or of the Sixth Mode. For example, a dominant of **A** (or 6) with a final on **D** (or 2) in place of **E** (or 3) outlines characteristic tones of the First Mode. Theorists mark some compositions as Mode IV because the final is **E** although most of the melody lies perfectly in the First Mode. An example of this may be found in *Credo VI.*

The Fourth Mode is frequently transposed a fifth higher. In this case **B** (or 7) is the final. Such is the case in *Kyrie XV* and *Kyrie XVIII.*

Since Mode IV is so irregular, its melodies may not be easy to read at sight. For the same reason, each composition should have a preintonation exercise personal to it. As a general preparation we may sing:

34 56 7. — 76 54 3. — 321 7̣12 3.

35 61̇ 6. 3. — 34 21 23 3. — 35 66 56 5. 3.

324 23 3. — 654 543 3.

For a transposed Fourth Mode melody we may sing:

$7\dot{1}\dot{2}\ \ \dot{3}.—\dot{3}\dot{2}\dot{1}\ \ 7.—7\ \ 65\ \ 65\ \ 67\ \ 7.$

$\dot{2}\dot{3}\dot{2}\ \ \dot{1}7\ \ 67\ \ 7.$

REVIEW QUESTIONS

1. Classify Mode IV.
2. To which mode is Mode IV related?
3. What is the range, pentachord, tetrachord, and final of Mode IV?
4. What is the ancient dominant of Mode IV? What is the modern dominant?
5. Mode IV often suggests Mode I. Why is this to be expected?
6. What is the transposed final of Mode IV?
7. Compare and contrast Modes III and IV.
8. Name a Fourth Mode composition you know.

Suggested Melodies

Mode III: Sanctus VI; Gloria XIV; Kyrie XVI (note the dominants); Kyrie II (note skips characteristic of Mode I); Pange Lingua

Mode IV: Sanctus and Agnus Dei III; Sanctus and Agnus Dei X; Gloria XII and XV; Credo II; Creator Alme Siderum

Mode IV transposed: Sanctus and Agnus Dei of Mass I; Kyrie XV and XVIII

Modes III and IV: Te Deum Laudamus

Mode V

Modes V and VI are regular in both their finals and their dominants. Mode V is built on **F**; **F** is also its final. The dominant of Mode V is the last tone of its pentachord, or **C′**.

F – G – A – B ⌣ (C′) – D′ – E′ ⌣ F′
x

4 – 5 – 6 – 7 ⌣ ($\dot{1}$) – $\dot{2}$ – $\dot{3}$ ⌣ $\dot{4}$
x

The **B-flat** is very often used in Fifth and Sixth Mode melodies. As we sing the scale of **F** with a **B-flat** we find that it sounds quite familiar. The Fifth Gregorian Mode with the **B-flat** has been used as our major scale; note that the pattern of whole and half steps is the same.

F – G – A ⌣ B♭ – (C′) – D′ – E′ ⌣ F′

4 – 5 – 6 ⌣ $\not{7}$ – ($\dot{1}$) – $\dot{2}$ – $\dot{3}$ ⌣ $\dot{4}$

1 – 2 – 3 ⌣ 4 – (5) – 6 – 7 ⌣ $\dot{1}$

If a Fifth Mode composition always has a **B-flat** or if it avoids the use of the **B** entirely, we may call **F**, "do" (or 1). In any case **F** is still the final and **C′** is still the dominant. Following the above plan in which **F** is called "do" (or 1), sing the *Sanctus* of Mass IX. What is its final, its dominant, its range?

A regular Fifth Mode melody with the **B-flat** is often transposed. In this case the final is placed on **C**, the dominant on **G**, and we have the major scale of **C** with its usual pattern of whole and half steps and its usual tonic and dominant.

C – D – E ⌣ F – (G) – A – B ⌣ C′

1 – 2 – 3 ⌣ 4 – (5) – 6 – 7 ⌣ $\dot{1}$

The *Salve Regina Mater Misericordiae* and the *Salve Mater Misericordiae* are examples of a transposed Fifth Mode.

REVIEW QUESTIONS

1. Classify Mode V.
2. Give the range, pentachord, tetrachord, final, and dominant of Mode V.
3. The Fifth Mode with the **B-flat** is our modern major scale. May we sing this modal scale as we would sing our modern major scale? Explain.
4. When a Fifth Mode melody is transposed, what is its range, pentachord, tetrachord, final, and dominant? Answer using both letter names and *sol-fa* syllables.
5. Name a Fifth Mode composition you know.

Mode VI

The plagal Sixth Mode has the same final and the same pentachord as Mode V. What are they? The dominant is in the center of the pentachord, that is, on **A** (or 6). The tetrachord is the **C – D – E ⌣ F** (1 – 2 – 3 ⌣ 4) below the pentachord.

B-flat makes a common appearance in Sixth Mode melodies. Again, if every **B** in the composition is flatted, or if the **B** is avoided completely, we may call **F**, "do" (or 1). Following this plan we have:

C – D – E ⌣ F – G – (A) ⌣ B♭ – C′

1 – 2 – 3 ⌣ 4 – 5 – (6) ⌣ $\not 7$ – $\dot{1}$

$\underset{\cdot}{5}$ – $\underset{\cdot}{6}$ – $\underset{\cdot}{7}$ ⌣ 1 – 2 – (3) ⌣ 4 – 5

The *Agnus Dei* of Mass IV is in Mode VI with a **B-flat.**

REVIEW QUESTIONS

1. Classify Mode VI.
2. Give the range, pentachord, tetrachord, final, and dominant of Mode VI.
3. May we call the final of this mode "do" (1) instead of "fa" (4)? Explain.
4. If so, what is the range, pentachord, tetrachord, final, and dominant? Answer in *sol-fa* syllables (or numbers).
5. Compare and contrast Modes V and VI.
6. Name a Sixth Mode composition you know.

Suggested Melodies

Mode V: Gloria VIII; Sanctus and Agnus Dei IX; Sanctus and Agnus Dei XVII; Credo III

Mode V transposed: Attende Domine; Adoro Te Devote; Salve Mater Misericordiae; Salve Regina Mater Misericordiae; Alma Redemptoris Mater (simple tone)

Mode VI: Agnus Dei IV; Sanctus and Agnus Dei VIII; Kyrie XVII; Introit and Kyrie of the Requiem Mass; the Hymn: Stabat Mater; Ave Verum; Regina Coeli Laetare; Ave Regina Coelorum

Mode VII

G is the remaining regular final. In the authentic Mode VII, the pentachord is **G – A – B ⌣ C′ – D′** (5 – 6 – 7 ⌣ $\dot{1}$ – $\dot{2}$). The place of the dominant is regular, that is, on the last note of the pentachord, or **D′** (or $\dot{2}$). The tetrachord is above the pentachord: **D′ – E′ ⌣ F′ – G′** ($\dot{2} - \dot{3} \smile \dot{4} - \dot{5}$).

G – A – B ⌣ C′ – (D′) – E′ ⌣ F′ – G′

$5 - 6 - 7 \smile \dot{1} - (\dot{2}) - \dot{3} \smile \dot{4} - \dot{5}$

To prepare for a composition in Mode VII, we may sing:

$56\ 7\dot{1}\ \dot{2}. — \dot{2}\dot{3}\dot{4}\ \dot{5}. — \dot{5}\dot{4}\dot{3}\ \dot{2}. — \dot{2}\dot{1}\ 76\ 5.$

$5.\ \dot{2}.\ 5. — 567\ \dot{1}65\ \dot{1}.\ \dot{2}. — 565\ 4.\ 5.$

In the *Gloria* of Mass IX we may find a regular Seventh Mode melody.

REVIEW QUESTIONS

1. Is Mode VII an authentic or a plagal mode?
2. Give the range, pentachord, tetrachord, final, and dominant of Mode VII.
3. Name a Seventh Mode composition you know.

Mode VIII

The pentachord of the plagal Mode VIII is the same as the pentachord of Mode VII; the final of these modes is also the same. The tetrachord is below the pentachord: **D – E ⌣ F – G** (2 – 3 ⌣ 4 – 5). The ancient dominant, **B**, is in the center of the pentachord. But for the same reason as in Mode III, the modern dominant is **C′** (or $\dot{1}$). This modern dominant is very common in Eighth Mode melodies.

D – E ⌣ F – G – A – B ⌣ (C′) – D′

$2 - 3 \smile 4 - 5 - 6 - 7 \smile (\dot{1}) - \dot{2}$

Let us prepare ourselves by singing:

$56\ 7\dot{1}\ \dot{2}. — \dot{2}\dot{1}\ 76\ 5. — 543\ 2. — 234\ 5.$

$56\ \dot{1}\dot{1}\ 76\ 5. — 5\dot{1}\ 5. — 54\ 345\ 5.$

$5\dot{1}6\ 53\ 45\ 5.$

The *Sanctus* of Mass IV is a lovely melody in Mode VIII.

Note that Mode I and Mode VIII have the same range but that these modes differ in every other characteristic point.

REVIEW QUESTIONS

1. Classify Mode VIII.
2. Give the range, pentachord, tetrachord, final, and the ancient and modern dominants of Mode VIII.
3. Compare and contrast Modes VII and VIII.
4. How is the Eighth Mode like the First Mode? Is it truly like the First Mode? Explain.
5. Name an Eighth Mode composition you know.

Suggested Melodies

Mode VII: Gloria IX; Asperges Me; In Paradisum; Ecce Panis Angelorum or the complete Lauda Sion

Mode VIII: Sanctus IV; Gloria X; Gloria VI; Sanctus and Agnus Dei VII; the Tract, Agnus Dei, and Communion of the Requiem Mass; Salva Nos Domine Vigilantes; Veni Creator Spiritus; Verbum Supernum; the Antiphon: Vespere Autem Sabbati; the Antiphon: Repleti Sunt Omnes

Modes VII and VIII: Kyrie VI; Gloria I from the "Cantus ad libitum"

Modulation

As we sang the suggested modal melodies, we noted the introduction of phrases, or bits of phrases, characteristic of other modes than the one designated. Changing from mode to mode within a composition is called modulation. This change may be effected in three ways. In each of the three ways the *final* is the most important factor.

A composer may modulate to a new mode by using the same dominant but a different final. There are three modes which have **A** (or 6) as the dominant, and three which have **C′** (or $\dot{1}$) as the dominant. A melody which has a dominant of **A** (or 6) may have an ending on **D** (or 2) which would then be Mode I, an ending on **E** (or 3) which would be Mode IV, or an ending on **F** (or 4) which would be Mode VI. A melody which has a dominant of C′ (or $\dot{1}$) and a final of **E** (or 3) is in Mode III; if it has a final of **F** (or 4) it is in Mode V; if it has a final of **G** (or 5) it is in Mode VIII.

The ending of a phrase is called a cadence. Modes have characteristic cadences with which we will become familiar as we sing them. Modulation from mode to mode may also be effected by using the characteristic cadence on the final of the new mode with or without introducing the new dominant.

Summarizing this we may say that modulation may be effected (1) by the use of the same dominant and a new final, (2) by introducing a new dominant and a new modal cadence on a new final, or (3) by introducing only a new modal cadence on a new final.

REVIEW QUESTIONS

1. What is meant by modulation?
2. What is meant by a cadence?
3. In what three ways may modulation be effected?

TABLE OF THE MODES

No.	*Name*	*Character*	*Final*	*Dominant*
I	Dorian	Authentic	**D** or 2	**A** or 6
II	Hypodorian	Plagal	**D** or 2	**F** or 4
III	Phrygian	Authentic	**E** or 3	**C′** or $\dot{1}$ (**B** or 7)
IV	Hypophrygian	Plagal	**E** or 3	**A** or 6 (**G** or 5)
V	Lydian	Authentic	**F** or 4	**C′** or $\dot{1}$
VI	Hypolydian	Plagal	**F** or 4	**A** or 6
VII	Mixolydian	Authentic	**G** or 5	**D′** or $\dot{2}$
VIII	Hypomixolydian	Plagal	**G** or 5	**C′** or $\dot{1}$ (**B** or 7)

SCHEME OF THE MODES

Mode I	D – E ‿ F – G – (A) – B ‿ C′ – D′
Mode I	2 – 3 ‿ 4 – 5 – (6) – 7 ‿ 1̇ – 2̇
Mode II	A, – B, ‿ C – D – E ‿ (F) – G – A
Mode II	6̣ – 7̣ ‿ 1 – 2 – 3 ‿ (4) – 5 – 6
Mode III	E ‿ F – G – A – B ‿ (C′) – D′ – E′
Mode III	3 ‿ 4 – 5 – 6 – 7 ‿ (1̇) – 2̇ – 3̇
Mode IV	B, ‿ C – D – E ‿ F – G – (A) – B
Mode IV	7̣ ‿ 1 – 2 – 3 ‿ 4 – 5 – (6) – 7
Mode V	F – G – A – B ‿ (C′) – D′ – E′ ‿ F′
Mode V	4 – 5 – 6 – 7 ‿ (1̇) – 2̇ – 3̇ ‿ 4̇
Mode VI	C – D – E ‿ F – G – (A) – B ‿ C′
Mode VI	1 – 2 – 3 ‿ 4 – 5 – (6) – 7 ‿ 1̇
Mode VII	G – A – B ‿ C′ – (D′) – E′ ‿ F′ – G′
Mode VII	5 – 6 – 7 ‿ 1̇ – (2̇) – 3̇ ‿ 4̇ – 5̇
Mode VIII	D – E ‿ F – G – A – B ‿ (C′) – D′
Mode VIII	2 – 3 ‿ 4 – 5 – 6 – 7 ‿ (1̇) – 2̇

CHAPTER IX

PSALMODY

A. Introduction

WE DO not know who wrote the 150 psalms although it is safe to claim that David was their principal author. However, since they are part of the Old Testament, we know that no matter who wrote them they are inspired by God Himself.

The psalms express in vivid and glowing terms the divine attributes of the Creator and the relationship which all creation, animate and inanimate, must necessarily ever bear toward Him. There is no state of soul nor any human emotion which cannot find release in the prayers given to us by the Holy Spirit of God. It is not surprising then that the Jews used the psalms in their personal and liturgical prayer life. It is not surprising either that the early Christians loved and sang them and that they have become part of the official prayer of the Church. As we ourselves pray the psalms, we, also, fall under their spell and find in them the expression of our own inmost thoughts and feelings.

Thus far, our attention has been particularly directed to the liturgy of the Mass because the Mass is the center of the liturgy and the prayer of the Church which we more ordinarily offer. Yet, as we have said, in the early days of the Church it was common for the followers of Christ to unite their own praise with His praise of the Father through the inspired words of the psalms. It is the desire of the Church that the laity return to what had been their practice for centuries.

In praying the psalms we are fulfilling the desire of God expressed in many places in both the Old and the New Testaments.

In the psalms themselves, God gives us not only the words in which He wishes us to express our praise of Him but He also exhorts us to offer Him this praise. In Psalm 49, He says through the Psalmist: "Offer to God the sacrifice of praise"; and later in the same psalm: "The sacrifice of praise shall glorify me" (Ps. 49:14, 23). Other psalms speak thus: "Sing ye a psalm to his name; give glory to his praise" (Ps. 65:2); "Ye that fear the Lord, praise him" (Ps. 21:24). Psalm 116, which we sing at the close of Benediction of the Most Blessed Sacrament, begins: "Praise the Lord all ye nations: praise him, all ye people" (Ps. 116:1). A later book of the Old Testament urges: "Sing to him, yea, sing praises to him: and relate all his wondrous works" (1 Para. 16:9). God, through St. Paul, reminds us that "we have not here a lasting city, but we seek one that is to come." The Epistle continues: "By him [that is, by Christ] therefore let us offer the sacrifice of praise always to God, that is to say, the fruit of lips confessing to his name" (Hebr. 13:14–15). St. John, recounting his vision of heaven, says: "And a voice came out from the throne, saying: Give praise to our God, all ye his servants; and you that fear him, little and great" (Apoc. 19:5).

The psalms form the chief part of the Divine Office, the official prayer of praise which the Church offers to God at the various hours of the day and night. The Church has arranged readings and prayers and has selected psalms which are particularly appropriate for each Hour. The night Hours are *Matins* (which has three divisions known as Nocturns) and *Lauds.* The day Hours begin with a morning prayer of praise called *Prime.* This is followed later by *Terce,* still later by *Sext,* then by *None,* and finally, in the late afternoon, by *Vespers. Compline* is our official night prayer.

As we noted in a preceding chapter, the spirit of each feast of the liturgical year, as well as the spirit of the year's successive seasons, is expressed completely in the Mass, but this spirit is expressed with greater elaboration in the Hours of the Divine Office. In the Hours which precede the Sacrifice of the Mass we prepare ourselves to offer It. Through the Hours which follow, we continue in the spirit in which we made our offering.

The word *Office* immediately brings to our mind a *work* to be done. The Divine Office is a divine work — the work of praise. Some of the faithful have dedicated themselves to offer this praise officially, that is, with Christ in their own name and in the name of all His members. Although we may not be of the number who have so dedicated themselves, it is our privilege to join ourselves with their work. Only as we pray the psalms will we begin to understand and appreciate what a gift they are to us. Only as we pray the Hours together will we begin to make the most of this fuller participation in Christ's liturgical action in His Church.

In Number 150 of the *Mediator Dei,* Pius XII reminds us that the laity do not have an obligation with regard to the Divine Office. Yet he asks that parish Sunday Vespers be restored wherever possible, and he urges the laity to "participate in reciting or chanting" it.[1] Before we prepare to sing the psalms of Vespers or any of the Hours, it is well that we discuss a few points with regard to their technique.

B. The Technique of Psalm Singing

Psalmody has been defined as the art and technique of psalm singing. It could be a long and profitable study if we investigated it fully. Here, however, we will discuss it only briefly. Dom Sunol's *Text Book of Gregorian Chant* or the lessons of Father Joseph Kush as found in the *C.C.C.,*[2] as well as other accessible works, make a more complete knowledge of psalmody easily obtainable. Our purpose here is not to learn all we can about psalmody itself, but to increase our appreciation of its importance in our Catholic heritage, and, above all, to prepare ourselves to participate actively in the corporate worship of the Church.

Every psalm is composed of verses in prose rhythm. Each verse is divided into halves. In the liturgical books, the break in the middle of each verse is marked by an asterisk. There are, generally speaking, three parts to the first half of the verse — an intonation,

[1] *Mediator Dei.* Read also Nos. 138–149.

[2] *Catholic Choirmasters Course,* Clifford Bennett, ed. (Toledo: Gregorian Institute of America, 1945).

a reciting tone, and a mediant cadence; and two parts to the second half of the verse—the reciting tone again, and the final cadence. In a very long verse, a flex may also be inserted after the reciting tone and before the cadence. This will be understood as we sing the psalm verses.

A psalm tone is not the same thing as a mode; for example, when we say the First Psalm Tone we do not mean the First Mode. However, psalm tones are related to each mode and Tone I is related to Mode I. It is on the dominant of Mode I that we recite in Tone I. Moreover, an antiphon meant to be sung in connection with a psalm is in the same mode as the tone of the psalm. (See the antiphon *Ego Sum* and the psalm *Benedictus Dominus Deus Israel,* as in the Kyriale). As a matter of fact, the psalm accommodates its tone to the mode of the sung antiphon. To some psalm tones there are several endings so that the connection between the psalms and the antiphons may be very smooth. Tone I has as many as ten endings. The ending that is considered the best is always marked in the liturgical books; we have only to sing them as directed. If the ending is marked with a large type, it means that the last note of the psalm tone is also the final of the corresponding mode. "Tone 8:G" reminds us that **G** is the final of Mode VIII. "Tone 8:c" reminds us that **c** is *not* the final of Mode VIII.

Although it is well to memorize the tones and their various endings, it is not necessary to do so for they may be found in liturgical books. It is very important, however, that we know *how* to sing the psalms and we must know this from memory.

DIRECTIONS FOR SINGING PSALMS

Father Kush, in his lessons on *Psalmody* in the *Catholic Choirmasters Course,* says:

> Every verse forms a fresh song, because all the verses differ in contents and meaning. The singer must learn gradually to recognize in the verses, songs from his own inward being, songs in which his own soul finds a long sought expression. God created man for the praise of Himself, He gave man the voice to utter that praise, and He also gave the psalms wherewith to formulate it. If professional soloists try to ingratiate them-

selves with their audience by convincing delivery, should the psalm singer do less when the audience is God Himself, the Author of the psalms, the Creator of the voice and the Master of the universe?[3]

And he continues:

While, on the one hand, theatricality is to be abhorred in all renditions of Gregorian Chant, and therefore of psalmody, still, on the other hand, one must shun the opposite extreme of unmusical insipidity as well. Worse yet is the disconcerting, barbaric, raucous mutilation resulting from the false notion that "chanting" is some sort of monstrous hybrid composed of simultaneous talking and singing. Music is unreal, lifeless unless allowed its proper expression, warmth and movement. Defects that are intolerable in other music should not be coddled "for tradition's sake" in God's music. Such defects are: careless phrasing, unintelligible diction, unjustifiable accelerandos or ritardandos, irrelevant bursts of volume, lack of ensemble, and so forth. The most besetting of all is the defect of eliding or near-eliding a vowel preceding another vowel, and of telescoping the dactyls.[4]

In the *Laudate Dominum omnes gentes,* for instance, we must see that the full time of each syllable is respected in such words as "populi, quoniam, misericordia, Domini, Gloria, Filio, Spiritui, principio, saecula, saeculorum."

Dom Johner[5] also gives some directions which may be of assistance to us:

(1) The intonation must be clear and distinct with regard to tone, tempo, and rhythm.
(2) The choir or class must have a uniform pronunciation of the Latin.
(3) The accent of every word must be given consideration but all must *lead to the climax* of the phrase. A climax is found in the musical accent of each cadence. [In an earlier chapter of this text, the movement in rhythm is compared to the movement in swinging. Following this comparison, we may say that we "pump" to the climax of the phrase and then "die down" to the pause at the asterisk; we "pump" again to the climax found in the second half of the psalm verse and finally "die down" to the end.]
(4) The climax of a phrase will always be found on a word accent, even

[3] Joseph T. Kush, "Psalmody," *Catholic Choirmasters Course,* Clifford A. Bennett, ed. (Toledo: Gregorian Institute of America, 1945), C.L., 106.

[4] *Ibid.*

[5] Dom Dominic Johner, *A New School of Gregorian Chant* (New York: Pustet, 1914), pp. 95–98.

though a change of melody may seem to bring out other syllables of the word.

(5) The last note is not to be cut off abruptly.

(6) The last syllable of a cadence must die away softly and gently.

(7) After an asterisk there must be a pause. [Dom Sunol says of this pause: "Approximately it equals the value of four ordinary syllables."[6] If one feels here and observes a silence equal to a full compound rhythm, there will be no break in the movement.]

(8) The pause after the final cadence of a verse is equal to at least two ordinary (word) syllables and may be longer. [Here we would suggest the observance of a silence equal to an elementary rhythm. Again, there should be no break in the movement.]

(9) The flex gives a lengthening of the last syllable of the word thus sung, but it does not permit a break in the tone.

Our singing of the psalms must be smooth and connected, but the words must remain clear cut and distinct. Father Kush urges us to "pursue the phraseological accent (bring to a boil)" and to "de-emphasize the final syllables of words, especially at dotted notes." He says further: "Haste and halt are equally destructive of good psalmody. Psalmody, in its effect, is comparable to two huge waves alternately bursting into a spray on the reef. An *up-surge,* a *momentary stalling,* a *back flow,* and then a *lull* while the cycle is repeated across the way."[7]

The correct and expressive reading of the Latin is very important, "for it is upon the text that the notes depend for their value and strength; the text it is which gives them life and energy and well-balanced phrasing."[8] "The mother tongue of worshipping Roman Catholics is Latin, when liturgical worship is concerned. No man cares to speak his mother tongue in a foreign accent. Respect the Roman pronunciation."[9]

Before one prepares to sing a melody with any psalm verse, one should be sure that the rendition of the text of the psalm verse is as perfect as he can make it. When reading the words alone, follow the suggestions herein listed for the singing of the psalms. The

[6] Sunol, *op. cit.,* p. 59. See all of his chapter on "The Singing of the Psalms," pp. 46–64.

[7] Kush, *Catholic Choirmasters Course,* C.L., 106.

[8] Sunol, *op. cit.,* p. 56.

[9] Kush, *loc. cit.*

singing itself will profit from this preparation of the text.

The *Laudate Dominum omnes gentes* in the various tones (with only one ending for each tone) is given below. In most hymnals, for the sake of convenience, the tones have been written on the staff in definite musical keys, and consequently the dominant or reciting tone does not always appear as we might expect. Here the tones have been placed on the staff in the key of **C** so that our eye will be satisfied. We should, however, sing the psalms in the key which is best for our voices.

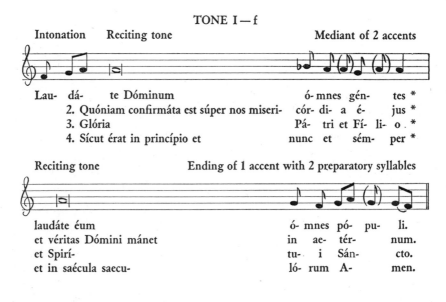

TONE I — f

Intonation Reciting tone Mediant of 2 accents

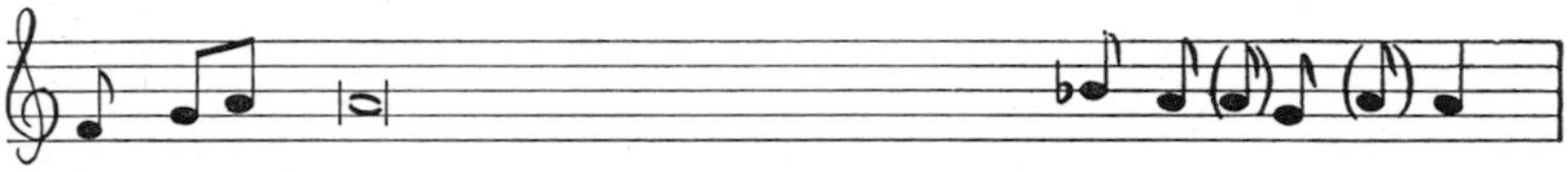

Lau- dá- te Dóminum ó- mnes gén- tes *
2. Quóniam confirmáta est súper nos miseri- cór- di- a é- jus *
3. Glória Pá- tri et Fí- li- o. *
4. Sícut érat in princípio et nunc et sém- per *

Reciting tone Ending of 1 accent with 2 preparatory syllables

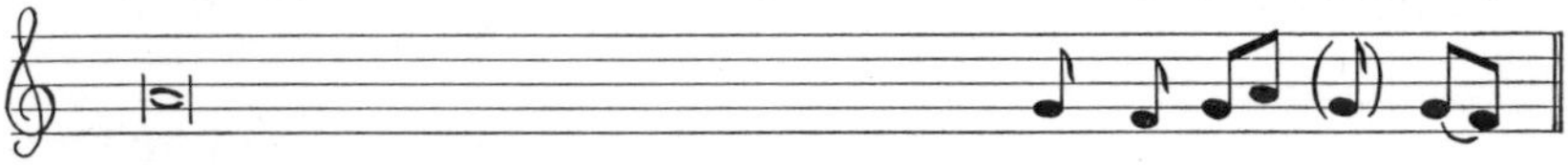

laudáte éum ó- mnes pó- pu- li.
et véritas Dómini mánet in ae- tér- num.
et Spirí- tu- i Sán- cto.
et in saécula saecu- ló- rum A- men.

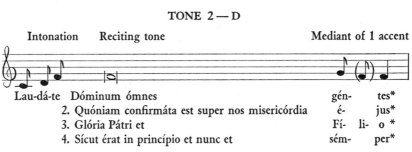

TONE 2 — D

Intonation Reciting tone Mediant of 1 accent

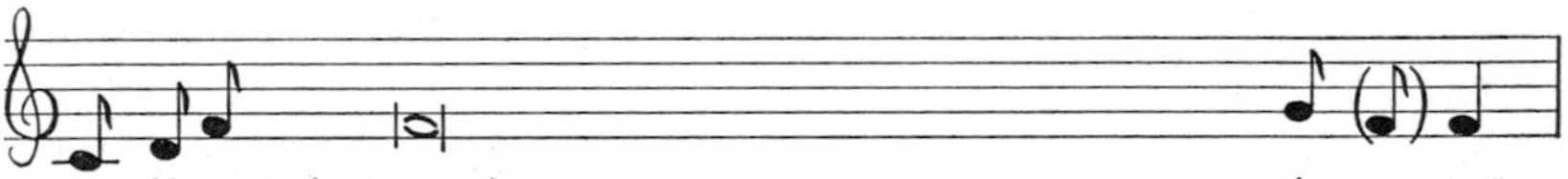

Lau-dá-te Dóminum ómnes gén- tes*
2. Quóniam confirmáta est super nos misericórdia é- jus*
3. Glória Pátri et Fí- li- o *
4. Sícut érat in princípio et nunc et sém- per*

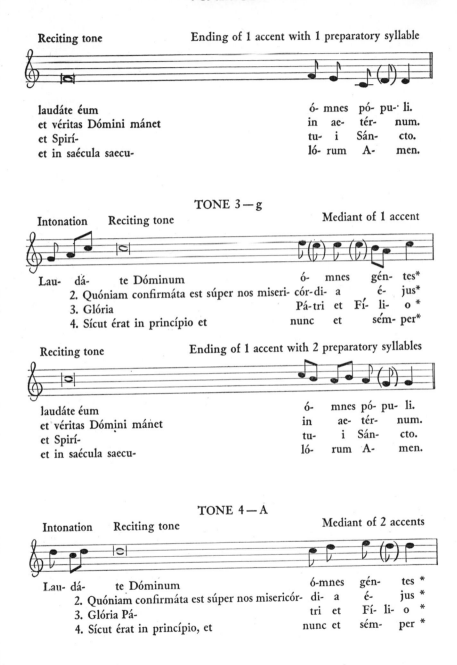

Reciting tone — Ending of 1 accent with 1 preparatory syllable

laudáte éum — ó- mnes pó- pu-· li.
et véritas Dómini mánet — in ae- tér- num.
et Spirí- — tu- i Sán- cto.
et in saécula saecu- — ló- rum A- men.

TONE 3—g

Intonation — Reciting tone — Mediant of 1 accent

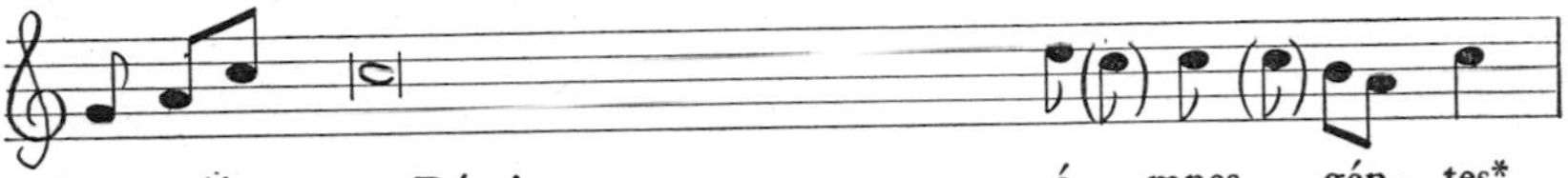

Lau- dá- te Dóminum — ó- mnes gén- tes*
2. Quóniam confirmáta est súper nos miseri- — cór-di- a é- jus*
3. Glória — Pá-tri et Fí- li- o *
4. Sícut érat in princípio et — nunc et sém- per*

Reciting tone — Ending of 1 accent with 2 preparatory syllables

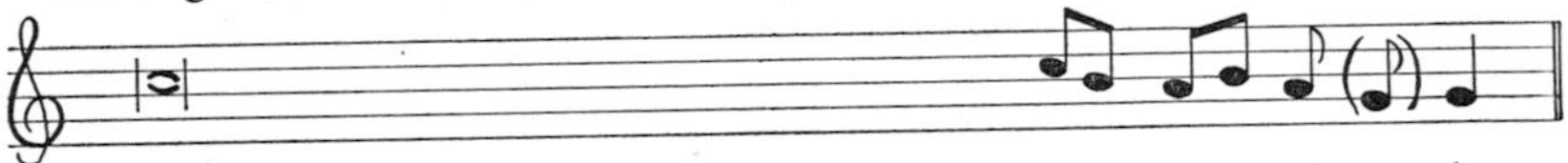

laudáte éum — ó- mnes pó- pu- li.
et véritas Dómini mánet — in ae- tér- num.
et Spirí- — tu- i Sán- cto.
et in saécula saecu- — ló- rum A- men.

TONE 4—A

Intonation — Reciting tone — Mediant of 2 accents

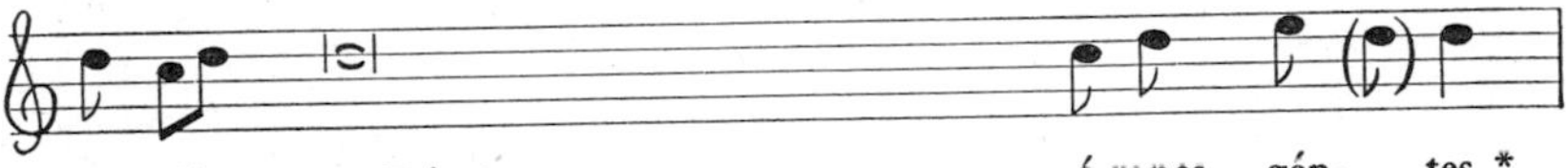

Lau- dá- te Dóminum — ó-mnes gén- tes *
2. Quóniam confirmáta est súper nos misericór- — di- a é- jus *
3. Glória Pá- — tri et Fí- li- o *
4. Sícut érat in princípio, et — nunc et sém- per *

Reciting tone — Ending of 1 accent with 3 preparatory syllables

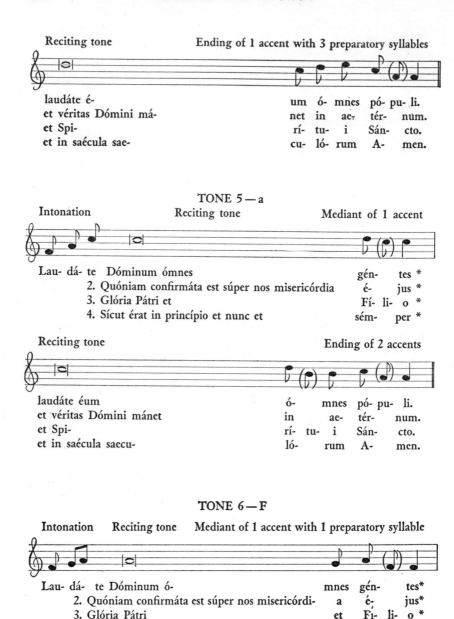

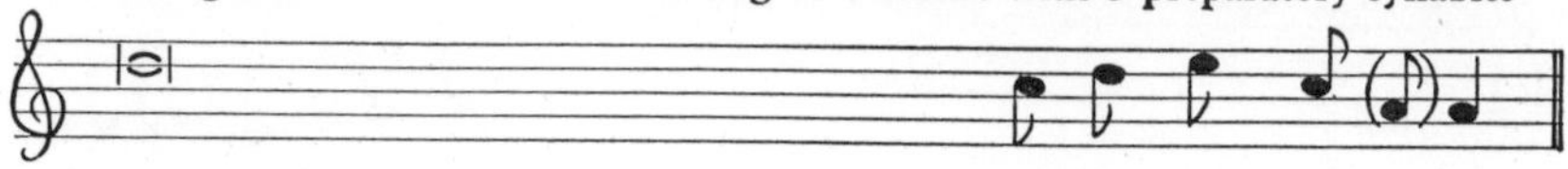

laudáte é- um ó- mnes pó- pu- li.
et véritas Dómini má- net in ae- tér- num.
et Spi- rí- tu- i Sán- cto.
et in saécula sae- cu- ló- rum A- men.

TONE 5—a

Intonation — Reciting tone — Mediant of 1 accent

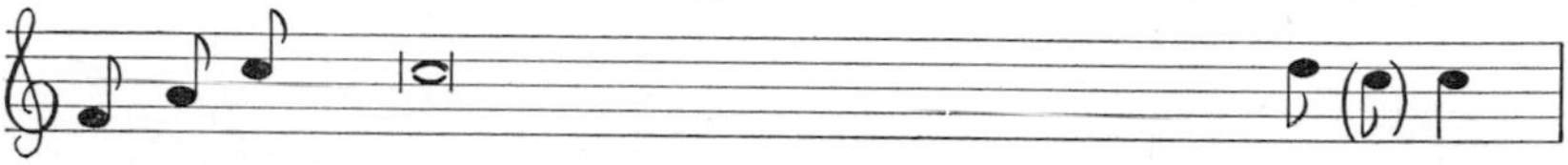

Lau- dá- te Dóminum ómnes gén- tes *
2. Quóniam confirmáta est súper nos misericórdia é- jus *
3. Glória Pátri et Fí- li- o *
4. Sícut érat in princípio et nunc et sém- per *

Reciting tone — Ending of 2 accents

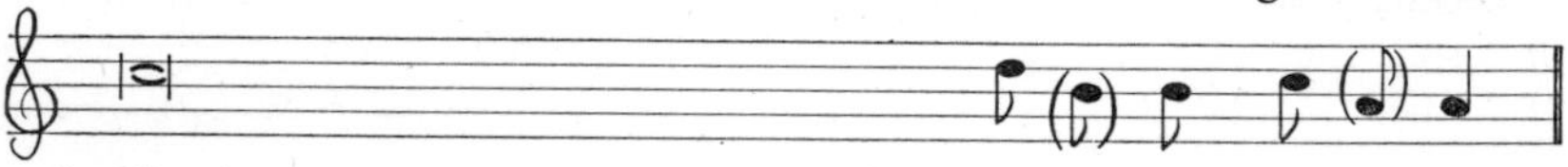

laudáte éum ó- mnes pó- pu- li.
et véritas Dómini mánet in ae- tér- num.
et Spi- rí- tu- i Sán- cto.
et in saécula saecu- ló- rum A- men.

TONE 6—F

Intonation — Reciting tone — Mediant of 1 accent with 1 preparatory syllable

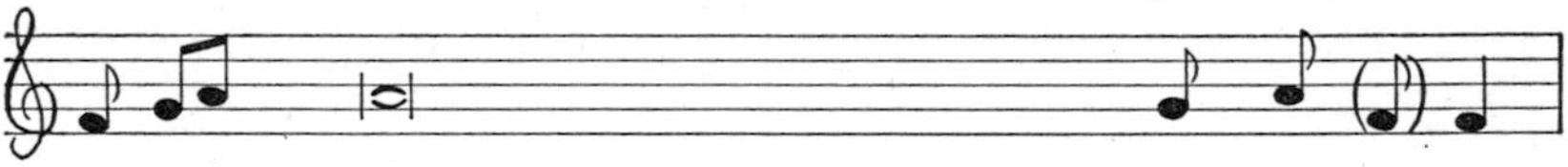

Lau- dá- te Dóminum ó- mnes gén- tes*
2. Quóniam confirmáta est súper nos misericórdi- a é- jus*
3. Glória Pátri et Fi- li- o *
4. Sícut érat in princípio et nunc et sém- per*

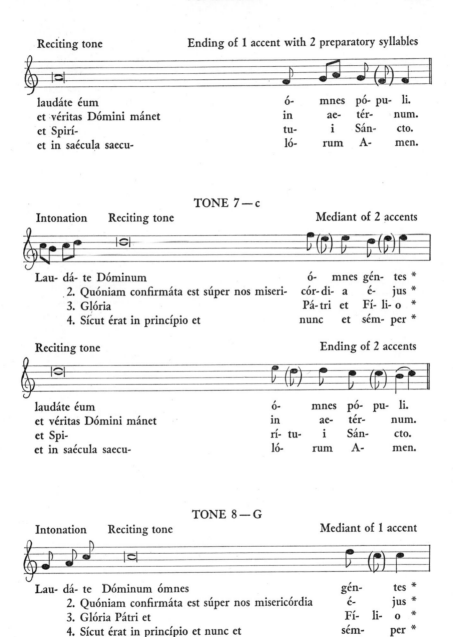

Reciting tone — Ending of 1 accent with 2 preparatory syllables

laudáte éum ó- mnes pó- pu- li.
et véritas Dómini mánet in ae- tér- num.
et Spirí- tu- i Sán- cto.
et in saécula saecu- ló- rum A- men.

TONE 7 — c

Intonation — Reciting tone — Mediant of 2 accents

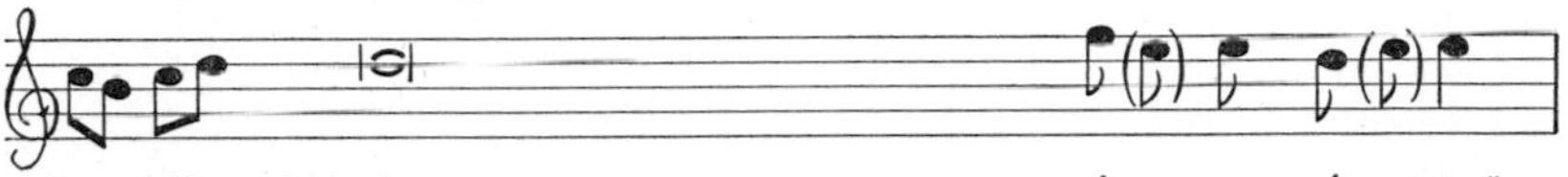

Lau- dá- te Dóminum ó- mnes gén- tes *
2. Quóniam confirmáta est súper nos miseri- cór- di- a é- jus *
3. Glória Pá- tri et Fí- li- o *
4. Sícut érat in princípio et nunc et sém- per *

Reciting tone — Ending of 2 accents

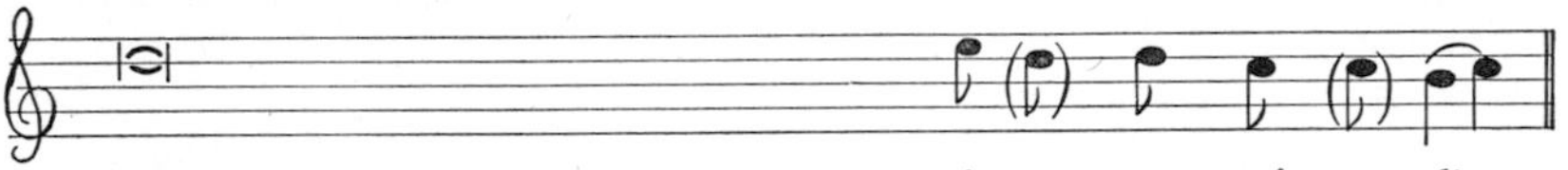

laudáte éum ó- mnes pó- pu- li.
et véritas Dómini mánet in ae- tér- num.
et Spi- rí- tu- i Sán- cto.
et in saécula saecu- ló- rum A- men.

TONE 8 — G

Intonation — Reciting tone — Mediant of 1 accent

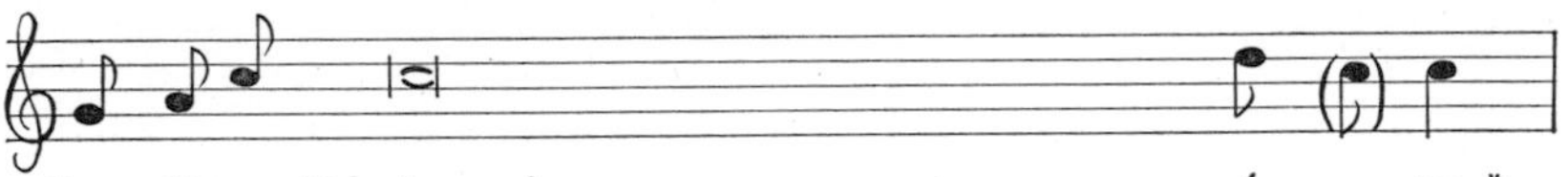

Lau- dá- te Dóminum ómnes gén- tes *
2. Quóniam confirmáta est súper nos misericórdia é- jus *
3. Glória Pátri et Fí- li- o *
4. Sícut érat in princípio et nunc et sém- per *

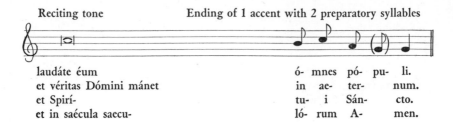

Reciting tone — Ending of 1 accent with 2 preparatory syllables

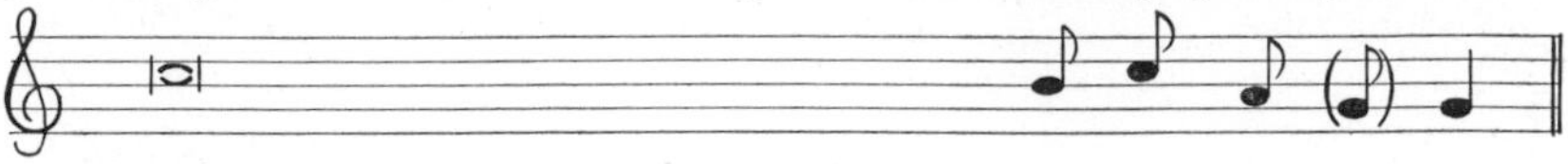

laudáte éum	ó- mnes	pó-	pu-	li.
et véritas Dómini mánet	in ae-	ter-		num.
et Spirí-	tu- i	Sán-		cto.
et in saécula saecu-	ló- rum	A-		men.

REVIEW QUESTIONS

1. Who wrote the 150 psalms? Who is their true Author?
2. How can we say that in praying the psalms we are fulfilling the desire of God Himself?
3. Name the Hours of the Divine Office.
4. Why do we study psalmody?
5. Name the parts of a psalm tone.
6. Why are there various endings to a psalm tone?
7. What is the meaning of "Tone 8:G"? "Tone 8:c"? "Tone 6:F"?
8. Under the following headings summarize the words of Father Kush concerning the singing of the psalms: (*a*) the use of the psalms in the praise of God, (*b*) general faults to be avoided in singing the psalms, and (*c*) special faults to be avoided in singing them.
9. This chapter notes nine directions given by Dom Johner for the rendition of the psalms. What are these directions?
10. What does Father Kush say of "haste and halt" in psalmody?
11. When preparing to sing a psalm, what should be our first step?
12. Prepare to read Psalm 116 as it should be read and sung.

CHAPTER X

A SUGGESTED COMPARATIVE STUDY

IN HIS *Motu Proprio on Sacred Music,* Pius X reminded us that music in the liturgy must have the same purpose as has the liturgy itself, namely, "the glory of God and the sanctification and edification of the faithful."[1] Sacred music "helps to increase the beauty and splendour of the ceremonies of the Church, and since its chief duty is to clothe the liturgical text, which is presented to the understanding of the faithful, with suitable melody, its object is to make that text more efficacious, so that the faithful through this means may be the more roused to devotion, and better disposed to gather to themselves the fruits of grace which come from the celebration of the sacred mysteries."[2]

The text of the liturgy voices the prayer of the whole Church; consequently, the music which develops, interprets, and expresses this text suitably must not cater to a purely personal interpretation. The "liturgy presupposes a fellowship of spirit."[3] There is not loss but gain for the individual in this unity of the Body of Christ.

As we have said elsewhere, the liturgy both prays and teaches. If we would learn from it, particularly if we would learn from the prayers the Holy Spirit has given us to address to the Godhead, we

[1] Pius X, *Motu Proprio,* No. 1. Translation and commentary by C. J. McNaspy, S.J. (Toledo: Gregorian Institute of America).

[2] *Ibid.* The *Apostolic Constitution* of Pius XI and the encyclical, *Mediator Dei,* of Pius XII voice the same sentiments.

[3] Dom Dominic Johner, *The Chants of the Vatican Gradual,* trans. by Monks of St. John's Abbey (1940), p. 9.

must be alert in soul and mind. This is what Zundel means when he says: "Psalmody *listens* even more than it sings."[4]

In this chapter we will attempt to show how the chant, as found in the Propers of the various feasts of the liturgical year, can be a means of grace not always realized. Dom Johner says: "One will never come to a correct understanding of a liturgical text unless one views it in connection with the melody which proceeds from its inmost spirit. The praying and singing of plainsong, and therefore of the liturgy in general, express more shades of meaning and a richer gradation of feeling than is generally recognized. Advent and Christmas joy, for instance, differ greatly from the exultation of Easter time."[5] The difference in this joy is subtly expressed in the plainsong Proper.

How are the melodies chosen for the Propers? Older Masses probably had melodies composed especially for their texts. Later Masses sometimes, although rarely, are treated in the same way. In most instances, melodies are borrowed or adapted from older Mass-formularies, either because of a similarity of thought, similarity of the expression of the thought (that is, the text), or simply because of a spiritual relationship in the feasts. In some cases, a melody was borrowed intact because it fitted a new text perfectly. Later the same melody was used for another newer feast because of its relationship with the second feast.

To trace, in the plainsong Propers, the textual and melodic references of one feast to another is inspirational. We are not surprised to find that the text and melody of the Offertory of the Common of Doctors, and the text and melody of the same Common have been taken from the Mass of St. John the Evangelist, the "Doctor" of the Divinity of Christ. We are impelled to consider what God thinks of virginity when we see, or hear, that the Introit of the second Mass of the Common of Virgins is the same as the Introit for the Feast of the Annunciation. The melody and text of the Gradual of the feast of the Transfiguration, "Thou are beautiful

[4] From *The Splendour of the Liturgy* by Maurice Zundel, p. 285. Copyright Sheed and Ward, Inc., New York.

[5] Johner, *Chants of the Vatican Gradual,* p. 28.

above the sons of men" (Ps. 44:3), is found in the Proper for the Sunday within the Octave of Christmas. Johner says: "On Christmas we consider above all else His human charm and entrancing beauty. To-day, however, we contemplate the divine element which transfigures the Son of Man. Never before did a human form radiate such supernatural beauty as did Christ on Tabor."[6] "Thou art beautiful above the sons of men!" Again, we note that the verse and melody of the Alleluia for the Paschal Votive Mass of the Sacred Heart is repeated at the Mass of All Saints, the Mass of those who heeded this invitation of the Sacred Heart: "Come to me, all you that labour, and are burdened, and I will refresh you" (Mt. 11:28).

On Holy Thursday we sing, "The right hand of the Lord hath wrought strength: the right hand of the Lord hath exalted me: I shall not die, but live: and shall declare the works of the Lord" (Ps. 117:16–17). "Who prays so?" asks Johner. Our thoughts turn first to Christ who is celebrating the Pasch with His disciples before His Passion. "Well does He know that the right hand of the Lord will exalt Him, as indeed the Gradual jubilantly announced in its verse. He does not die, but in death obtains eternal life for Himself and for all the world."[7] Considering this text in the light of the Eucharist, we may also hear the Church singing it, for "He that eateth my flesh, and drinketh my blood, hath everlasting life" (Jn. 6:55). "Hence the Church and with her the Christian soul sings . . . 'I shall not die, but live.' . . . Finally, this song may also be placed in the mouths of the penitents who to-day are again received into the church."[8] All this is brought to our minds again as we sing the same melody and text after the Gospel of the Third Sunday after the Epiphany, that Gospel "in which the Lord in such a loving manner stretches forth His hand and heals the man stricken with leprosy":[9] "The right hand of the Lord hath exalted me," hath stretched toward me in pardon and in love. "I shall not die, but live: and shall declare the works of the Lord."

[6] *Ibid.*, p. 418.
[7] *Ibid.*, p. 165.
[8] *Ibid.*, p. 166.
[9] *Ibid.*, p. 385.

This same Offertory and the Holy Thursday Introit, "But it behooves us to glory in the cross of our Lord Jesus Christ in Whom is our salvation, life, and resurrection; by Whom we are saved and delivered," are sung with the same melodies on the feast of the Finding of the Holy Cross, May 3. As Johner remarks, what on Holy Thursday is a prophecy is now on May 3 commemorated as a reality.[10] Surely, "it behooves us to glory in the cross of our Lord," for because of it "I shall not die but live and declare the works of the Lord."

We need not infer from what we have been saying that the plainsong always repeats the melody if it repeats a text. For example, the treatment of the text, "The Lord will overshadow thee with his shoulders, and under his wings thou shalt trust" (Ps. 90:4), differs in the Offertory and in the Communion of the First Sunday of Lent. We are tracing melodic and textual references and are not discussing other possible treatments of text.

It is not surprising that the Offertory and the Communion of the Mass for the feast of the Annunciation is that of the Fourth Sunday of Advent. Incidentally, this particular melodic treatment of the Offertory "Ave Maria" is one of the most lovely of plainsong compositions.

We already spoke of the Gradual for the feast of the Annunciation and its incorporation in the Mass of a Virgin. Do we note, as we sing it, the melodic reference in this Mass to the second Mass of Christmas, to the Epiphany, and to the feast of the Annunciation?

It is this use of melodic reference, either complete or in part, that most joins the spirit and significance of feasts, even when the texts differ. Thus the Gradual of the feast of SS. Peter and Paul melodically recalls to our minds the feast of the Holy Trinity, the Godhead whom they represented on earth. Thus also the feasts of Christmas, of the Holy Family, and of Christ the King are joined in the melody of their Offertories. On the Sunday within the Octave of Corpus Christi, we sing "Alleluia, O Lord my God, in Thee have I put my trust" (Ps. 7:2). Its melody is used for the Alleluia verse for the

[10] *Ibid.*, p. 385.

feast of the Holy Name of Jesus, reminding us that in the name of Jesus is our hope and our trust.

But no feast seems commemorated as often as the feast of the Epiphany, the feast of the manifestation of Christ. The Introit for this feast begins with the melody sung in each High Mass as an introduction to the Canon, the "Per omnia saecula saeculorum" of the Preface. This Introit melody is borrowed in full for the Introit of the Blessed Mother's Mass, "Salve sancta parens." We agree with Johner that it is fitting to use the same melody to hail Him each day at Mass and also that "we greet with the same song both the royal Child and the queen Mother."[11] The melody of the Gradual of the feast of Christ the King fittingly borrows the melody of the Gradual of the Epiphany, which was for years regarded as the feast of Christ the King. The Alleluia melody of the third Mass of Christmas is heard again on the Epiphany as it is heard on the feasts of St. John the Baptist His precursor, St. John the Apostle and proclaimer of His divinity, St. Stephen His first martyr, and SS. Peter and Paul the foundation stones of His Church. The Epiphany Offertory is recalled in the Votive Mass for the Propagation of the Faith.

In the Communion-song for the Monday after the Fourth Sunday of Lent we sing: "From my secret sins cleanse me, O Lord" (Ps. 18:13). On May 3 we sing to the same melody: "By the sign of the cross from our enemies deliver us, O Thou our God." It is through the cross of Christ that we may expect deliverance from our enemies, our sins.

The feast of Christ the King chants "His power is an everlasting power, that shall not be taken away: and His kingdom that shall not be destroyed," to a song we heard on the Fourth Sunday after Easter where we rejoiced with the "Prince of Life" as the Sequence calls Him: "Christ, rising again from the dead, dieth now no more: death shall no more have dominion over Him. Alleluia" (Rom. 6:9).

Melodically, we connect Christ's coming to earth, as an effective example to us, with His ascension into heaven, from whence He

[11] *Ibid.*, p. 81.

sends His Holy Spirit to abide with us to the consummation of the world. Thus we recognize identical melodies in the Alleluia of the Third Sunday of Advent, of the feast of the Ascension, and of the feast of Pentecost.

The Introit of the Solemnity of St. Joseph borrows the melody of its second and third phrases from the third Christmas Mass and thus brings to our minds the place of St. Joseph in the life of the Word made flesh.

We have already said that the Mass of our Lady uses the Epiphany Introit. Nor is St. Joseph forgotten, for the Gradual in our Blessed Mother's Masses uses the Gradual for March 19.

That a melody is used for many feasts does not lessen the implication of spiritual relationship between some of them. It may be a matter of astonishment that the Gradual of the Requiem Mass is the melody of the first Mass of Christmas, the Resurrection Mass, and the Nuptial Mass. The Son of God becomes Man, and after giving His all for us in His life and death rises again by His own power, thus destroying the power of death over Himself and over all those souls who have been brought into the world through the Sacrament of Marriage and are "other Christs" in sanctifying grace.

It would not be our way to sing the same melody on Christmas and Easter and at a Requiem Mass. "For my thoughts are not your thoughts: nor your ways my ways, saith the Lord" (Isa. 55:8). This is very evident in the Mass of Midnight on Christmas. Johner notes that we have in the plainsong melodies "no singing contest with the angels."[12] Again we quote him: "With what childlike joy our folksongs speak of the Christchild! They try to please Him, to coax a smile from His rosy lips. They speak to us in a fresh, direct, intimate way. Not so the texts and the plainsong melodies of the Midnight Mass. That Child, lying so poor and helpless and mute in His rude manger, is the one great Word spoken by the heavenly Father before all time, begotten of His own essence. This Child is equal in greatness, holiness, sublimity, and beauty to the Father Himself."[13] "The Lord said to me: Thou art my Son, this

[12] *Ibid.*, p. 49. [13] *Ibid.*, p. 45.

day have I begotten thee" (Ps. 2:7). In the Communion of this Mass we "once again hear expressions of the eternal generation of the Word from the Father. In the Introit and in the Alleluia-verse the Newborn One Himself spoke of it. In the first part of the Gradual" and in the Communion chant "the Father is the speaker."[14] This difference between the Divine Persons speaking is subtly and delicately indicated in the plainsong.

The melodies to which are sung the least understood part of our sung Mass — the Gradual and Alleluia — should be given particular thought. Monsignor Hellriegel says that in the Kyrie we knock at the door of God's Heart nine times, three times at the Heart of each Person.[15] God the Father answers us in the Epistle or Prophecy, God the Son speaks in the Gospel, and God the Holy Spirit speaks, through the Church in which He abides, in the sermon. However, as we have said, God's influence on us greatly depends on the receptivity of our souls. This is the very purpose of the Gradual and the Alleluia with its verse, that through meditation looking back to the thought of the Epistle and forward to the coming Testament, we prepare ourselves to accept Him and His teachings wholeheartedly as He greets us in His Gospel and through His Church. The plainsong melodies of the Gradual and Alleluia, clothing and making more effective these proper texts, are meant to assist us to prepare our souls for Him.

Anyone who sings the chant to any extent will agree that "it is meant to be sung and not just listened to." This is to be expected if we realize that our purpose in singing is to glorify God particularly by impressing the spirit of the text on our hearts so that we may the more fully receive Christ and His grace. Even we, who so often think of music as an exteriorization of some sentiment, will realize and accept the fact that the better music of the liturgy will have little exteriorization but will attempt to influence the interior of the singer himself.

As we study the texts of the liturgy and their melodies, we are

[14] *Ibid.*, p. 49.

[15] Martin B. Hellriegel, *The Holy Sacrifice of the Mass* (St. Louis: Pio Decimo Press, 1944), p. 31.

struck afresh with the wonderful goodness of God in bringing us, His members, into the inner circle of His own life. We realize more how it is that His glory is bound up with the real happiness of His creatures. We are impressed anew with the oneness of worship in the worship of His Church, the oneness of His Life and Passion with His Resurrection and Glory, the oneness of the Sacrifice of Calvary with the Eucharistic and heavenly Sacrifice,[16] the oneness of the God-Man with each member of His Body. And we see that "it is truly meet and just, right and availing unto salvation, that we should at all times and in all places give thanks to Thee, O holy Lord, Father almighty, everlasting God, through Christ our Lord."[17] We feel forced to sing with the heavenly choir "in common joy, in unison, in unceasing praise: Holy, Holy, Holy Lord God of Hosts. Heaven and earth are full of Thy glory. Hosanna in the Highest!"[18]

REVIEW QUESTIONS

1. What is the purpose of the music of the liturgy?
2. "Psalmody *listens* even more than it sings." Discuss.
3. How does the plainsong Proper assist us to understand the liturgical text?
4. How are melodies chosen for the Proper of a new feast?
5. Cite at least four feasts whose Proper texts and melodies recall other feasts.
6. Trace melodic references in the Propers of at least six feasts which you did not mention under Number 5.
7. "The chant is meant to be sung, not listened to." Discuss.
8. What reaction is to be expected in one who contemplates the graces which come to us from the liturgy? Has he an effective expression of gratitude?

[16] Maurice de la Taille, *The Mystery of Faith,* translated by Rev. Joseph Carroll (New York: Sheed and Ward, 1940), Chap. V.

[17] Preface of the Mass.

[18] *Ibid.*

BIBLIOGRAPHY

Authors and Editions Cited

The Holy Bible, Douay-Rheims (Belgium: Etabl. Brepols, 1938). Issued by The E. M. Lohmann Co.

The New Testament of Our Lord and Saviour Jesus Christ, Ronald A. Knox (New York: Sheed and Ward, 1945).

Pius X, St., *Motu Proprio on Sacred Music.* George V. Predmore, *Sacred Music and the Catholic Church* (Boston: McLaughlin and Reilly, 1936).

——— *Motu Proprio of Church Music,* translation and commentary by C. J. McNaspy, S.J. (Toledo: Gregorian Institute of America, 1950).

Pius XI, *Apostolic Constitution.* George V. Predmore, *Sacred Music and the Catholic Church* (Boston: McLaughlin and Reilly, 1936).

Pius XII, *Mystici Corporis,* with Introductory Analysis, Study Outline, Review Questions, Selected Bibliography prepared by Joseph J. Bluett, S.J. (New York: The America Press, 1943).

——— *Mediator Dei,* with Introduction and Notes by Gerald Ellard, S.J. (New York: The America Press, 1948).

Adam, Karl, *Christ Our Brother,* translated by Dom Justin McCann (New York: The Macmillan Company, 1931).

Aigrain, Rene, *Religious Music,* translated by Rev. C. Mulcahy (London: Sands and Company, n.d.).

Augustine, St., *The Confessions of St. Augustine,* translated by F. J. Sheed (New York: Sheed and Ward, 1943).

Beauduin, Dom Lambert, *Liturgy the Life of the Church,* translated by Dom Virgil Michel, 2 ed. (Collegeville: The Liturgical Press, 1929).

Benedictine of Stanbrook, *A Grammar of Plainsong* (Liverpool: Rushworth and Dreaper, 1934).

Bewerunge, H., "Plain Chant," *Catholic Encyclopedia,* 1913 edition, XII: 144–148.

Brennan, Robert E., *The Apostolate of the Liturgy, A Commentary on Mediator Dei* (Washington, D. C.: N.C.W.C., 1948).

Brown, Beatrice Bradshaw, "The Sacrifice of Cain," *The Catholic Choirmaster,* Vol. XXVIII: 155–157.

Cabrol, Dom Fernand, O.S.B., *The Books of the Latin Liturgy,* translated by the Benedictines of Stanbrook (London: Sands and Company, 1932).

——— *The Mass of the Western Rites,* translated by C. M. Antony (St. Louis: B. Herder Company, 1934).

——— *The Prayer of the Early Christians,* translated by Dom Ernest Graf (London: Burns, Oates and Washbourne, 1930). Issued in U. S. by Benziger Brothers.

The Catholic Choirmaster (New York: Society of St. Gregory of America).

The Catholic Choirmasters Course, Clifford Bennett, editor (Toledo: The Gregorian Institute of America, 1945).

Dickinson, Edward, *Music in the History of the Western Church* (New York: Scribner's Sons, 1902).

Douglas, Winfred, *Church Music in History and Practice* (New York: Charles Scribner's Sons, 1937).

Ellard, Gerald, S.J., *Christian Life and Worship* (Milwaukee: The Bruce Publishing Company, 1940).

——— *The Dialog Mass* (New York: Longmans, Green and Company, 1942).

——— *The Mass of the Future* (Milwaukee: The Bruce Publishing Company, 1948).

Elwell, Clarence, and others, editors, *Our Goal and Our Guides,* textbook for high school religion, 4 vols. (Chicago: Mentzer, Bush and Company, 1945).

Finney, Theodore M., *A History of Music* (New York: Harcourt, Brace and Company, 1935).

Fortescue, Adrian, *The Mass* (London: Longmans, Green and Company, 1912, 1950).

Gajard, Dom Joseph, O.S.B., *The Rhythm of Plainsong,* translated by Dom Aldhelm Dean (London: Rushworth and Dreaper, 1943).

Gavin, M., *The Sacrifice of the Mass* (London: Burns, Oates and Washbourne, Ltd., 1903).

Graf, Dom Ernest, O.S.B., *The Church's Daily Prayer* (London: Burns, Oates and Washbourne, Ltd., 1938).

Graham, E. P., editor, *The New Psalter* (New York: Pustet, 1935).

Hayes, Carlton J. H., *A Political and Cultural History of Modern Europe,* 2 vols. (New York: The Macmillan Company, 1932).

Hellriegel, Martin B., *The Holy Sacrifice of the Mass* (St. Louis: Pio Decimo Press, 1944).

Hillenbrand, Reynold, "The Meaning of the Liturgy," *National Liturgical Week* (Conception: Liturgical Conference, 1942).

Howell, Clifford, S.J., "The Blessed Virgin in the Liturgy," *Orate Fratres,* XXIV, No. 1:1–8.

Hudleston, G. Roger, "Gregory I," *Catholic Encyclopedia,* 1913 edition.

Hugle, Dom P. Gregory, O.S.B., *The Spotlight on Catholic Church Music* (Boston: McLaughlin and Reilly, 1935).

Johner, Dom Dominic, O.S.B., *A New School of Gregorian Chant,* 2 English ed., translated by Rev. W. A. Hofler (New York: Pustet, 1914).

——— *The Chants of the Vatican Gradual,* translated by the Monks of St. John's Abbey (Collegeville: St. John's Abbey Press, 1940).

Johnson, George, "Education For Life," *Guiding Growth in Christian Social Living,* Sister M. Joan, O.P., and Sister M. Nona, O.P., Vol. II (Washington, D. C.: The Catholic University of America Press, 1946).

Jungmann, Joseph Andreas, S.J., *The Mass of the Roman Rite,* translated by Francis A. Brunner, C.SS.R., Vols. I and II (New York: Benziger Brothers, 1951, 1952).

——— "The Pastoral Effects of the Liturgy," *Orate Fratres,* XXIII: 489.

Klarmann, Andrew F., *Gregorian Chant* (Toledo: Gregorian Institute of America, 1945).

Klauser, Theodor, "A Brief History of the Liturgy in the West," *Orate Fratres,* XXIII: 1–4.

Kush, Joseph, "Psalmody," *Catholic Choirmasters Course* (Toledo: Gregorian Institute of America, 1945).

Lang, Paul Henry, *Music in Western Civilization* (New York: W. W. Norton and Company, Inc., 1941).

La Taille, de, Maurice, S.J., *The Mystery of Faith,* Book I, translated by Rev. Joseph Carroll (New York: Sheed and Ward, 1940).

Lefebvre, Dom Gaspar, O.S.B., *Catholic Liturgy* (London: Sands and Company, 1924).

——— *Daily Missal* (Bruges: Desclée, 1934).

Marmion, Dom Columba, O.S.B., *Christ in His Mysteries,* translated from the French by a Nun of Tyburn Convent (London: Sands and Company, 1931; St. Louis: B. Herder).

Masure, Eugene, *The Christian Sacrifice,* translated from the French by Dom Illtyd Trethowan (London: Burns, Oates and Washbourne, Ltd., 1944; New York: Kenedy, 1947).

McGarrigle, Francis J., S.J., *My Father's Will* (Milwaukee: The Bruce Publishing Company, 1944).

Michel, Dom Virgil, O.S.B., *The Liturgy of the Church According to the Roman Rite* (New York: The Macmillan Company, 1939).

——— *Our Life in Christ* (Collegeville: The Liturgical Press, 1939).

O'Connell, Laurence J., *The Book of Ceremonies* (Milwaukee: The Bruce Publishing Company, 1943).

Parsch, Pius, *The Liturgy of the Mass,* translated by Rev. Frederic C. Eckhoff (St. Louis: B. Herder, 1940).

Pierik, Marie, *The Spirit of Gregorian Chant* (Boston: McLaughlin and Reilly, 1939).

Reese, Gustave, *Music in the Middle Ages* (New York: W. W. Norton and Company, 1940).

Rooney, Richard, S.J., *Light on the Liturgy,* Parts I and II (St. Louis: The Queen's Work, 1945).

Rudloff, D. Leo, O.S.B., "Meaning of Participation in the Mass," *National Liturgical Week* (Conception: Liturgical Conference, 1942).

Scheeben, Matthias Joseph, *The Mysteries of Christianity,* translated by Cyril Vollert, S.J. (St. Louis: B. Herder, 1946).

Steuart, R. H. J., S.J., *Temples of Eternity* (New York: Longmans, Green and Company, 1931).

Sunol, Dom Gregory, O.S.B., *Text Book of Gregorian Chant,* translated from the sixth French edition by G. M. Dunford (Boston: McLaughlin and Reilly, No. 988).

Thibault, Ethelbert, "Rhythm and Chironomy," *Catholic Choirmasters Course,* Clifford Bennett, ed. (Toledo: Gregorian Institute of America, 1945).

Thomas Aquinas, St., *The Summa Theologica,* translated by the Fathers of the English Dominican Province, 3 ed. (London: Burns, Oates and Washbourne, 1941; New York: Benziger Brothers).

Thuis, Dom Stephen, O.S.B., *Gregorian Chant A Barometer of Religious Fervor* (St. Meinrad, Ind.: St. Meinrad Abbey Press, 1931).

——— "Parish Worship, Its Artistic Expression," *National Liturgical Week* (Conception: Liturgical Conference, 1942).

Thurston, Herbert, "Calendar," *Catholic Encyclopedia,* Vol. III.

Vann, Gerald, O.P., *The Sorrow of God* (Oxford: Blackfriars Publication, 1946).

Van Waesberghe, Jos. Smits, *Gregorian Chant and Its Place in the Catholic Liturgy,* translated by W. A. G. Doyle-Davidson (Stockholm: Continental Book Company, n.d.).

Wagner, Peter, *Introduction to the Gregorian Melodies,* translated by Agnes Orme and E. G. P. Wyatt, 2 ed. (London: Plainsong and Medieval Society, 1901).

Ward, Justine B., "The Reform of Church Music," reprinted in *The Chant of the Church* (Collegeville: The Liturgical Press, 1930).

Weinmann, Karl, *History of Church Music* (Boston: McLaughlin and Reilly, n.d.).

Young, Karl, *The Drama of the Medieval Church,* 2 vols. (Oxford, Clarendon Press, 1933).

Zundel, Maurice, *The Splendour of the Liturgy* (New York: Sheed and Ward, 1944).

Further Bibliography

Adam, Karl, *The Spirit of Catholicism,* translated by Dom Justin McCann, O.S.B., rev. ed. (New York: The Macmillan Company, 1943).

Apel, Willi, *Harvard Dictionary of Music* (Cambridge: Harvard University Press, 1944).

——— *The Notation of Polyphonic Music, 900–1600* (Cambridge: The Medieval Academy of America, 1942; third corrected edition, 1945).
Apel, Willi, and Archibald Davidson, *Historical Anthology of Music* (Cambridge: Harvard University Press, 1947).
Attwater, Donald, *The Catholic Eastern Churches,* rev. ed. (Milwaukee: The Bruce Publishing Company, 1937).
——— *The Dissident Eastern Churches* (Milwaukee: The Bruce Publishing Company, 1937).

Batiffol, Pierre Henry, *History of the Roman Breviary,* translated from the third French edition (New York: Longmans, Green and Company, 1912).
——— *Primitive Catholicism,* translated by Henri L. Brianceau (New York: Longmans, Green and Company, 1911).
——— *St. Gregory the Great,* translated by John L. Stoddard (New York: Benziger Brothers, 1929).
Bazin, Rene, *Pius X,* translated from the second edition of the Benedictines of Talacre (London: Sands and Company, 1928).
Boylan, M. Eugene, O.C.R., *The Mystical Body* (Westminster, Md.: Newman Book Shop, 1948).
Britt, Matthew, O.S.B., *The Hymns of the Breviary and the Missal* (New York: Benziger Brothers, 1922, 1936).

Cabrol, Dom Fernand, O.S.B., *Liturgical Prayer,* translated by a Benedictine of Stanbrook (London: Burns, Oates and Company, 1925).
The Caecilia, "A Review of Liturgical Music" (Boston: McLaughlin and Reilly).
Cagin, Dom Paul, O.S.B., *Plain Chant and Solesmes* (London: Burns and Oates, 1940).
Coventry, John, S.J., *The Breaking of Bread* (New York: Sheed and Ward, 1950).

Duchesne, Mgr. Louis, *Early History of the Christian Church,* 3 vols., translated from the French fourth edition (London: John Murray, 1909, 1933).
——— *Christian Worship,* translated from the third French edition by M. L. McClure (London: Society for Promoting Christian Knowledge, 1904).

Gihr, Nicholas, *The Holy Sacrifice of the Mass,* 13 rev. ed., translated from the German (St. Louis: B. Herder, 1939).
Giordani-Tobin, *Pius X, A Country Priest* (Milwaukee: The Bruce Publishing Company, 1954).
Gradenwitz, Peter, *The Music of Israel* (New York: W. W. Norton, 1949).
Gruden, John C., S.T.L., *The Mystical Christ* (St. Louis: B. Herder, 1938).
Gueranger, Dom Prosper, O.S.B., *Liturgical Year* in 15 vols., translated by Dom L. Shepherd, O.S.B. (Westminster: Newman Press, 1948).

Hadow, W. H., Buck, Percy, and others, editors, *Oxford History of Music,* 8 vols., 2 ed. (London: Oxford University Press, 1929, 1934).

Henry, P., S.M., *The Liturgical Year* (Milwaukee: The Bruce Publishing Company, 1940).

Herzog, Charles, S.J., *Channels of Redemption* (New York: Benziger Brothers, 1931).

Idelssohn, Abraham Zebi, *Jewish Liturgy and Its Development* (New York: Henry Holt and Company, 1932).

——— *Jewish Music in Its Historical Development* (New York: Henry Holt and Company, 1929).

Kellner, K. A. Heinrich, *Heortology,* translated from the German (St. Louis: B. Herder, 1908).

Kurth, Godefroid, *The Church at the Turning Points of History,* translated from the French by Rt. Rev. Monsignor Day (Helena: Rt. Rev. Victor Day, 1918).

Marmion, Dom Columba, O.S.B., *Christ the Life of the Soul,* translated from the French by a Nun of Tyburn Convent (St. Louis: B. Herder, 1931).

Martindale, C. C., S.J., *Towards Loving the Psalms* (New York: Sheed and Ward, 1940).

McGarry, William J., S.J., *He Cometh* (New York: The America Press, 1942).

——— *Paul and the Crucified* (New York: The America Press, 1939).

——— *Unto the End* (New York: The America Press, 1941).

McKinney, Howard D., and Anderson, W. R., *Music in History* (New York: American Book Company, 1940).

Mersch, Emile, S.J., *Morality and the Mystical Body,* translated by Daniel Ryan, S.J. (New York: P. J. Kenedy, 1939).

——— *The Theology of the Mystical Body,* translated by Cyril Vollert, S.J. (St. Louis: B. Herder, 1951).

——— *The Whole Christ,* translated from the second French edition by John R. Kelly, S.J. (Milwaukee: The Bruce Publishing Company, 1938).

Mocquereau, Dom Andre, O.S.B., *Le Nombre Musical Gregorien,* Tomes I and II (Tournai: Desclée & Cie, 1928).

——— *Le Nombre Musical Gregorien,* translated by Aileen Tone, Vol. I, Part I (Tournai: Desclée and Company, 1932).

Mourret, Fernand, S.S., *History of the Catholic Church,* 6 vols., translated by Newton Thompson, S.T.D. (St. Louis: B. Herder, 1936).

Music and Liturgy, Dom Gregory Murray, editor (Bath: Downside Abbey).

Nef, Karl, *An Outline of the History of Music,* translated by Carl F. Pfatteicher (New York: Columbia University Press, 1935).

Nemmers, Erwin Esser, *Twenty Centuries of Catholic Church Music* (Milwaukee: The Bruce Publishing Company, 1949).

Nielen, Joseph M., *Earliest Christian Liturgy* (St. Louis: B. Herder, 1941).

Orate Fratres (Worship), Monks of St. John's Abbey, editors (Collegeville: The Liturgical Press).

Perkins, Mary, *Your Catholic Language* (New York: Sheed and Ward, 1940).

Proceedings for National Liturgical Week (Conception: The Liturgical Conference).

Puniet, de, Dom Jean, O.S.B., *The Mass Its Origin and History* (London: Burns, Oates and Washbourne, 1931).

Saminsky, Lazare, *Music of the Ghetto and the Bible* (New York: Bloch Publishing Company, 1934).

Schopp, Ludwig, and others, editors, *The Fathers of the Church.*

Schuster, Dom Ildefons, O.S.B., *The Sacramentary,* translated from the Italian by Arthur Levelis-Marke (London: Burns, Oates and Washbourne, 1924), 5 vols.

Sheen, Fulton J., *The Mystical Body* (New York: Sheed and Ward, 1935).

Sicard, Abbé A., *The Soul of the Sacred Liturgy,* translated by R. J. Benson and S. A. Raemers (St. Louis: B. Herder, 1924).

Strasser, Bernard, O.S.B., *With Christ Through the Year* (Milwaukee: The Bruce Publishing Company, 1947).

Suhard, Emmanuel Cardinal, *The Church Today* (Chicago: Fides Publishers, 1953).

Sunol, Dom Gregory, O.S.B., *Introduction a la Paleographie Musicale Gregorienne* (Tournai: Desclée & Cie, 1935).

Terry, Richard, *Music of the Roman Rite* (London: Burns, Oates, 1931).

V. G. L., *The Chant, A Simple and Complete Method for Teachers and Students* (St. Louis: B. Herder, 1938).

——— *Legendo, A Simple Approach to the Latin of the Liturgy* (New York: J. Fischer).

Von Hildebrand, Dietrich, *Liturgy and Personality* (New York: Longmans, Green and Company, 1943).

Williams, C. F. Abdy, *The Story of Notation* (New York: Scribner's Sons, 1903).

Wooldridge, H. E., *The Oxford History of Music, Polyphonic Period,* 2 vols., 2 rev. ed. (London: Oxford University Press, 1932).

APPENDIX I

TOPICS SUGGESTED FOR SPECIAL STUDY AND CLASS REPORT

1. My place in the worship of the Mystical Body.
2. Women's share in liturgical worship.
3. The *Motu Proprio* of St. Pius X.
4. The *Apostolic Constitution, "Divini cultus sanctitatem."*
5. Our Holy Father's encyclical on the Mystical Body.
6. The *Mediator Dei* of Pope Pius XII.
7. Religious worship — liturgical and devotional.
8. Corporate and individual worship in the liturgy.
9. Choral worship. (See Father Ellard's *Christian Life and Worship.*)
10. "Each hath his part." (See *Christian Life and Worship.*)
11. How to render the chant.
12. Liturgical song. (Why the chant is pre-eminently the song of the Church.)
13. Beauty in worship. (The "beautiful" versus the "pretty.")
14. Christianity, a perfect religion. (See *Christian Life and Worship.*)
15. The sequence as an art form.
16. One religion, one worship, one song — source of unity among peoples.
17. The liturgical work of St. Ambrose.
18. The liturgical work of Pope St. Gregory the Great.
19. Liturgical processions and their chants.
20. The musical interlude of the Mass.
21. Responsorial and antiphonal chants in the liturgy.
22. Forerunners of the *Motu Proprio.*

23. The work of the Solesmes monks.
24. "Through Christ Our Lord" — my liturgy and my devotion. (See Karl Adam's *Christ Our Brother*.)
25. Liturgical greetings.
26. Liturgy and song — melody and the Mass.
27. The Church and its liturgy.
28. Reform in Church music — its need and its result.
29. What choir membership can mean to me — its place in the plan of the Church.
30. Organists and choir directors — their privilege and responsibility.
31. The sung liturgy, the heritage of the common people.
32. The place of the altar in sacrifice.
33. Christ's sacrifice in our liturgy.
34. The sacrifice of the Church in our liturgy.
35. Our Lady in the liturgy.
36. "Human elements" in the liturgy — present-day modifications.
37. Modern liturgical conferences.
38. Modern music — liturgical music.
39. The Liturgy, the basis of Catholic Action.
40. Catholic Action in the liturgy.
41. The true Christian spirit, of which active participation in the liturgy is the primary and indispensable source.

APPENDIX II

INTERLINEAR TRANSLATIONS

IF WE have the opportunity to study the Latin language, we are, of course, greatly assisted in our understanding of the prayers of the Church as they are expressed in the liturgy. But if we do not have this opportunity, we can still assist ourselves in following the thoughts thus expressed if we build up a liturgical vocabulary. For this reason there are in this section a number of prayers and hymns accompanied by an interlinear translation. Below each Latin word is the English equivalent. In this the Latin order of the words is followed. Often we will have to adjust the order of the words to obtain a logical English translation.

Gloria

Glória	**in**	**excélsis**	**Déo.**	**Et**	**in**	**térra**	**pax**	**homínibus**
Glory	in	the-highest	to-God.	And	on	earth	peace	to-men

bónae	**voluntátis.**	**Laudámus**	**te.**	**Benedícimus**	**te.**	**Adorámus**
of-good	will.	We-praise	Thee.	We-bless	Thee.	We-adore

te.	**Glorificámus**	**te.**	**Grátias**	**ágimus**	**tíbi**	**própter**
Thee.	We-glorify	Thee.	Thanks	we-give	to-Thee	for

mágnam	**glóriam**	**túam.**	**Dómine**	**Déus,**	**Rex**	**caeléstis,**	**Déus**
great	glory	Thy.	Lord	God,	King	heavenly,	God

Páter	**omnípotens.**	**Dómine**	**Fíli**	**unigénite**	**Jésu**	**Chríste.**
Father	all-powerful.	Lord	Son	Only-Begotten	Jesus	Christ.

Dómine	**Déus,**	**Ágnus**	**Déi**	**Fílius**	**Pátris.**		**Qui**
Lord	God,	Lamb	of-God	Son	of-the-Father.	(Thou)	Who

tóllis	**peccáta**	**múndi**	**miserére**	**nóbis.**		**Qui**
takest-away	the-sins	of-the-world,	have-mercy	on-us.	(Thou)	Who

tóllis peccáta múndi, súscipe deprecatiónem nóstram.
takest-away the-sins of-the-world, receive prayer our.

Qui sédes ad déxteram Pátris, miserére
(Thou) Who sitteth at the-right-hand of-the-Father, have-mercy

nóbis. Quóniam tu sólus sánctus. Tu sólus
on-us. For Thou alone (art) holy. Thou alone (art)

Dóminus. Tu sólus Altíssimus, Jésu Chríste. Cum
Lord. Thou alone (art) Most-High, Jesus Christ. With

Sáncto Spíritu in glória Déi Pátris. Ámen.
the-Holy Spirit in the-glory of-God the-Father. So-be-it.

Credo

Crédo in únum Déum Pátrem omnipoténtem, factórem
I-believe in one God, the-Father Almighty, Creator

caéli et térrae, visibílium ómnium, et invisibílium.
of-heaven and of-earth, of-visible-things all, and of-invisible.

Et in únum Dóminum Jésum Chrístum, Fílium
And (I believe) in one Lord Jesus Christ, Son

Déi unigénitum. Et ex Pátre nátum ánte ómnia
of-God the-Only-Begotten. And of the-Father born before all

saécula. Déum de Déo, lúmen de lúmine, Déum vérum de Déo
ages. God of God, light of light, God true of God

véro. Génitum non fáctum, consubstantiálem Pátri:
true. Begotten not made, consubstantial with-the-Father:

per quem ómnia fácta sunt. Qui própter nos hómines,
through Whom all-things made were. Who for us men,

et própter nóstram salútem descéndit de caélis.
and for our salvation descended from the-heavens.

Et incarnátus est de Spíritu Sáncto ex María
And (He) incarnate was of the-Spirit Holy from Mary

Vírgine: et hómo fáctus est. Crucifíxus étiam pro
the-Virgin: and man made was. (He was) crucified also for

nóbis sub Póntio Piláto: pássus et sepúltus est. Et
us under Pontius Pilate: (He) suffered and He-was-buried. And

resurréxit tértia díe, secúndum scriptúras. Et
He-rose the-third day, according-to the-Scriptures. And

ascéndit in caélum: sédet ad déxteram Pátris.
He-ascended into Heaven: He-sits at the-right-hand of-the-Father.

Et íterum ventúrus est cum glória, judicáre vívos et
And again to-come He-is with glory, to-judge the-living and

mórtuos: cújus régni non érit fínis.
the-dead: of-Whose kingdom no there-shall-be end.

Et in Spíritum Sánctum, Dóminum, et vivificántem:
And (I believe) in the-Spirit Holy, Lord, and life-Giver:

qui ex Pátre Filióque procédit. Qui cum Pátre
Who from the-Father and-the-Son proceeds. Who with the-Father

et Fílio símul adorátur, et conglorificátur: qui
and the-Son together is-adored, and glorified: Who

locútus est per Prophétas. Et únam
spoke through the-prophets. And (I believe in) one

sánctam cathólicam et apostólicam Ecclésiam. Confíteor únum
holy catholic and apostolic Church. I-confess one

baptísma in remissiónem peccatórum. Et expécto resurrectiónem
baptism for the-remission of-sins. And I-await the-resurrection

mortuórum. Et vítam ventúri saéculi.
of-the-dead. And life everlasting (literally: of-the-coming-ages).

Ámen.
So-be-it.

Pater Noster

(And Preceding Prayer)

Orémus: Praecéptis salutáribus móniti, et divína
Let-us-pray: By-precepts salutary taught, and by-divine

institutióne formáti, audémus dícere: Páter nóster qui es
institution strengthened, we-dare to-say: Father our who art

in caélis: Sanctificétur nómen túum: Advéniat régnum túum:
in heaven: hallowed-be name thy: come kingdom thy:

Fíat volúntas túa sícut in caélo, et in térra. Pánem
be-done Will thy, as in heaven, so on earth. Bread

nóstrum quotidiánum da nóbis hódie: et dimítte nóbis
our daily give us this-day: and forgive us

débita nóstra, sícut et nos dimíttimus debitóribus nóstris, Et
trespasses our, as also we forgive trespassers our, And

ne nos indúcas in tentatiónem, (R) Sed líbera nos a
not us lead into temptation, But deliver us from

málo. Ámen.
evil. So-be-it.

Prayers at Communion

Pánem caeléstem accípiam, et nómen Dómini
Bread heavenly I-shall-take, and the-name of-the-Lord

invocábo. Dómine, non sum dígnus ut íntres
I-will-call-upon. Lord, not I-am worthy that Thou-shouldst-enter

sub téctum méum: sed tántum dic vérbo, et
under roof my: but only speak in-a-word, and

sanábitur ánima méa. Córpus Dómini nóstri Jésu Chrísti
shall-be-healed soul my. The-Body of-Lord our Jesus Christ

custódiat ánimam méam (or túam) in vítam aetérnam. Ámen.
may-keep soul my (*or* your) into life eternal. So-be-it.

Asperges Me

(Antiphon and Psalm Sung Before a Solemn Mass Outside Paschal Time.)

Aspérges me Dómine, hyssópo, et mundábor:
Thou-shalt-sprinkle me, O-Lord, with-hyssop, and I-shall-be-cleansed:

lavábis me, et súper nívem dealbábor.
thou-shalt-wash me, and more-than snow I-shall-be-made-white.

Psalm 50: Verse 1.

Miserére méi, Déus, secúndum mágnam misericórdiam
Have-mercy on-me, O-God, according-to great mercy

túam.
Thy.

Vidi Aquam

(Antiphon and Psalm Sung Before a Solemn Mass During Paschal Time.)

Vídi	**áquam**	**egrediéntem**	**de**	**témplo,**	**a**	**látere**	**déxtro,**
I-saw	water	flowing-out	from	the-temple,	from	the-side	right,

allelúia:
alleluia:

et	**ómnes,**	**ad**	**quos**	**pervénit**	**áqua**	**ísta,**	**sálvi**	**fácti**	**sunt**	**et**
and	all	to	whom	comes	water	this,	safe	made	were	and

dícent,	**allelúia,**	**allelúia.**
said,	alleluia,	alleluia.

Psalm 117: Verse 1.

Confitémini	**Dómino**	**quóniam**		**bónus:**	**quóniam**
Give-praise-to	the-Lord	for	(He is)	good:	for

in	**saéculum**		**misericórdia**	**éjus.**
in	all-ages	(is)	mercy	His.

Responses

1. ℣.	**Dóminus**	**vobíscum.**	℟.	**Et**	**cum**	**spíritu**	**túo.**
	The-Lord	with-thee.		And	with	spirit	thy.

2. ℣.	**Per**	**Chrístum**	**Dóminum**	**nóstrum.**	℟.	**Ámen.**
	Through	Christ	Lord	our.		So-be-it.

3. ℣.	**Pax**	**Dómini**	**sit**	**sémper**	**vobíscum.**	℟.	**Et**	**cum**
	The-peace	of-the-Lord	be	always	with-thee.		And	with
	spíritu	**túo.**						
	spirit	thy.						

4. ℟.	**Glória**	**tíbi,**	**Dómine.**
	Glory	to-Thee,	Lord.

5. ℟.	**Laus**		**tíbi,**	**Chríste.**
	Praise	(be)	to-Thee,	Christ.

6. ℣.	**Oráte,**	**frátres,**	**ut**	**méum**	**ac**	**véstrum**	**sacrifícium**	**acceptábile**
	Pray,	brethren,	that	my	and	your	sacrifice	acceptable
	fíat	**ápud**	**Déum**	**Pátrem**	**omnipoténtem.**			
	may-be	with	God	the-Father	almighty.			

℟. **Suscípiat Dóminus sacrifícium de mánibus túis ad**
May-receive the-Lord the-sacrifice from hands thy to

láudem et glóriam nóminis súi, ad utilitátem quóque
the-praise and glory of-name His, to profit also

nóstram, totiúsque Ecclésiae súae sánctae. (Ámen.)
our, and-of-all Church His holy. (So-be-it.)

7. ℣. **Súrsum córda.** ℟. **Habémus ad Dóminum.**
Lift-up (your) hearts. We-have (lifted them) to the-Lord.

℣. **Grátias agámus Dómino Déo nóstro.**
Thanks let-us-give to-the-Lord God our.

℟. **Dígnum et jústum est.**
Worthy and just it-is.

8. ℣. **Déus, in adjutórium méum inténde.**
God, to help my come (literally: direct-your-efforts).

℟. **Dómine, ad adjuvándum me féstina.**
Lord, to assistance my hasten.

9. ℣. **Dómine, exáudi oratiónem méam.** ℟. **Et clámor méus ad**
Lord, hear prayer my. And cry my unto

te véniat.
Thee let-come.

10. ℣. **Ora pro nóbis, sáncta Déi Génitrix,**
Pray for us, O-holy of-God Mother,

℟. **Ut dígni efficiámur promissiónibus Christi.**
That worthy we-may-be-made of-the-promises of-Christ.

11. ℣. **Pánem de coélo praestitísti éis. (Allelúia.)**
Bread from heaven Thou-hast-given to-them. (Alleluia.)

℟. **Omne delectaméntum in se habéntem. (Allelúia.)**
All sweetness in itself having. (Alleluia.)

The Bishop's Blessing

℣. **Sit nómen Dómini benedíctum.**
Be the-name of-the-Lord blessed.

℟. **Ex hoc nunc et úsque in saéculum.**
From this moment and constantly through-all-ages.

℣.	**Adjutórium**	**nóstrum**		**in**	**nómine**	**Dómini.**		
	Help	our	(is)	in	the-name	of-the-Lord.		

℟.	**Qui**	**fécit**	**caélum**	**et**	**térram.**
	Who	made	heaven	and	earth.

℣.	**Benedícat**	**vos**	**omnípotens**	**Déus:**	**Páter,**	**et**	**Fílius,**	**et**	
	May-bless	you	almighty	God:	Father,	and	Son,	and	

Spíritus	**Sánctus.**	℟.	**Ámen.**
Spirit	Holy.		So-be-it.

CHANTS FOR THE DEAD

Gradual of the Requiem Mass

Réquiem	**aetérnam**	**dóna**	**éis**	**Dómine:**	**et**	**lux**	**perpétua**
Rest	eternal	give	to-them	O-Lord:	and	light	perpetual

lúceat	**éis.**	℣.	**In**	**memória**	**aetérna**	**érit**	**jústus:**
let-shine	on-them.		In	remembrance	eternal	will-be	the-just:

ab	**auditióne**	**mála**	**non**	**timébit.**
from	report	evil	not	he-shall-fear.

Tract of the Requiem Mass

Absólve,	**Dómine,**	**ánimas**	**ómnium**	**fidélium**	**defunctórum**	**ab**
Free,	Lord,	the-souls	of-all	the-faithful	departed	from

ómni	**vínculo**	**delictórum.**	℣.	**Et**	**grátia**	**túa**	**íllis**	**succurrénte,**
every	bond	of-sin.		And	with-grace	Thy	them	help,

	mereántur	**evádere**	**judícium**	**ultiónis.**	℣.	**Et**
(that)	they-may-merit	to-escape	the-judgment	of-vengeance.		And

lúcis	**aetérnae**	**beatitúdine**	**pérfrui.**
of-light	eternal	the-beatitude	to-enjoy.

Offertory of the Requiem Mass

Dómine	**Jésu**	**Chríste,**	**Rex**	**glóriae,**	**líbera**	**ánimas**	**ómnium**
Lord	Jesus	Christ,	King	of-glory,	free	the-souls	of-all

fidélium	**defunctórum**	**de**	**poénis**	**inférni,**	**et**	**de**
the-faithful	departed	from	the-punishment	of-hell,	and	from

profúndo	**lácu:**	**líbera**	**éas**	**de**	**óre**	**leónis,**	**ne**
the-deep	lake:	free	them	from	the-mouth	of-the-lion,	lest

absórbeat éas tártarus, ne cádant in obscúrum:
absorb them the-infernal-regions, lest they-fall into obscurity:

sed sígnifer sánctus Míchael repraeséntet éas in
but the-standard-bearer holy Michael may-lead them into

lúcem sánctam: * Quam ólim Ábrahae promisísti,
the-light holy: Which formerly to-Abraham Thou-didst-promise,

et sémini éjus. ℣. Hóstias et préces tíbi Dómine
and to-offspring his. Sacrifices and prayers to-thee Lord

láudis offérimus: tu súscipe pro animábus íllis,
of-praise we-offer: (do) Thou receive (them) for souls those,

quárum hódie memóriam fácimus: fac éas, Dómine,
of-whom today a-remembrance we-make: grant them, Lord,

de mórte transíre ad vítam. * Quam ólim Ábrahae
from death to-pass to life. Which formerly to-Abraham

promisísti, et sémini éjus.
Thou-didst-promise, and to-offspring his.

Communion of the Requiem Mass

Lux aetérna lúceat éis, Dómine: Cum Sánctis túis in
Light eternal let-shine on-them, Lord: With saints Thy in

aetérnum, quía píus es. ℣. Réquiem aetérnam dóna
eternity, because kind Thou-art. Rest eternal give

éis, Dómine, et lux perpétua lúceat éis.
to-them, Lord, and light perpetual let-shine on-them.

Subvenite

Subveníte Sáncti Déi, occúrrite Ángeli
Come-to-assist (him) Saints of-God, run-to-meet (him) Angels

Dómini, * Suscipiéntes ánimam éjus, * Offeréntes éam in
of-the-Lord, Receiving soul his, offering it in

conspéctu Altíssimi. ℣. Suscípiat te Chrístus, qui
the-sight of-the-Most-High. May-receive thee Christ, who

vocávit te, et in sínum Ábrahae ángeli dedúcant
called thee, and into the-bosom of-Abraham the-angels may-lead

te.
thee.

Responsory — Libera Me

Líbera me, Dómine, de mórte aetérna, in díe ílla treménda:
Free me, Lord, from death eternal, on day that terrible:

*** Quándo caéli movéndi sunt et térra:**
When the-heavens are-to-be-moved and earth:

*** Dum véneris judicáre saéculum per ígnem.**
When Thou-shalt-come to-judge the-race by fire.

℣. **Trémens fáctus sum égo, et tímeo,**
Trembling have-been-made I, and I-am-in-fear, (of the time)

dum discússio vénerit, átque ventúra
when the-examination shall-take-place, and (of) the-coming

íra.
wrath.

℣. **Díes ílla, díes írae, calamitátis et misériae,**
(O) day that, day of-wrath, of-misfortune and of-distress,

díes mágna et amára válde.
day great and bitter exceedingly.

℣. **Réquiem aetérnam dóna éis, Dómine: et lux perpétua**
Rest eternal give to-them, O-Lord: and light perpetual

lúceat éis.
let-shine on-them.

Antiphon — In Paradisum

In paradísum dedúcant te ángeli: in túo advéntu
Into paradise may-lead thee the-angels: at thy coming

suscípiant te Mártyres, et perdúcant te in civitátem
may-receive thee the-Martyrs, and may-they-lead thee into the-city

sánctam Jerúsalem. Chórus Angelórum te suscípiat, et
holy Jerusalem. The-chorus of-angels thee may-receive, and

cum Lázaro, quóndam páupere aetérnam hábeas
with Lazarus, once a-poor-man, eternal mayest-thou-have

réquiem.
rest.

Antiphon — Ego Sum

Égo sum resurréctio et víta: qui crédit in me,
I am the-resurrection and the-life: (he) who believes in Me,

étiam si mórtuus fúerit, vívet: et ómnis qui vívit et
even if dead he-shall-be, he-shall-live: and all who live and

crédit in me, non moriétur in aetérnum.
believe in Me, not shall-die forever.

SEQUENCES

Dies Irae

Sequence of the Requiem Mass

Attributed to Thomas of Celano — Thirteenth Century

1a.

Díes írae, díes ílla Sólvet saéclum
Day of-wrath, day that (on which) shall-dissolve the-world

in favílla,
in ashes,

Téste Dávid cum Sibylla.
according-to-the-witness of-David with the-Sibyl.

1b.

Quántus trémor est futúrus, Quándo júdex est ventúrus
How-great a-trembling there-will-be, when the-Judge will-come

Cúncta strícte discussúrus.
everything with-strictness to-investigate.

2a.

Túba, mírum spárgens sónum Per sepúlcra
The-trumpet, a-wonderful scattering sound through the-graves

regiónum
of-all-regions

Cóget ómnes ánte thrónum.
shall-compel (to come) all before the-throne.

2b.

Mors stupébit et natúra Cum resúrget creatúra
Death will-be-stunned and nature when shall-rise the-creature

Judicánti responsúra.
to-the-Judge to-answer.

3a.

Líber scríptus proferétur, In quo tótum continétur
The-book written shall-be-brought, in which everything is-contained

Unde múndus judicétur.
whence the-world shall-be-judged.

3b.

Júdex érgo cum sedébit, Quídquid látet, apparébit,
The-Judge then when shall-sit, whatever hides, shall-appear,

Nil inúltum remanébit.
nothing unavenged shall-remain.

4a.

Quid sum míser tunc dictúrus? Quem patrónum
What am-I poor-wretch, then going-to-say? Whom as-a-patron

rogatúrus
shall-I-call

Cum vix jústus sit secúrus?
when scarcely the-just-man is secure?

4b.

Rex treméndae majestátis, Qui salvándos sálvas grátis,
(O) King of-terrible majesty, Who those-to-be-saved saves freely,

Sálva me, fons pietátis.
save me, fountain of-kindness.

5a.

Recordáre, Jésu píe, Quod sum cáusa túae
Remember, Jesus kind, that I-am the-cause of-Thy

víae:
life (literally: journey):

Ne me pérdas ílla díe.
do-not me destroy on-that day.

5b.

Quaérens me, sedísti lássus, Redemísti crúcem
Seeking me Thou-didst-sit weary, Thou-didst-redeem (me) the-cross

pássus:
having-suffered:

Tántus lábor non sit cássus.
so-much labor not do-let-be voided.

6a.

Júste júdex ultiónis, Dónum fac remissiónis,
Just Judge of-vengeance, a-gift make of-remission,

Ánte díem ratiónis.
before the-day of-reckoning.

6b.

Ingemísco, támquam réus, Cúlpa rúbet vúltus méus,
I-groan, as one-condemned, guilt reddens face my,

Supplicánti párce, Déus.
the-suppliant spare, O-God.

7a.

Qui Maríam absolvísti, Et latrónem exaudísti,
(Thou) Who Mary didst-absolve, and the-thief didst-hear,

Míhi quóque spem dedísti.
to-me also hope hast-given.

7b.

Préces méae non sunt dígnae: Sed tu bónus
Prayers my not are worthy: but Thou (Who art) good

fac benígne,
grant kindly,

Ne perénni crémer ígne.
that-not in-eternal I-be-burned fire.

8a.

Inter	**óves**	**lócum**	**praésta,**	**Et**	**ab**	**haédis**	**me sequéstra**
Among	the-sheep	a-place	give,	and	from	the-goats	me separate

Státuens	**in**	**párte**	**déxtra.**
placing-me	in	the-section	on-the-right.

8b.

Confutátis	**maledíctis,**		**Flámmis**	**ácribus**	**addíctis,**
Having-been-silenced	the-wicked,	(and)	to-flames	bitter	assigned,

Vóca	**me**	**cum**	**benedíctis.**
call	me	with	the-blessed.

9a.

Oro	**súpplex**	**et**	**acclínis,**		**Cor**	**contrítum**	**quási**	**cínis:**
I-pray	kneeling	and	prostrate,	(my)	heart	crushed	like	ashes:

Gére	**cúram**	**méi**	**fínis.**
Take	care	of-my	ending.

10.

Lacrimósa	**díes**	**ílla,**	**Qua**	**resúrget**	**ex**	**favílla**
Tearful	day	that	on-which	shall-rise	from	glowing-ashes

11.

Judicándus	**hómo**	**réus.**	**Húic**	**érgo**	**párce**	**Déus.**
To-be-judged	man	guilty.	Him	then	spare,	God.

12.

Píe	**Jésu,**	**Dómine,**	**Dóna**	**éis**	**réquiem.**	**Ámen.**
Kind	Jesus,	Lord,	give	them	rest.	So-be-it.

Victimae Paschali

Sequence for Easter Week

Ascribed to Wipo — Eleventh Century

1.

Víctimae	**Pascháli**	**láudes**	**ímmolent**	**Christiáni.**
To-the-Victim	Paschal	of-praise	let-offer-sacrifices	Christians.

2a.

Ágnus	**redémit**	**óves:**	**Chrístus**	**ínnocens**	**Pátri**
The-lamb	has-redeemed	the-sheep:	Christ	the-innocent	to-the-Father

Reconciliávit	**peccatóres.**
has-reconciled	sinners.

2b.

Mors	**et**	**víta**	**duéllo**	**Conflixére**	**mirándo:**
Death	and	life	in-a-battle	have-struggled	wonderful:

Dux	**vítae**		**mórtuus,**	**régnat**	**vívus.**
The-Prince	of-life	(although)	dead,	reigns	living.

3a.

Dic	**nóbis,**	**María,**	**Quid**	**vidísti**	**in**	**vía?**
Tell	us,	Mary,	what	did-you-see	on	the-way?

Sepúlcrum	**Chrísti**	**vivéntis,**	**Et**	**glóriam**	**vídi**
The-tomb	of-Christ	the-living,	and	the-glory	I-saw

resurgéntis:	
of-the-Risen	(One):

3b.

Angélicos	**téstes,**	**Sudárium,**	**et**	**véstes.**
Angelic	witnesses,	the-napkin,	and	the-linencloths.

Surréxit	**Chrístus**	**spes**	**méa:**	**Praecédet**	**súos**
Has-risen	Christ	hope	my:	He-shall-go-before	His-own

in	**Galilaéam.**
into	Galilee.

4.

Scímus	**Chrístum**	**surrexísse**	**A**	**mórtuis**	**vére:**
We-know	Christ	to-have-risen	from	the-dead	truly:

Tu	**nóbis,**	**víctor**	**Rex,**	**miserére.**	**Ámen.**	**Allelúia.**
Thou	on-us,	victorious	King,	have-mercy.	So-be-it.	Alleluia.

Veni Sancte Spiritus

Sequence for Pentecost and Its Octave
Probably Composed by Innocent III (1161–1216)

1a.

Véni, Sáncte Spíritus, Et emítte caélitus
Come, Holy Spirit, and send-forth heavenly
Lúcis túae rádium.
light of-Thy the-rays.

1b.

Véni páter páuperum, Véni dátor múnerum,
Come, Father of-the-poor, come, Giver of-gifts,
Véni lúmen córdium.
come, Light of-hearts.

2a.

Consolátor óptime, Dúlcis hóspes ánimae,
Consoler best, sweet Guest of-the-soul,
Dúlce refrigérium.
sweet Coolness.

2b.

In labóre réquies, In aéstu tempéries,
In labor Rest, in heat Tempering (Refreshment),
In flétu solátium.
in tears Solace.

3a.

O lux beatíssima, Réple córdis íntima
O light most-blessed, fill of-the-hearts the-intimate-recesses
Tuórum fidélium.
of-Thy faithful.

3b.

Síne túo númine, Níhil est in hómine,
Without Thy divine-assistance, nothing is in man,

Níhil est innóxium.
nothing is harmless.

4a.

Láva quod est sórdidum, Ríga quod est áridum,
Wash-away what is base, bedew what is arid,

Sána quod est sáucium.
heal what is wounded.

4b.

Flécte quod est rígidum, Fóve quod est frígidum,
Bend what is rigid, warm what is cold,

Rége quod est dévium.
guide what is astray.

5a.

Da túis fidélibus, In te confidéntibus,
Give to-Thy faithful, in Thee confiding,

Sácrum septenárium.
(Thy) holy (gifts) sevenfold.

5b.

Da virtútis méritum, Da salútis éxitum,
Give of-virtue a-reward, give of-safety a-death,

Da perénne gáudium.
give eternal joy.

ANTIPHONS OF OUR LADY

Alma Redemptoris Mater

Antiphon From Vespers of the Saturday Before the First Sunday of Advent to the Feast of the Purification Inclusive

Hermann Contractus (1015–1054)

Álma Redemptóris Máter, quae pérvia caéli
Gracious of-the-Redeemer Mother, who the-accessible of-heaven

Pórta mánes et stélla máris, succúrre cadénti,
gate remaineth and star of-the-sea, aid (thy) falling,

Súrgere qui cúrat, pópulo: tu quae genuísti,
to-rise who strive, people: thou who didst-beget

Natúra miránte, túum sánctum Genitórem,
while-nature marvelled, thy holy Creator,

Vírgo príus ac postérius, Gabriélis ab óre
a-virgin before and after, of-Gabriel from the-mouth

Súmens íllud Áve, peccatórum miserére.
receiving that "Ave," on-(us)-sinners have-pity.

Ave Regina Caelorum

Antiphon From Compline of the Feast of the Purification Until Holy Thursday

Authorship and Date Uncertain — It Has Been in Use Since the Twelfth Century

Áve Regína caelórum, Dómina Áve angelórum:
Hail Queen of-heaven, hail Lady of-the-angels:

Sálve, rádix, sálve, pórta, Ex qua múndo lux est
Hail, root, hail, door, from which for-the-world light is

órta:
arisen:

Gáude, Vírgo gloriósa, Súper ómnes speciósa,
Rejoice, O-Virgin glorious, above all lovely,

Vále, o válde decóra, Et pro nóbis Chrístum exóra.
Hail, o exceedingly beautiful, and for us Christ entreat.

Regina Caeli Laetare

Antiphon From Compline of Holy Saturday to None of the Saturday After Pentecost Inclusive

Authorship and Date Uncertain — Found in a Fourteenth-Century Manuscript

Regína caéli laetáre, allelúia,
O-Queen of-heaven rejoice, alleluia,

Quía quem meruísti portáre, allelúia,
For He-whom thou-didst-merit to-bear, alleluia,

Resurréxit, sícut díxit, allelúia,
Has-risen, just-as He-said, alleluia,

Ora pro nóbis Déum, allelúia.
Pray for us (to) God, alleluia.

Salve Regina Mater Misericordiae

Antiphon From the First Vespers of the Feast of the Holy Trinity Until None of the Saturday Before the First Sunday of Advent

Attributed to Hermann Contractus (1013–1054)

Sálve Regína, máter misericórdiae, Víta, dulcédo et spes
Hail Queen, Mother of-mercy, life, sweetness and hope

nóstra, sálve. Ad te clamámus, éxsules fílii Hévae. Ad te
our hail. To thee do-we-cry, exiled children of-Eve. To thee

suspirámus, geméntes et fléntes in hac lacrimárum válle.
do-we-sigh, mourning and weeping in this of-tears vale.

Éia érgo, advocáta nóstra, íllos túos misericórdes óculos
Behold therefore, advocate our, those thine of-mercy eyes

ad nos convérte. Et Jésum, benedíctum frúctum véntris túi,
to us turn. And Jesus, the-blessed fruit of-womb thy,

nóbis post hoc exsílium osténde. O clémens, O pía, O dúlcis
to-us after this exile show. O clement, O loving, O sweet

Vírgo María.
Virgin Mary.

HYMNS

Ave Maria

Áve María, grátia pléna, Dóminus técum, benedícta
Hail Mary, grace full, the-Lord (is) with-thee, blessed (art)

tu in muliéribus, et benedíctus frúctus véntris túi,
thou among women, and blessed (is) the-fruit of-womb thy,

Jésus. Sáncta María, Máter Déi, óra pro nóbis peccatóribus,
Jesus. Holy Mary, Mother of-God, pray for us sinners,

nunc et in hóra mórtis nóstrae. Ámen.
now and in the-hour of-death our. So-be-it.

Veni Domine Jesu

Advent Responsorial

Véni Dómine Jésu, Véni Dómine Jésu, Véni, Véni, Véni,
Come Lord Jesus, come Lord Jesus, come, come, come,

Et nóli tardáre.
and do-not delay.

Creator Alme Siderum

Vesper Hymn for Advent

Ambrosian Hymn — Seventh Century

1.

Creátor álme síderum, Aetérna lux credéntium,
O-Creator kind of-the-stars, eternal light of-the-believing,

Jésu, Redémptor ómnium, Inténde vótis súpplicum.
Jesus, Redeemer of-all, listen-to the-prayers of-suppliants.

2.

Qui daémonis ne fráudibus Períret
(O Thou) Who of-the-devil lest through-the-deceits should-be-lost

órbis, ímpetu
the-world, by-the-impulse

Amóris áctus, lánguidi Múndi medéla fáctus es.
Of-love moved, for-the-languid world a-remedy became.

5.

Te deprecámur, últimae Mágnum diéi Júdicem,
Thee we-pray, of-the-last great day Judge,

Ármis supérnae grátiae Defénde nos ab hóstibus.
With-the-arms of-heavenly grace defend us from (our) enemies.

6.

Vírtus, hónor, laus, glória Déo Pátri cum Fílio,
All-power, honor, praise, glory (be) to-God the-Father with the-Son

Sáncto símul Paráclito, In saeculórum saécula. Ámen.
To-the-holy also Paraclete, forever-and-ever. So-be-it.

Rorate Caeli

Advent Responsory

Roráte caéli désuper, et núbes plúant
Drop-dew ye-heavens, from-above, and the-clouds let-rain

jústum.
the-Just-One.

Ecce Nomen Domini

Écce nómen Dómini Emmánuel! Quod annuntiátum est
Behold the-name of-the-Lord Emmanuel! which was-announced

per Gábriel,
through Gabriel,

Hódie appáruit in Ísrael, Per Maríam Vírginem est natus
To-day appeared in Israel. Of Mary the-Virgin was born

Rex.
the-King.

Éia! Vírgo Déum génuit, Ut divína vóluit cleméntia.
Behold! A-virgin God gave-birth-to, as divine willed clemency.

In Béthlehem nátus est Et in Jerúsalem vísus est,
In Bethlehem He-was-born, and in Jerusalem He-was-seen,

Et in ómnem térram honorificátus est, Rex Ísrael!
and in all the-earth He-was-honored, the-King of-Israel!

Jesu Redemptor Omnium

Hymn for Vespers and Matins of Christmas
Ambrosian Hymn — Sixth Century

1.

Jésu, Redémptor ómnium, Quem lúcis ánte oríginem
Jesus, Redeemer of-all, whom of-light before the-beginning

Párem patérnae glóriae Páter suprémus édidit.
the-equal-of the-Father's glory the-Father sovereign begot.

3.

Meménto, rérum Cónditor, Nóstri quod ólim córporis,
Remember, of-(all)-things Creator, of-our that formerly body,

Sacráta ab álvo Vírginis Nascéndo, fórmam
the-sacred from the-womb of-the-Virgin in-being-born, the-form

súmpseris.
Thou-didst-assume.

7.

Jésu, tíbi sit glória, Qui nátus es de Vírgine,
Jesus, to-Thee be glory, Who wert-born of a-Virgin,

Cum Pátre, et álmo Spíritu
with the-Father, and (with) the-life-giving Spirit

In sempitérna saécula.
forever-and-ever.

Jesu Dulcis Memoria

Hymn for the Feast of the Holy Name of Jesus
Attributed to St. Bernard (1091–1153)

1.

Jésu, dúlcis memória, Dans véra córdis gáudia:
Jesus, sweet thought, giving true of-heart joy:

Sed súper mel, et ómnia, Éjus dúlcis praeséntia.
But above honey, and all (sweetness is) His sweet presence.

2.

Nil cánitur suávius, Nil áuditur jucúndius,
Nothing can-be-sung more-sweet, nothing can-be-heard more-pleasing,

Nil cogitátur dúlcius, Quam Jésus Déi Fílius.
Nothing can-be-thought more-lovely, than Jesus of-God the-Son.

3.

Jésu, spes poeniténtibus, Quam píus es peténtibus,
O-Jesus, hope of-penitents, how kind Thou-art to-those-who-pray,

Quam bónus te quaeréntibus, Sed quid inveniéntibus?
How good Thee to-those-who-seek, but what to-those-who-find?

4.

Nec língua válet dícere, Nec líttera exprímere:
Neither tongue is-able to-say, nor written-word to-express:

Expértus pótest crédere Quid sit Jésum dilígere.
(Only) the-experienced is-able to-know what it-means Jesus to-love.

5.

Sis Jésu, nóstrum gáudium, Qui es futúrus praémium:
Be-Thou, O-Jesus, our joy, Who art our-future reward:

Sit nóstra in te glória, Per cúncta sémper saécula.
May-be our in Thee glory, through all always eternity.

Jesu Rex Admirabilis

Hymn for Matins of the Feast of the Holy Name of Jesus
Attributed to St. Bernard — (1091–1153)

1.

Jésu, Rex admirábilis, Et triumphátor nóbilis,
Jesus, King admirable, and conqueror noble,

Dulcédo ineffábilis, Tótus desiderábilis.
Sweetness ineffable, wholly desirable.

2.

Quándo cor nóstrum vísitas, Tunc lúcet éi véritas,
When heart our Thou-visitest, then illuminates it truth,

Múndi viléscit vánitas, Et íntus
Of-the-world becomes-contemptible the-vanity, And within

férvet cáritas.
glows charity.

3.

Jésu, dulcédo córdium, Fons vívus, lúmen méntium,
O-Jesus, sweetness of-the-heart, fountain living, light of-minds,

Excédens ómne gáudium, Et ómne desidérium.
Exceeding all joy, and all desire.

4.

Jésum ómnes agnóscite, Amórem éjus póscite:
Jesus everyone may-confess, love His earnestly-seek:

Jésum ardénter quaérite Quaeréndo inardéscite.
Jesus zealously seek, (and) in-seeking be-enkindled

5.

Te nóstra Jésu vox sónet, Nóstri te móres éxprimant,
Thee our, Jesus, voices may-praise, our Thee days may-give-testimony-of,

Te córda nóstra díligant, Et nunc, et in perpétuum.
Thee hearts our may-love, both now, and forever.

Crudelis Herodes Deum

Hymn for Vespers of the Feast of the Epiphany

Attributed to Sedulius — Fifth Century

1.

Crudélis Heródes, Déum Régem veníre quid tímes?
Cruel Herod, God the-King to-come why do-you-fear?

Non éripit mortália, Qui régna dat coeléstia.
Not he-does-take-away mortal, who kingdoms gives heavenly.

2.

Íbant Mági, quam víderant, Stéllam sequéntes praéviam:
Proceed the-Magi, which they-saw, the-star following going-before-them:

Lúmen requírunt lúmine: Déum faténtur múnere.
The-Light they-seek by-the-light: God they-acknowledge with-gifts.

5.

Jésu,	**tíbi**	**sit**	**glória,**	**Qui**	**apparuísti**	**Géntibus,**
Jesus,	to-Thee	be	glory,	Who	didst-appear	to-the-Gentiles,

Cum	**Pátre,**	**et**	**álmo**	**Spíritu,**	**In sempitérna saécula.**
With	the-Father,	and	the-life-giving	Spirit,	forever-and-ever.

Attende Domine

Lenten Responsory

Atténde	**Dómine,**	**et**	**miserére,**	**quía**	**peccávimus**
Attend	Lord,	and	have-mercy,	because	we-have-sinned

tíbi.
against-Thee.

Parce Domine

Lenten Responsorial

Párce	**Dómine,**	**párce**	**pópulo**	**túo;**	**ne**	**in**	**aetérnum**	**irascáris**
Spare	Lord,	spare	people	Thy;	not	forever		do-be-angry

nóbis.
with-us.

Vexilla Regis

Hymn for Vespers From Passion Sunday to Wednesday of Holy Week and on Feasts of the Holy Cross

The First Five Verses Are Attributed to Fortunatus (530–609)

1.

Vexílla	**Régis**	**pródeunt:**	**Fúlget**	**crúcis**	**mystérium,**
The-banners	of-the-King	go-forth:	gleams	of-the-cross	the-mystery,

Quae	**víta**	**mórtem**	**pértulit,**	**Et**	**mórte**	**vítam**	**prótulit.**
On-which	life	death	suffered,	and	by-death	life	produced.

2.

	Quae	**vulneráta**	**lánceae**	**Mucróne**	**díro,**
(That Life)	Which	was-wounded	of-a-lance	by-a-point	cruel,

críminum
of-sin

Ut nos laváret sórdibus, Manávit únda
That us It-might-cleanse from-the-defilements, flowed in-water

et sánguine.
and in-blood.

3.

Impléta sunt quae cóncinit Dávid fidéli cármine,
Those-things-are-fulfilled which foretold David in-faithful song,

Dicéndo natiónibus: Regnávit a lígno Déus.
Saying to-the-nations: has-reigned from a-tree God.

4.

Árbor decóra et fúlgida, Ornáta régis
O-tree beautiful and resplendent, adorned of-the-King

púrpura,
with-the-purple,

Eléeta dígno stípite Tam sáncta mémbra tángere.
Chosen on-(thy)-worthy trunk so holy limbs to-touch.

5.

Beáta, cújus bráchiis Prétium pepéndit
O-blessed (Tree) from-whose branches the-ransom hung

saéculi,
of-the-world,

Statéra fácta córporis, Tulítque
The-balance (which) was-made of-the-body, and-(which)-stole-away

praédam tártari.
the-prey of-hell.

6.

O Crux áve, spes única, Hoc Passiónis témpore
O Cross hail, (our) hope only, in-this of-Passion time

Píis adáuge grátiam, Reísque déle crímina.
In-the-just increase grace, and-for-sinners blot-out sins.

7.

Te, fons salútis Trínitas, Colláudet ómnis spíritus:
Thee, fount of-salvation O-Trinity, may-praise every spirit:

Quíbus Crúcis victóriam Largíris, ádde
(To those) to-whom of-the-Cross the-victory Thou-givest, give-also

praémium.
the-reward.

Hosanna Filio David

Antiphon for Palm Sunday

Hosánna fílio Dávid: benedíctus qui vénit in nómine
Hosanna to-the-son of-David: blessed who comes in the-name

Dómini. Rex Ísrael: Hosánna in excélsis.
of-the-Lord. King of-Israel: Hosanna in the-highest.

Pueri Hebraeorum

Antiphon Sung During the Distribution of the Palms on Palm Sunday

1.

Púeri Hebraeórum, portántes rámos olivárum,
Children of-the-Hebrews, carrying branches of-olive-trees,

obviavérunt Dómino, clamántes, et dicéntes, Hosánna in
went-before the-Lord, shouting, and saying, Hosanna in

excélsis.
the-highest.

2.

Púeri Hebraeórum vestiménta prosternébant in via,
Children of-the-Hebrews garments cast-down in the-road,

et clamábant dicéntes: Hosánna fílio Dávid:
and shouted saying: Hosanna to-the-son of-David:

benedíctus qui vénit in nómine Dómini.
blessed (is he) who comes in the-name of-the-Lord.

Gloria Laus et Honor

Responsory for the Palm Sunday Procession

Attributed to Theodulf, Bishop of Orleans (760–821)

Glória, laus, et hónor tíbi sit, Rex Chríste
Glory, praise, and honor to-Thee be, King, Christ, (and)

Redémptor:
Redeemer:

Cúi	**pueríle**	**décus**	**prómpsit**	**Hosánna**	**píum.**
To-whom	youthful	beauty	has-uttered	Hosanna	a-loving.

Veni Creator

Hymn for Vespers and Terce of Pentecost and Throughout the Octave

Also Used as an Invocation to the Holy Spirit

Authorship Variously Ascribed to Rabanus Maurus, Charlemagne, St. Ambrose, and St. Gregory the Great

1.

Véni	**Creátor**	**Spíritus,**	**Méntes**	**tuórum**		**vísita,**
Come	Creator	Spirit,	the-souls	of-Thy	(children)	visit,

Ímple	**supérna**	**grátia**	**Quae**	**tu**	**creásti**	**péctora.**
Fill	with-heavenly	grace	which	Thou	hast-created	the-hearts.

2.

Qui	**díceris**	**Paráclitus,**	**Altíssimi**	**dónum**	**Déi,**
Thou-Who	art-called	the-Paraclete,	the-most-High	gift	of-God,

Fons	**vívus,**	**ígnis,**	**cáritas,**	**Et**	**spiritális**	**únctio.**
The-fountain	living,	fire,	love,	and	spiritual	unction.

3.

Tu	**septifórmis**	**múnere,**	**Dígitus**	**patérnae**	**déxterae,**
Thou	sevenfold	in-gifts,	the-finger	of-the-Father's	right-hand,

Tu	**ríte**	**promíssum**	**Pátris,**	**Sermóne**	**dítans**	**gúttura.**
Thou	fitly	the-promise	of-the-Father,	with-words	enriching	throats.

4.

Accénde	**lúmen**	**sénsibus:**	**Infúnde**	**amórem**	**córdibus:**
Kindle	light	in-our-senses:	pour	love	into-our-hearts:

Infírma	**nóstri**	**córporis**	**Virtúte**	**fírmans**	**pérpeti.**
The-weaknesses	of-our	body	strength	strengthening	with-perpetual.

5.

Hóstem	**repéllas**	**lóngius,**	**Pacémque**	**dónes**
The-enemy	mayest-Thou-drive-back	afar,	and-peace	give

prótinus:
straightway:

Ductóre	**sic**	**te**	**praévio,**		**Vitémus**	**ómne**
As-a-Guide	so	with-Thee	going-before	(us)	we-will-avoid	everything

nóxium.
evil.

6.

Per	**te**	**sciámus**	**da**		**Pátrem,**	**Noscámus**
Through	Thee	we-may-know	grant	(that)	the-Father,	we-may-know

átque	**Fílium,**
and-also	the-Son,

Téque	**utriúsque**	**Spíritum**	**Credámus**	**ómni**	**témpore.**
And-in-Thee	of-both	the-Spirit	may-we-believe	for-all	time.

7.

Déo	**Pátri**	**sit**	**glória,**	**Et**	**Fílio**	**qui**	**a**	**mórtuis**
To-God	the-Father	be	glory,	and	to-the-Son	who	from	the-dead

Surréxit,	**ac**	**Paráclito,**	**In saeculórum saécula.**	**Ámen.**
Rose,	and	to-the-Paraclete,	forever-and-ever.	So-be-it.

O Beata Trinitas

O	**beáta**	**Trínitas!**	**Córdis**	**Jésu**	**cháritas,**
O	blessed	Trinity!	of-the-heart	of-Jesus	love,

Imménsae		**cleméntiae,**	**Imménsae**	**sint**		**grátiae,**
boundless	(Thy)	mercy,	boundless	let-be	(Thy)	graces,

Aetérna	**sit**		**glória.**	**Ámen**	**dícant**	**ómnia.**	**Ámen.**
eternal	may-be	(Thy)	glory.	So-be-it	let-say	all.	So-be-it.

Pange Lingua

Hymn for Vespers of the Feast of Corpus Christi

Also Used as a Procession Hymn of the Blessed Sacrament

The Last Two Verses Are Sung at Benediction of the Blessed Sacrament

Composed by St. Thomas Aquinas (1227–1274)

1.

Pánge	**língua**	**gloriósi**	**Córporis**	**mystérium,**
Sing,	O-tongue,	of-the-glorious	Body	the-mystery,

Sanguinísque	**pretiósi,**	**Quem**	**in**	**múndi**	**prétium**
and-of-the-Blood	Precious,	which	in	of-the-world	ransom

Frúctus	**véntris**	**generósi**	**Rex**	**effúdit**	**Géntium.**
Fruit	of-a-womb	noble	the-King	shed	of-the-Gentiles.

2.

Nóbis	**dátus,**	**nóbis**	**nátus**	**Ex**	**intácta**	**Vírgine,**
To-us	given,	for-us	born	of	a-chaste	Virgin,

Et	**in**	**múndo**	**conversátus,**	**Spárso**	**vérbi**
and	in	the-world	living,	having-been-scattered	of-the-word

sémine,
the-seed,

Súi	**móras**	**incolátus**	**Míro**	**cláusit**	**órdine.**
His	delays-of-dwelling (earthly-days)		in-a-marvellous	He-closed	manner.

3.

In	**suprémae**	**nócte**	**coénae**	**Recúmbens**	**cum**	**frátribus,**
On	of-the-Last	the-night	Supper	reclining	with (His)	brethren,

Observáta	**lége**	**pléne**	**Cíbis**	**in**
having-been-observed	the-law	fully	nourishment	in-regard-to

legálibus,
legal,

Cíbum	**túrbae**	**duodénae**	**Se**	**dat**
as-food	to-the-assembly	twelve-in-number	Himself	He-gave

súis	mánibus.
with-His-own	Hands.

4.

Vérbum		cáro,	pánem	vérum	Vérbo
The-Word	(made)	flesh,	bread	true	by-(His)-Word

	cárnem	éfficit:
(His)	flesh	makes:

Fítque	Sánguis	Chrísti	mérum,	Et	si	sénsus
and-also-becomes	the-Blood	of-Christ	the-wine,	and	if	the-senses

déficit,
fail,

Ad	firmándum	cor	sincérum	Sóla	fídes	súfficit.
for	strengthening	the-heart	sincere	alone	faith	suffices.

5.

Tántum	érgo	Sacraméntum	Venerémur	cérnui:
So-great	therefore	a-Sacrament	let-us-venerate	prostrate:

Et	antíquum	documéntum	Nóvo	cédat	rítui:
and	the-old	pattern	to-new	let-give-way	rites:

Praéstet	fídes	suppleméntum	Sénsuum	deféctui.
let-furnish	faith	a-supplement	of-the-senses	to-the-weakness.

6.

Genitóri,	Genitóque	Laus	et	jubilátio,
To-the-Father,	and-to-the-Son	praise	and	glory,

Sálus,	hónor,	vírtus	quóque	Sit	et	benedíctio:
salvation,	honor,	power	also	be	and	benediction:

Procedénti	ab	utróque	Cómpar	sit	laudátio.	Ámen.
to-Him-Who-proceeds	from	Both-and	equal	be	praise.	So-be-it.

O Salutaris

Last Two Verses of "Verbum Supernum" Composed by St. Thomas Aquinas (1227–1274)

1.

O Salutáris Hóstia, Quae caéli pándis óstium,
O Saving Victim, Who of-heaven openest the-gate,

Bélla prémunt hostília, Da róbur, fer auxílium.
Attacks oppress-us hostile, Give (us) strength, bring (us) aid.

2.

Uni trinóque Dómino Sit sempitérna glória,
To-the-One and-Triune God Be eternal glory,

Qui vítam síne término Nóbis dónet in pátria.
Who life without end To-us gives in (our) native-land.

Ecce Panis Angelorum

Last Four Verses of the Sequence — "Lauda Sion"
Composed by St. Thomas Aquinas (1227–1274)

1.

Ecce pánis Angelórum Fáctus cíbus viatórum:
Behold the-bread of-angels is-made the-food of-pilgrims:

Vére pánis filiórum, Non mitténdus cánibus.
Truly (it is) the-bread of-children, not to-be-given to-dogs.

2.

In figúris praesignátur, Cum Isáac immolátur,
In figures it-was-prefigured, when Isaac was-immolated,

Agnus Páschae deputátur,
(When) the-lamb of-the-Pasch was-sacrificed, (and when)

Dátur mánna pátribus.
was-given manna to-the-fathers.

3.

Bóne Pástor, pánis vére, Jésu, nóstri miserére:
(O) Good Shepherd, Bread true, Jesus, on-us have-mercy:

Tu nos pásce, nos tuére, Tu nos
(Do) Thou us feed, (and) us protect, (Do) Thou us

bóna fac vidére In térra vivéntium.
good-things make to-see in the-land of-the-living.

4.

Tu qui cúncta scis et váles, Qui nos páscis
(O) Thou Who all-things knows and can-do, Who us feeds

hic mortáles:
here mortals:

Túos íbi commensáles, Cohaerédes et sodáles
Thy there guests, the-co-heirs and the-intimate-friends

Fac sanctórum cívium. Ámen.
make (us to be) of-the-holy (heavenly) citizens. So-be-it.

O Sacrum Convivium

Antiphon From the Office of the Blessed Sacrament

Composed by St. Thomas Aquinas (1227–1274)

O Sácrum convívium in quo Chrístus súmitur, recólitur
O sacred banquet in which Christ is-received, is-recalled

memória passiónis éjus, mens implétur grátia,
the-memory of-passion His, the-soul is-filled with-grace,

et futúrae glóriae nóbis pígnus dátur.
and of-future glory to-us a-pledge is-given.

Panis Angelicus

The Last Two Verses of "Sacris Solemnis" — Hymn for Matins of the Feast of Corpus Christi

Composed by St. Thomas Aquinas (1227–1274)

1.

Pánis angélicus fit pánis hóminum;
The-bread of-angels becomes the-bread of-men;

Dat pánis caélicus figúris términum:
Puts (literally: furnishes) Bread heavenly to-figures an-end:

O res mirábilis, mandúcat Dóminum
O thing wonderful, eats (his) Lord

Páuper, sérvus, et húmilis.
The-poor, the-servant, and the-lowly (man).

2.

Te trína Déitas únaque póscimus,
Thee Three Godhead and-One we-beseech,

Sic nos tu vísita, sícut te cólimus:
That-so us Thou visit as Thee we-adore:

Per túas sémitas duc nos quo téndimus
By Thy ways lead us whither we tend

Ad lúcem quam inhábitas.
To (that) light which Thou-dwellest-in.

Adoro Te Devote

Hymn Composed by St. Thomas Aquinas (1227–1274)

1.

Adóro te devóte, látens Déitas,
I-adore Thee devoutly, hidden Deity,

Quae sub his figúris vére látitas:
Who under these figures truly liest-hidden:

Tíbi se cor méum tótum súbjicit,
To-Thee itself heart my completely subjects,

Quía te contémplans, tótum déficit.
For Thee in-contemplating wholly it-is-lost.

5.

O memoriále mórtis Dómini,
O memorial of-the-death of-the-Lord,

Pánis vívus vítam praéstans hómini,
O-Bread living, life giving to-man,

Praésta méae méntis de te vívere,
Grant to-my soul on Thee to-live,

Et te ílli sémper dúlce sápere.
And (grant that) Thou to-it ever sweet taste.

7.

Jésu, quem velátum nunc aspício:
O-Jesus, Whom veiled now I-see:

Oro fíat íllud, quod tam sítio:
I-pray may-be that, which so I-thirst-for:

Ut te reveláta cérnens fácie,
That Thee unveiled seeing with-(Thy)-countenance,

Vísu sim beátus túae glóriae. Ámen.
With-the-vision I-may-be blessed of-Thy glory. So-be-it.

Ego Sum Panis

Ego sum pánis vívus, qui de coélo descéndi.
I am the-Bread living, which from heaven came-down.

Si quis manducáverit ex hoc páne vívet in aetérnum.
If anyone shall-have-eaten of this Bread he-shall-live forever.

Ave Verum

Probably Composed by Pope Innocent VI

Ave vérum Córpus nátum De María Vírgine,
Hail true Body born of Mary the-Virgin,

Vére pássum, immolátum In crúce pro hómine,
(Which) truly suffered, (and was) immolated on the-cross for man,

Cújus látus perforátum Flúxit áqua et sánguine,
Whose side pierced streamed with-water and with-blood,

Esto nóbis praegustátum Mórtis in exámine,
Be to-us a-foretaste (of heaven) of-death in the-testing,

O Jésu dúlcis! O Jésu píe! O Jésu fíli Maríae.
O Jesus sweet! O Jesus loving! O Jesus Son of-Mary.

O Esca Viatorum

1.

O ésca viatórum, O pánis angelórum, O mánna coélitum!
O food of-travelers, O bread of-angels, O manna heavenly!

Esuriéntes cíba, Dulcédine non príva córda
The-hungry feed, of-sweetness not do-deprive hearts

quaeréntium.
of-seekers.

2.

O lýmpha fóns amóris Qui púro Salvatóris E
O clear-water, fount of-love which pure of-the-Saviour from

córde prófluis,
the-heart flows,

Te sitiéntes póta, Haec sóla nóstra vóta
Thee those-thirsting-for absorb, these only our offerings

His úna sùfficis.
in-these (gifts) in-a-singular-way Thou-fulfillest.

3.

O Jésu, túum vúltum Quem cólimus occúltum Sub
O Jesus, Thy countenance which we-adore (is) hidden under

pánis spécie:
of-bread the-species:

Fac ut, remóto vélo, Post, líbera
Grant that, being-removed the-veil, afterwards, free (us)

in coélo, Cernámus fácie. Ámen.
in heaven, (that) we-may-see Thy-face. So-be-it.

Adoro Te O Panis Caelice

1.

Adóro te, O Pánis caélice, O Dómine, O Déus máxime.
I-adore Thee, O Bread heavenly, O Lord, O God most-great.

Chorus

Sánctus, Sánctus, Sánctus, síne fíne Sánctus,
Holy, holy, holy, without end holy,

Sémper tíbi glória sácra sit sub hóstia.
Always to-You glory Sacred be in the-Host.

2.

Nos fámulos, O Déus, réspice, Et grátia nos sémper
Us (Your) servants, O God, care-for, and with-grace us always

réfice.
strengthen.

O Panis Dulcissime

1.

O pánis dulcíssime, O fidélis ánimae Vitális
O Bread most-sweet, O faithful (and) of-the-soul vital

reféctio!
refreshment!

O Paschális víctimae, Agne mansuetíssime, Legális oblátio!
O Paschal victim, Lamb most-gentle, Legal Oblation!

2.

Suméntem, cum súmeris, Quía non
The-one-who-receives-Thee, when Thou-art-received because not

consúmeris, Aetérne vivíficas.
Thou-art-consumed, eternally Thou-dost-vivify.

Nam reátum scéleris, Dóno tánti múneris,
For, a-person-accused of-sin, with-a-gift of-such-great value,

Cleménter puríficas.
mercifully Thou-dost-purify.

O Quam Suavis Est

O quam suávis est, Dómine, spíritus túus! Qui
O how sweet is, O-Lord, spirit Thy! (Thou) Who

ut dulcédinem túam in fílios
in-order-that sweetness Thy to (Thy) sons-and-daughters

demonstráres, páne suavíssimo de coélo praéstito,
Thou-mightest-show, in-Bread most-sweet from heaven coming,

esuriéntes réples bónis, fastidiósos, dívites,
the-hungry fillest with-good-(things), fastidious, sumptuous,

dimíttens inánes.
leaving-aside (and) vain-(things).

O Cor Amoris

1.

O cor amóris víctima,
O heart of-love the-victim,

Caéli perénne gáudium,
of-heaven the-unceasing joy,

Mortálium solátium,
of-mortals the-solace,

Mortálium spes última.
of-mortals hope the-last.

2.

Tu Trinitátis glória,
Thou of-the-Trinity glory,

Júngit tíbi se Fílius,
joins to-Thee Himself the-Son,

In te quiéscit Spíritus,
in Thee reposes the-(Holy)-Spirit,

In te Pátri sunt gáudia.
in Thee of-the-Father are the-joys.

3.

Cor dúlce, Cor amábile,
Heart sweet, Heart worthy-of-love,

Amóre nóstri sáucium,
for-love our wounded,

Amóre nóstri lánguidum,
for-love our longing

Fac sis míhi placábile.
bring-to-pass (that) Thou-be to-me propitious.

Ave Mundi Gloria

1.

Ave, múndi glória, Vírgo, máter álma, Ave, benigníssima!
Hail, of-the-world glory, Virgin, Mother gracious, Hail, most-kindly-one!

Chorus

Ave, Ave María, Ave, Ave María!
Hail, hail Mary, Hail, hail Mary!

2.

Ave pléna grátia, Angelórum Dómina, Ave praeclaríssima!
Hail full of-grace, of-the-angels Queen, Hail most-noble-one!

3.

Ave, décus vírginum, Ave, sálus hóminum, Ave,
Hail, glory of-virgins, Hail, salvation of-men, Hail,

potentíssima!
most-powerful-one!

4.

Ave, máter Dómini, Génitrix Altíssimi, Ave,
Hail, Mother of-the-Lord, Mother of-the-Most-High, Hail,

prudentíssima!
most-prudent-one!

Salve Mater Misericordiae

Sálve máter misericórdiae, Máter Déi, et máter
Hail Mother of-mercy, Mother of-God, and Mother

véniae,
of-forgiveness,

Máter spéi, et máter grátiae, Máter pléna sánctae
Mother of-hope, and Mother of-grace, Mother full of-holy

laetítiae, O María!
joy, O Mary!

1.

Sálve décus humáni géneris, Sálve Vírgo dígnior
Hail glory of-the-human race, Hail Virgin more-honorable-than

céteris,
others,

Quae vírgines ómnes transgréderis, Et áltius sédes
Who virgins all surpasseth, And higher sitteth

in súperis, O María!
in the-heavens, O Mary!

2.

Sálve félix Vírgo puérpera: Nam qui sédet in
Hail happy Virgin Mother: For He-Who sitteth at

Pátris déxtera,
of-the-Father the-right-hand

Caélum régens, térram et aéthera, Intra túa se cláusit
Heaven ruling, earth and sky, Within thy Himself hid

víscera, O María!
womb, O Mary!

Ave Virgo Virginum

1.

Ave, Vírgo vírginum, Ave, lúmen lúminum, Ave, stélla
Hail, Virgin of-virgins, Hail, light of-lights, Hail, star

praévia!
leading-the-way!

Chorus

Ave, Ave María, Ave, Ave María!
Hail, Hail Mary, Hail, Hail Mary!

2.

Benedícta Fília, Tóta pléna grátia, Tóta síne
Blessed Daughter, Wholly full of-grace, Wholly without

mácula!
stain!

3.

Mediátrix hóminum, Ablutríxque críminum, Ave, Vírgo régia!
Mediatrix of-men, And-purifier of-offenses, Hail, Virgin royal!

Salve Regina Caelitum

Sálve Regína caélitum, O María! Tuórum spes fidélium,
Hail Queen heavenly, O Mary! Of-thy hope faithful,

O María!
O Mary!

Exsultáte, chérubim, jubiláte, séraphim, Sálve, Sálve, Sálve Regína!
Exult, cherubim, rejoice seraphim, Hail, hail, hail Queen!

Maria Mater Gratiae

María Máter grátiae, dúlcis párens cleméntiae,
Mary Mother of-grace, sweet Mother of-mercy,

Tu nos ab hóste prótege, et mórtis hóra
(Do) Thou us from the enemy protect, and of-death in-the-hour

súscipe.
receive-(us).

Te Joseph Celebrent

Hymn for Vespers of the Feast of St. Joseph and of the Solemnity of St. Joseph

Author Unknown — Seventeenth Century

1.

Te, Jóseph, célebrent ágmina coélitum,
Thee, Joseph, let-praise the-hosts heavenly,

Te cúncti résonent christiádum chóri,
Thee all let-praise christian choirs,

Qui clárus méritis, júnctus es ínclytae
Who renowned for-merits, were-joined to-the-glorious

Cásto foédere Vírgini.
In-chaste bond Virgin.

5.

Nóbis, súmma Trías, párce precántibus,
On-us, sovereign Trinity, have-mercy (Thy) suppliants,

Da Jóseph méritis sídera scándere:
Grant of-Joseph by-the-merits the-heavens to-ascend-to:

Ut tándem líceat nos tíbi pérpetim
That finally it-may-be-permitted-to us to-Thee forever

Grátum prómere cánticum.
A-grateful to-sing canticle.

Tu Es Petrus

Tu es Pétrus et súper hanc pétram aedificábo Ecclésiam
Thou art Peter and upon this rock I-will-build Church

méam.
My.

Oremus pro Pontifice

Orémus pro Pontífice nóstro, (Pió). Dóminus consérvet
Let-us-pray for Pontiff our, (Pius). The-Lord may-preserve

éum, et vivíficet éum, et beátum fáciat éum in
him, and may-He-give-life-to him, and blessed make him on

térra, et non trádat éum in ánimam inimicórum éjus.
earth, and not deliver him to the-will of-enemies his.

Jesu Corona Virginum

Hymn for Vespers and Lauds of the Common of Virgins

Attributed to St. Ambrose (340–397)

1.

Jésu, coróna Vírginum, Quem máter ílla cóncipit,
O-Jesus, crown of-virgins, Whom Mother that conceived,

Quae sóla Vírgo párturit: Haec vóta
Who alone as-a-Virgin gave-birth-to-a-Child: these prayers

clémens áccipe.
graciously receive.

2.

Qui pérgis ínter lília, Séptus choréis
(O Thou) Who walkest among the-lilies, surrounded with-choirs

Vírginum,
of-virgins,

Spónsus decórus glória, Sponsísque réddens
As-a-Spouse fittingly-adorned with-glory, and-to-the-brides giving

praémia.
gifts.

3.

Quocúmque téndis, Vírgines Sequúntur, átque láudibus
Wherever Thou-goest, virgins follow, and in-praise

Post te canéntes cúrsitant, Hymnósque dúlces pérsonant.
After Thee singing hasten, and-hymns sweet make-resound.

4.

Te deprecámur súpplices; Nóstris ut áddas sénsibus,
Thee we-pray as-suppliants; to-our that grant senses,

Nescíre prórsus ómnia Corruptiónis vúlnera.
They-be-ignorant-of completely all of-corruption the-wounds

5.

Vírtus, hónor, laus, glória Déo Pátri cum Fílio,
Virtue, honor, praise, glory (be) to-God the-Father with the-Son,

Sáncto símul Paráclito, In saeculórum saécula.
with-the-Holy together Paraclete, forever-and-ever.

Salva Nos Domine Vigilantes

Sálva nos, Dómine, vigilántes, custódi nos dormiéntes:
Save us, Lord, as-we-watch, guard us as-we-sleep:

Ut vigilémus cum Chrísto et requiescámus in páce.
That we-may-watch with Christ and may-rest in peace.

Ultima in Mortis Hora

Ultima in mórtis hóra Fílium pro nóbis óra:
The-last in of-death hour (Thy) Son for us entreat:

Bónam mórtem ímpetra, Vírgo, Máter, Dómina.
A-good death obtain (for us), Virgin, Mother, Lady.

Ecce Sacerdos Magnus

Ecce sacérdos mágnus, qui in diébus súis plácuit Déo:
Behold a-priest great, who in days his pleased God:

Ideo jurejurándo fécit íllum Dóminus créscere in
Therefore by-an-oath made him the-Lord to-increase among

plébem súam.
people His.

℣. **Benedictiónem ómnium géntium dédit ílli, et**
The-blessing of-all nations He-gave him, and

testaméntum súum confirmávit súper cáput éjus.
covenant His He-confirmed upon head his.

Te Deum Laudamus

1.

Te Déum laudámus: te Dóminum confitémur.
Thee God we-praise: Thee the-Lord we-acknowledge.

2.

Te aetérnum Pátrem ómnis térra venerátur.
Thee eternal Father all the-earth reverences.

3.

Tíbi ómnes Angeli, tíbi caéli, et univérsae
To-Thee all the-angels, to-Thee the-heavens, and all

potestátes:
the-Powers:

4.

Tíbi Chérubim et Séraphim incessábili vóce
To-Thee the-Cherubim and Seraphim with-unceasing voice

proclámant:
proclaim:

5.

Sánctus, Sánctus, Sánctus Dóminus Déus Sábaoth.
Holy, Holy, Holy Lord God of-the-hosts (of heaven).

6.

Pléni sunt caéli et térra majestátis glóriae túae.
Full are the-heavens and earth of-the-majesty of-glory Thy.

7.

Te gloriósus Apostolórum chórus,
Thee the-glorious of-Apostles choir,

8.

Te	**Prophetárum**	**laudábilis**	**númerus,**
Thee	of-the-Prophets	the-laudable	number,

9.

Te	**Mártyrum**	**candidátus**	**láudat**	**exércitus.**
Thee	of-the-Martyrs	white-robed	praises	the-army.

10.

Te	**per**	**órbem**	**terrárum**	**sáncta**	**confitétur**	**Ecclésia,**
Thee	through	the-circle	of-the-earth	the-holy	acknowledges	Church,

11.

Pátrem	**imménsae**	**majestátis,**
The-Father	of-great	majesty,

12.

Venerándum	**túum**	**vérum**	**et**	**únicum**	**Fílium,**
Honored,	Thy	true,	and	only	Son,

13.

Sánctum	**quóque**	**Paráclitum**	**Spíritum,**
Holy	and-also	the-Paraclete	the-Spirit.

14.

Tu		**Rex**	**glóriae**	**Chríste.**
Thou	(art)	the-King	of-glory	O-Christ.

15.

Tu	**Pátris**	**sempitérnus**	**es**	**Fílius.**
Thou	of-the-Father	the-everlasting	art	Son.

16.

Tu	**ad**	**liberándum**	**susceptúrus**	**hóminem:**
Thou	to	free	when-about-to-take-upon-Thyself	man:

non	**horruísti**	**Vírginis**	**úterum.**
not	didst-abhor	of-the-Virgin	the-womb.

17.

Tu	**devícto**	**mórtis**	**acúleo:**	**aperuísti**
Thou	having-subjugated	of-death	the-sting:	didst-open

credéntibus	**régna**	**caelórum.**
to-those-believing	the-kingdom	of-heaven.

18.

Tu	**ad**	**déxteram**	**Déi**	**sédes,**	**in**	**glória**	**Pátris.**
Thou	at	the-right-hand	of-God	sitteth,	in	the-glory	of-the-Father.

19.

Júdex	**créderis**	**ésse**		**ventúrus.**
The-Judge	Thou-art-believed	to-be	(who)	art-to-come.

20.

Te	**érgo**	**quaésumus,**	**túis**	**fámulis**	**súbveni:**	**quos**
Thee,	therefore,	we-beseech,	Thy	servants	help:	whom

pretióso	**sánguine**	**redemísti.**
with-(Thy)-Precious	Blood	Thou-hast-redeemed.

21.

Aetérna	**fac**		**cum**	**sánctis**	**túis**	**in**	**glória**
Everlasting	make	(them)	with	saints	Thy	in	glory

numerári.
to-be-numbered.

22.

Sálvum	**fac**	**pópulum**	**túum**	**Dómine,**	**et**	**bénedic**	**haereditáti**
Safe	make	people	Thy,	Lord	and	bless	inheritance

túae.
Thy.

23.

Et	**rége**	**éos,**	**et**	**extólle**	**íllos**	**úsque**	**in**	**aetérnum.**
And	rule	them,	and	exalt	them	continuously	forever.	

24.

Per	**síngulos**	**díes,**	**benedícimus**	**te.**
Through	each	day,	we-bless	Thee.
	(Day by day)			

25.

Et laudámus nómen túum in saéculum, et in saéculum saéculi.
And we-praise name Thy forever, and forever-and-ever.

26.

Dignáre Dómine díe ísto síne peccáto nos custodíre.
Deign Lord on-day this without sin us to-lead.

27.

Miserére nóstri Dómine, miserére nóstri.
Have-mercy on-us Lord, have-mercy on-us.

28.

Fíat misericórdia túa Dómine súper nos, quemádmodum
Let-be mercy Thy, Lord, upon us, in-the-manner-that

sperávimus in te.
we-have-hoped in Thee.

29.

In te Dómine sperávi: non confúndar
In Thee, Lord, I-have-hoped: (do) not let-me-be-confounded

in aetérnum.
forever.

℣. **Benedicámus Pátrem et Fílium cum Sáncto**
Let-us-bless (God) the-Father and the-Son with the-Holy

Spíritu.
Spirit.

℟. **Laudémus et superexaltémus éum in saécula.**
Let-us-praise and let-us-exalt Him forever.

℣. **Benedíctus es Dómine in firmaménto caéli.**
Blessed art-Thou, Lord, in the-firmament of-heaven.

℟. **Et laudábilis, et gloriósus, et superexaltátus in saécula.**
And praiseworthy, and glorious, and exalted forever.

℣. **Dómine exáudi oratiónem méam.**
Lord, hear prayer my.

℟. **Et clámor méus ad te véniat.**
And cry my to Thee let-come.

℣. **Dóminus vóbiscum.**
The-Lord with-you.

℟. **Et cum spíritu túo.**
And with spirit thy.

Orémus.
Let us pray.

Déus, cújus misericórdiae non est númerus, et
O-God, of-whose mercy no there-is number, and

bonitátis infinítus est thesáurus: piíssimae majestátis
of-whose-goodness infinite is the-treasure: to-most-holy majesty

túae pro collátis dónis grátias ágimus, túam sémper
Thy for given the-gifts thanks we-give, Thy always

cleméntiam exorántes; ut qui peténtibus
mercy asking; inasmuch-as of-those-who-entreat (Thee)

postuláta concédis, eósdem non déserens, ad
the-requests Thou-grantest, the-same not deserting, (but) for

praémia futúra dispónas. Per Chrístum
rewards future Thou-preparest (them). Through Christ

Dóminum nóstrum. ℟. **Ámen.**
Lord our. So-be-it.

INDEX